THE I

BIG WORD PUZZLES

Over 400 synonym scrambles, crossword conundrums, word searches & other brain-tickling word games

by David L. Hoyt

with **Colin Morgan**

and the Editors at **Merriam-Webster**

WORKMAN PUBLISHING • NEW YORK

Library of Congress Cataloging-in-Publication Data is available.

ISBN 978-0-7611-8088-3

Puzzles created by David L. Hoyt and Colin Morgan

Designed by Janet Vicario
Pencil photo on cover and interior by Aleskss/fotolia

Workman books are available at special discounts when purchased in bulk for premiums and sales promotions as well as for fundraising or educational use. Special editions or book excerpts can also be created to specification. For details, please contact special.markets@hbgusa.com.

Workman Publishing Co., Inc., a subsidiary of Hachette Book Group, Inc.
1290 Avenue of the Americas
New York, NY 10104
workman.com
WORKMAN is a registered trademark of Workman Publishing Co., Inc., a subsidiary of Hachette Book Group, Inc.

Printed in China on responsibly sourced paper.

First printing July 2015

10 9 8 7 6 5 4

CONTENTS

INTRODUCTION

In *The Little Book of Big Word Puzzles,* we've put together a dazzling collection of more than 425 word games and puzzles to grow your mind and your vocabulary. Here, you'll find old favorites with a new twist—like word searches to find pairs of synonyms, and crosswords with scrambled-up clues—as well as brand-new puzzle types that are appearing for the first time in print.

These light, fun puzzles take a lot of their clues and concepts straight out of the Merriam-Webster dictionary. You'll find yourself puzzling over definitions, parts of speech, and more. In Antonym Unscramble you straighten out pairs of jumbled-up antonyms, while Word Winder sends you off seeking adjectives, or adverbs, or even four-syllable words hidden in a letter grid. To solve Syllabary, you'll link word segments to create complete words, and Dictionary Cross'd Words will have you filling in crossword puzzles aided only by the dictionary definitions. Grammar has never been so much fun!

Unlike a lot of word game books, this book is printed in full color, and many of the puzzles in this book make use of color not just for decoration but as an integral part of the puzzle. In Prism Cross'd Words, for example, the clues aren't numbered, but rather grouped by color, challenging you to determine which red answer goes in which red part of the crossword grid.

Color Word Chains challenge players to not only figure out words based on their definition, but then figure out how to use those words to connect like-colored squares. These puzzles, and more like them, would simply not be possible in a black-and-white book, and we're very pleased to be able to offer you some truly unique word game experiences.

There are 20 different types of puzzles in this book, so every page brings a fresh new challenge. The puzzles are rated for difficulty from 1 to 10, and each puzzle also features a spot to record how long it took to solve. The book starts off easy and gets progressively harder, but there are some stumpers sprinkled around early in the book, as well as a few "breathers" later on. If variety is the spice of life, we think you'll find that this book has plenty!

We hope you enjoy *The Little Book of Big Word Puzzles*. We're sure these puzzles will have you thinking, smiling, and turning the pages for more.

Sincerely,
David L. Hoyt
Colin Morgan
and the editors at Merriam-Webster

PUZZLES

1 | DIFFICULTY: ●○○○○○○○○○ COMPLETION: ☐ TIME: ______

PRISM WORD FINDER

Using the color-coded clues below, find and circle the words in the letter grid.

L	K	H	O	R	S	E	Y	H	C	T
M	Y	O	U	N	G	S	T	E	R	J
A	T	T	R	A	C	T	I	V	E	N
S	V	L	K	M	G	V	Y	G	N	G
N	I	L	O	I	O	T	D	L	T	O
O	E	M	P	V	T	O	A	L	E	R
I	S	C	I	E	E	M	S	D	R	G
T	U	J	R	L	I	L	I	E	T	E
A	O	P	C	N	A	K	Y	W	A	O
L	M	Z	A	X	K	R	O	L	I	U
E	J	A	R	E	A	C	P	H	N	S

Find five three-syllable words starting with an orange letter ○○○○○

Find five one-syllable mammals starting with a blue letter ○○○○○

Find four synonyms of "beautiful" starting with a purple letter ○○○○

Find two synonyms of "child" starting with a red letter ○○

2 | DIFFICULTY: ●○○○○○○○○○
COMPLETION: ☐ TIME: ________

SYNONYM UNSCRAMBLE

Unscramble the letters below to form pairs of SYNONYMS. Watch out—some words can be unscrambled more than one way!

O W G R = A N E D P X

V R A B E = L O B D

R Y O E J U N = R P T I

A R H M = G M A A D E

M U N A H = R E N O S P

N O T G R S = R U S E C E

N U Y F N = M A C C O I L

3 | DIFFICULTY: ●○○○○○○○○○
COMPLETION: ☐ TIME: ______

DEFINITION FINDER

Using the clues below, find and circle the words concealed in the letter grid.

X	D	A	N	C	E	W	T	T
S	I	L	V	E	R	I	H	H
B	U	N	D	L	E	T	E	G
Z	M	O	R	A	L	T	A	I
J	Q	U	A	R	T	Y	T	A
T	H	R	O	U	G	H	E	R
P	E	R	F	U	M	E	R	T
M	I	D	W	I	F	E	Z	S

○ Marked by or full of clever humor *(adjective)*
○ Free from bends, curves, or angles *(adjective)*
○ Fluid preparation that emits a pleasing odor *(noun)*
○ Relating to principles of right and wrong *(adjective)*
○ Unit of capacity equal to 1/4 of a gallon *(noun)*
○ Person who assists women in childbirth *(noun)*
○ Soft grayish-white metal that is very valuable *(noun)*
○ Into one side and out the other *(preposition)*
○ Group of things that are tied together *(noun)*
○ To move rhythmically with music *(verb)*
○ Building where plays are performed *(noun)*

4 | DIFFICULTY: ●○○○○○○○○○
COMPLETION: ☐ TIME: ______

SYNONYM FINDER

Find and circle the seven pairs of SYNONYMS divided between the letter grids below.

D	E	B	G	X	Y	P	R
E	R	K	N	K	M	M	F
F	U	Z	R	U	I	C	R
E	T	E	L	A	B	J	E
A	P	P	L	N	Q	C	T
T	A	C	G	Y	M	W	S
L	C	O	N	C	I	S	E
A	Y	D	H	T	P	X	P

J	P	T	Y	H	D	T	R
A	Z	O	E	P	C	W	E
U	P	B	R	A	K	F	U
N	L	P	P	T	S	N	Q
T	Q	M	L	T	L	E	N
Y	O	E	C	A	Z	Y	O
C	H	R	M	K	U	B	C
J	Z	G	Y	E	A	D	X

○○○○○○○

5 | DIFFICULTY: ●○○○○○○○○○
COMPLETION: ☐ TIME: ______

DICTIONARY UNSCRAMBLE

Unscramble the letters below to form words that match the Merriam-Webster definitions.

transitive verb
To place so as to stay

ELETTS= ☐☐☐☐☐☐

noun
Any of numerous basic monetary units (as in the U.S.)

LDLORA= ☐☐☐☐☐☐

adjective
Of primary importance: ESSENTIAL, PRINCIPAL

ATRENLC= ☐☐☐☐☐☐☐

adverb In a manner or measure or to a degree or number that strictly conforms to a fact or condition

TELACYX= ☐☐☐☐☐☐☐

adjective
Of great value or high price

SCRUPIOE= ☐☐☐☐☐☐☐☐

noun An open container with a handle that is used especially to hold and carry water and other liquids

TCEBKU= ☐☐☐☐☐☐

6 | DIFFICULTY: ●○○○○○○○○○ COMPLETION: ☐ TIME: ______

MIXED-UP DEFINITION

Unscramble the letters below to reveal the definition of the given word.

ac · tive *adjective* \'ak-tiv\

niodg tgshin taht qiereru plachsiy mnetevmo adn greyen

☐☐☐☐☐ ☐☐☐☐☐☐

☐☐☐☐ ☐☐☐☐☐☐☐

☐☐☐☐☐☐☐☐

☐☐☐☐☐☐☐☐

☐☐☐ ☐☐☐☐☐☐

7 | DIFFICULTY: ●○○○○○○○○○ COMPLETION: ☐ TIME: ______

SYNONYM FINDER

Find and circle the six pairs of SYNONYMS, one on each side, in the letter grids below.

H	F	T	U	R	N
E	D	X	A	T	E
P	Q	E	I	D	G
M	L	U	I	G	A
C	Q	O	A	C	R
G	V	W	R	L	L

=

B	M	A	T	C	H
E	R	Y	X	N	R
S	M	I	I	E	C
A	N	P	G	W	P
E	S	N	T	H	R
C	A	Z	M	Y	T

○○○○○○

8 | DIFFICULTY: ●○○○○○○○○○○
COMPLETION: ☐ TIME: ______

ANTONYM FINDER

Find and circle the seven pairs of ANTONYMS divided between the letter grids below.

```
S H A L L O W N
M E R R Y E O T
E L Z Q R I T S
A W X A T L G I
G N L S U Z X S
E G E S T P K R
R U N L D Q Y E
Q I X M Z J R P
```

```
P R A C B J K N
R R E N E L X P
L Z O S S A U Z
A Q Z F P W S E
V P J X O E E E
I W Q W B U C R
S H A D E G N T
H Q X V J Q V D
```

○ ○ ○ ○ ○ ○ ○

9 | DIFFICULTY: ●○○○○○○○○○
COMPLETION: ☐ TIME: ______

PRISM CROSS'D WORDS

Use the color-coded clues below to find words that fit in the like-colored portions of the puzzle grid below.

- ○ Desire for what others have (2-syllable verb)
- ○ Brief written message (2-syllable noun)
- ○ Not happening often (3-syllable adjective)

- ○ Use offensive words (1-syllable verb)
- ○ Highest amount that is possible (3-syllable noun)

- ○ Large flightless bird (2-syllable noun)
- ○ Opinion or belief (3-syllable noun)

- ○ A sudden, strong desire (2-syllable noun)
- ○ Great in quantity (1-syllable adjective)

- ○ Parts of a living thing (4-syllable noun)
- ○ Examine superficially (1-syllable verb)

10 | DIFFICULTY: ●○○○○○○○○○ COMPLETION: ☐ TIME: ______

DICTIONARY WORD WINDER

Use the clues below to help you find the answers word-winding their way through the grid. Each answer will connect one side of the grid to the other—left to right, top to bottom, right to left, and bottom to top.

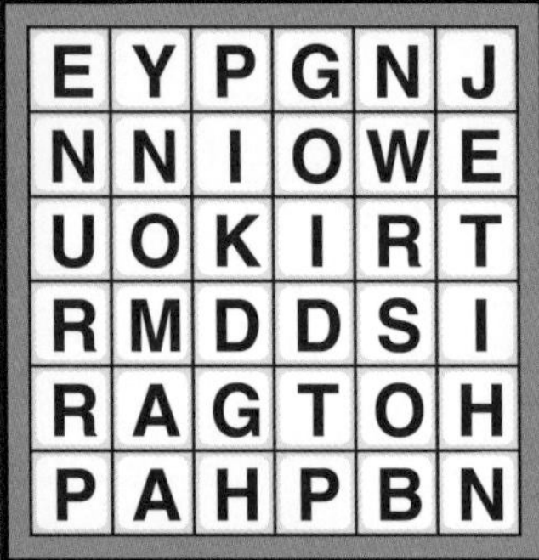

→ The pungent, usually crisp, root of a widely cultivated Eurasian plant of the mustard family usually eaten raw ______

↓ An individual's part or share of something ______

← A machine for converting any of various forms of energy into mechanical force and motion ______

↑ The combination of simultaneous musical notes in a chord ______

11 | DIFFICULTY: ●○○○○○○○○○ COMPLETION: ☐ TIME: ______

ANTONYM UNSCRAMBLE

Unscramble the letters below to form pairs of ANTONYMS. Note: Some words can be unscrambled more than one way!

L U L F ≠ P E T M Y

R A T M S ≠ L O I F O H S

V A E B O ≠ W E O B L

A S R I E ≠ W O R L E

N I L E S C E ≠ S I E N O

V A L E E ≠ R A V I E R

T E X E C D I ≠ R E D O B

12 | DIFFICULTY: ●○○○○○○○○○
COMPLETION: ☐ TIME: ______

CROSS'D WORDS UNSCRAMBLE

Unscramble the letters in each clue to fill in the puzzle grid below.

1				2		3				4
		5						6		
7						8				
9				10		11				12
		13								
14						15				

ACROSS

1 MWARS *(one-syllable word)*
3 VPOER *(one-syllable word)*
5 SRAPPIN *(two-syllable word)*
7 OHTTO *(one-syllable word)*
8 UMAES *(two-syllable word)*
9 SFHER *(one-syllable word)*
11 BGOUM *(two-syllable word)*
13 UNTAQBE *(two-syllable word)*
14 LMIYD *(two-syllable word)*
15 WORNF *(one-syllable word)*

DOWN

1 RISKT *(one-syllable word)*
2 CRAMH *(one-syllable word)*
3 NAADP *(two-syllable word)*
4 LEEGA *(two-syllable word)*
5 VOPBRER *(two-syllable word)*
6 MULTPEM *(two-syllable word)*
9 OFDLO *(one-syllable word)*
10 DAYHN *(two-syllable word)*
11 RFGFU *(one-syllable word)*
12 FEONT *(two-syllable word)*

13 | DIFFICULTY: ●○○○○○○○○○
COMPLETION: ☐ TIME: ______

MAKE THE CONNECTION

Fill in the boxes with common two-word phrases with the help of the clues below. The last word in each pair will be the first word in the following pair.

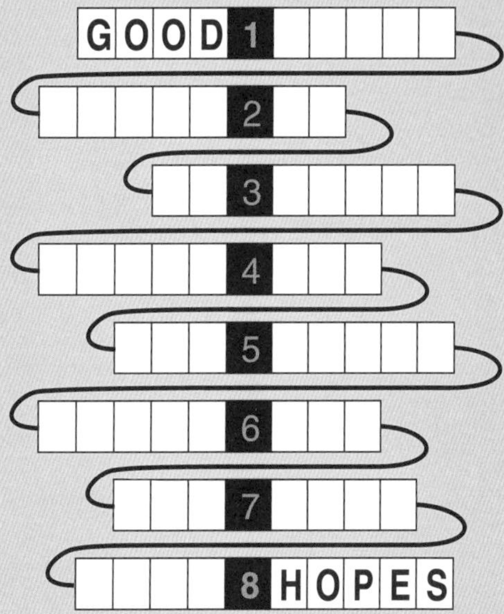

1 Fine physical condition
2 Lose weight, exercise, start to eat right, etc.
3 New York City, to Miami
4 Belgium border
5 Member of the pipefish family
6 Biting insect
7 Be full of hope or elation
8 Optimistic expectations

14 | DIFFICULTY: ●○○○○○○○○○○
COMPLETION: ☐ TIME: ______

MISSING DEFINITIONS FINDER

Using the clues below, find and circle the words concealed in the letter grid.

X	E	F	F	E	C	T	S	Z	G
W	O	R	K	I	N	G	Q	V	O
R	Z	B	R	O	C	K	S	X	O
E	X	H	E	A	T	V	Z	Q	D
T	I	M	E	Z	S	P	E	E	D
S	W	L	A	V	A	P	A	T	H
A	Q	B	L	O	C	K	S	X	Z
F	Z	V	X	L	I	G	H	T	K

ac·cel·er·ate *verb* \ik-ˈse-lə-ˌrāt\
to move ________ : to gain ________

ben·e·fi·cial *adjective* \ˌbe-nə-ˈfi-shəl\
producing ________ or helpful results or ________

erupt *verb* \i-ˈrəpt\
to send out ________, ash, ________, etc., in a sudden explosion

lei·sure *noun* \ˈlē-zhər, ˈle-, ˈlā-\
________ when you are not ________

ob·sta·cle *noun* \ˈäb-sti-kəl, -ˌsti-\
something that ________ your ________

so·lar *adjective* \ˈsō-lər, -ˌlär\
produced by or using the sun's ________ or ________

15 | DIFFICULTY: ●○○○○○○○○○
COMPLETION: ☐ TIME: ______

SYNONYM UNSCRAMBLE

Unscramble the letters below to form pairs of SYNONYMS. Watch out—some words can be unscrambled more than one way!

C T S K I D R E A E H

R E P V O F E Y V I R

R O W E P C R O E F

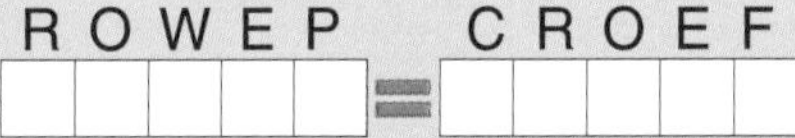

T O N N I A C R Y T O U N

D R A E O V O E L

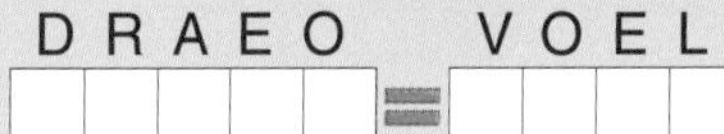

D R U B S A P U D S I T

S R H U R H Y R U

16 | DIFFICULTY: ●○○○○○○○○○ COMPLETION: ☐ TIME: ______

WORD WINDER

Use the clue to help you find the answers word-winding their way through the grid. Each answer will connect the top of the grid to the bottom.

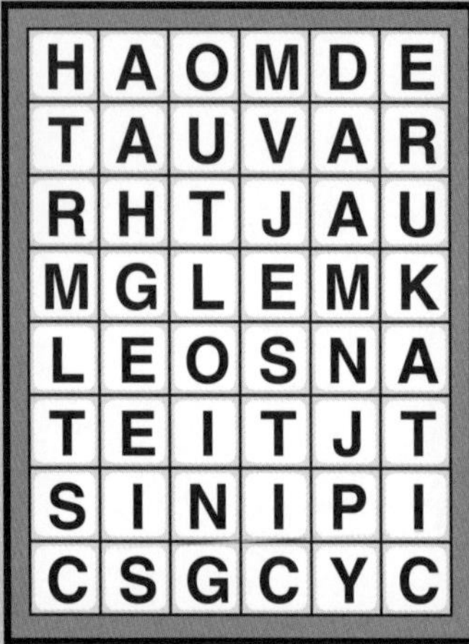

H	A	O	M	D	E
T	A	U	V	A	R
R	H	T	J	A	U
M	G	L	E	M	K
L	E	O	S	N	A
T	E	I	T	J	T
S	I	N	I	P	I
C	S	G	C	Y	C

Find five adjectives word-winding their way from top to bottom.

17 | DIFFICULTY: ●○○○○○○○○○
COMPLETION: ☐ TIME: ______

SYLLABARY

Link word segments together in the grid below to create words, and enter them in the blanks.

I	GENT	DO	LY	COM
DIL	PE	CIAL	MES	MU
ES	SUR	VI	TIC	NI
EN	AG	VOR	TY	FY
COUR	ING	IN	TEN	SI

Four-Syllable Verb: _ _ _ E _ _ _ _ _

Four-Syllable Noun: _ _ _ _ _ N _ _ _

Three-Syllable Adjective: _ O _ _ _ _ _ _

Four-Syllable Adverb: _ _ _ _ _ _ _ _ _ Y

Three-Syllable Adjective: _ _ _ _ _ E _ _

Three-Syllable Noun: _ _ _ _ I _ _ _

Four-Syllable Adjective: _ _ _ O _ _ _ _ _ _ _

18 | DIFFICULTY: ●○○○○○○○○○
COMPLETION: ☐ TIME: ______

ANTONYM FINDER

Find and circle the six pairs of ANTONYMS, one on each side, in the letter grids below.

S	F	W	N	D	P
L	M	C	R	Y	T
B	M	A	A	H	D
O	H	L	R	L	I
L	E	Q	J	T	M
D	P	D	R	D	K

T	I	M	I	D	Y
R	A	P	C	R	B
A	M	N	R	N	M
E	B	U	G	W	U
L	H	T	C	R	D
C	S	O	F	T	Y

○○○○○○

19 | DIFFICULTY: ●○○○○○○○○○
COMPLETION: ☐ TIME: ______

COLOR WORD CHAINS

Use the clues and letters below to make word paths between like colors to fill the board.

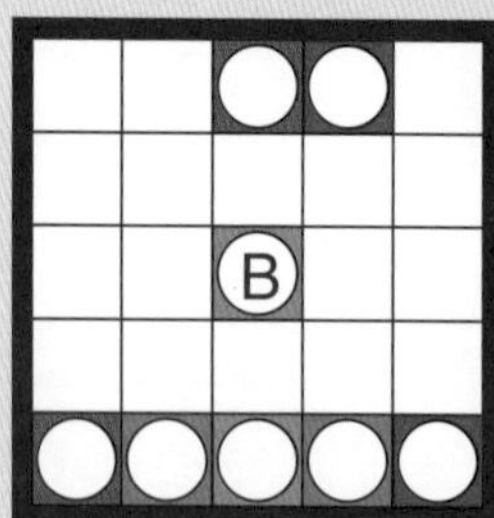

- Furniture for sleeping on
- To put into a trance
- A very tall African animal
- In a manner not likely to involve harm or danger

A	A	D	E	E	E
E	F	F	F	G	H
I	I	L	N	O	P
R	S	T	Y	Y	Z

20 | DIFFICULTY: ●○○○○○○○○○
COMPLETION: ☐ TIME: ______

CROSS'D WORD CONNECTIONS

The crosswords below share common letters as indicated by the colored boxes. Use the clues to solve the puzzles.

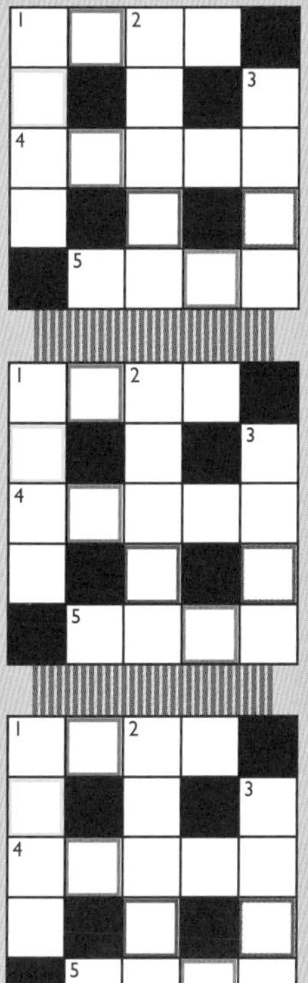

ACROSS
1 Skeletal material
4 Small pepper with a hot flavor
5 Someone who will inherit

DOWN
1 The rear part of the body
2 A loud or unpleasant sound
3 A structure that goes out from a shore into the water

ACROSS
1 A hard, black substance used as fuel
4 To emit rays of light
5 Blood vessel

DOWN
1 Hard covering for a broken bone
2 To get up after sleeping
3 Someone between childhood and adulthood

ACROSS
1 A small, burrowing animal with tiny eyes
4 The form or outline of an object
5 Mix with a spoon

DOWN
1 A large quantity, amount, or number
2 Smallest in amount or degree
3 Buck or doe

21 | DIFFICULTY: ● ○ ○ ○ ○ ○ ○ ○ ○ ○ ○
COMPLETION: ☐ TIME: ______

PRISM WORD FINDER

Using the color-coded clues below, find and circle the words in the letter grid.

Z	E	B	R	A	A	B	I	D	E	E
W	R	A	B	B	I	T	H	B	E	G
L	T	Q	G	J	B	S	G	T	Z	A
K	C	V	M	I	O	I	E	H	J	L
P	F	N	S	O	R	L	S	E	P	F
E	R	R	H	T	P	A	G	O	E	U
E	A	W	E	M	O	L	F	R	N	O
V	E	G	O	E	U	O	U	F	Z	M
E	B	C	H	D	Z	D	G	J	E	A
D	N	G	N	T	N	E	P	E	D	C
I	J	I	W	E	P	E	R	M	I	T

Find five synonyms for "tolerate" starting with an orange letter ○ ○ ○ ○ ○

Find four six-letter one-syllable words starting with a blue letter ○ ○ ○ ○

Find four two-syllable animals starting with a purple letter ○ ○ ○ ○

Find two ten-letter three-syllable words starting with a red letter ○ ○

22 | DIFFICULTY: ●○○○○○○○○○
COMPLETION: ☐ TIME: ______

SYLLABARY

Link word segments together in the grid below to create words, and enter them in the blanks.

CO	SAR	Y	NATE	DED
ES	OP	ER	I	CI
NEC	A	OUS	CA	FAS
TION	OR	BUR	AM	TION
RIG	GER	EX	HAM	INE

Three-Syllable Verb: _ _ A _ _ _ _

Three-Syllable Noun: _ _ _ _ _ R _ _ _

Five-Syllable Noun: _ _ O _ _ _ _ _ _ _ _

Four-Syllable Adjective: _ _ _ _ S _ _ _ _

Three-Syllable Verb: _ _ _ _ _ N _ _ _

Four-Syllable Noun: _ _ _ _ _ _ _ I _ _

Three-Syllable Adjective: _ _ _ O _ _ _ _

23 | DIFFICULTY: ● ○ ○ ○ ○ ○ ○ ○ ○ ○
COMPLETION: ☐ TIME: ______

DICTIONARY UNSCRAMBLE

Unscramble the letters below to form words that match the Merriam-Webster definitions.

noun A tropical forest where plants and trees grow very thickly

LUGEJN= ☐☐☐☐☐☐

adverb
Almost all or almost completely

SLOYMT= ☐☐☐☐☐☐

adjective
Higher in quality

TREEBT= ☐☐☐☐☐☐

adjective
Kept from knowledge or view

SCETRE= ☐☐☐☐☐☐

adverb
To a great degree

GYHHIL= ☐☐☐☐☐☐

transitive verb To become aware of (something or someone) by seeing, hearing, etc.

ONECTI= ☐☐☐☐☐☐

24 | DIFFICULTY: ●○○○○○○○○○
COMPLETION: ☐ TIME: ______

DICTIONARY CROSS'D WORDS

Fill in the puzzle using the Merriam-Webster definition clues below.

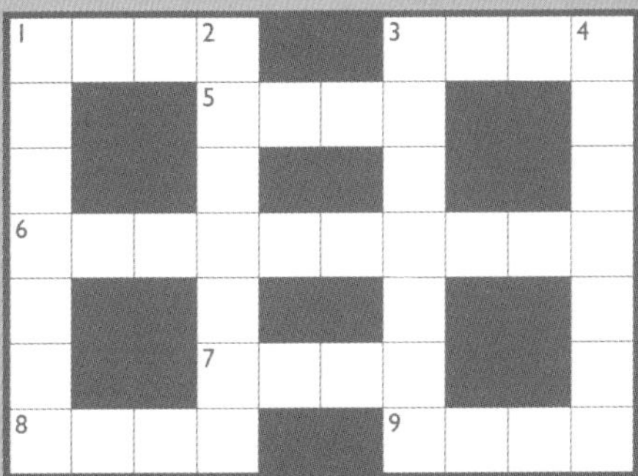

Across
1 To spring into the air (1-syllable verb)
3 Free from harm or risk (1-syllable adjective)
5 Any subterranean plant part (1-syllable noun)
6 Sudden shaking of the ground (2-syllable noun)
7 The cutting side of a blade (1-syllable noun)
8 To make a sudden, loud cry (1-syllable verb)
9 A device that produces light (1-syllable noun)

Down
1 Decorative objects that people wear (3-syllable noun)
2 Long, thin bread often shaped like a knot (2-syllable noun)
3 German pastry made of thin dough (2-syllable noun)
4 To completely enclose or surround (3-syllable verb)

25 | DIFFICULTY: ●●○○○○○○○○
COMPLETION: ☐ TIME: ______

SYNONYM UNSCRAMBLE

Unscramble the letters below to form pairs of SYNONYMS. Watch out—some words can be unscrambled more than one way!

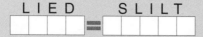

L I E D = S L I L T

T R A Y D = T A E L

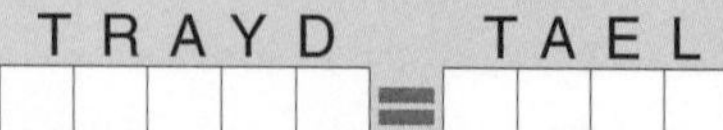

L E T L = V E E R L A

A B D = K I D W E C

V I L D E U G = F R I M O N

C R O E U S = I G R I N O

C E I T D = E R E D E C

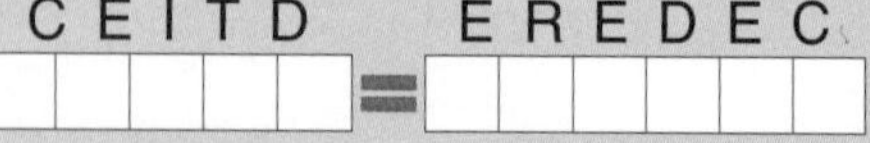

26 | DIFFICULTY: ●○○○○○○○○○○
COMPLETION: ☐ TIME: ______

WORD WINDER

Use the clue to help you find the answers word-winding their way through the grid. Each answer will connect the top of the grid to the bottom.

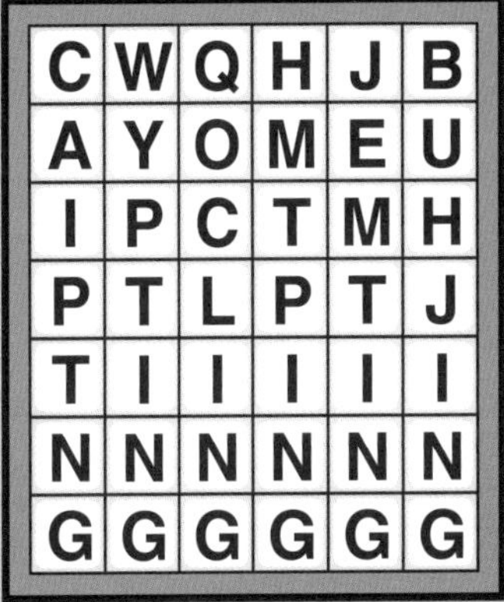

C	W	Q	H	J	B
A	Y	O	M	E	U
I	P	C	T	M	H
P	T	L	P	T	J
T	I	I	I	I	I
N	N	N	N	N	N
G	G	G	G	G	G

Find at least five verbs ending in "ING" word-winding their way from top to bottom.

27 | DIFFICULTY: ●○○○○○○○○○
COMPLETION: ☐ TIME: ______

DEFINITION FINDER

Using the clues below, find and circle the words concealed in the letter grid.

E E A R L Y Z W D
L H J S T E A K I
C A C O B R A Z P
Y M X U S U A L L
C M B I T T E R O
I E Q A W A R D M
N R S E A R C H A
U X V S C H O O L

- ○ To give (a reward or prize) to someone *(verb)*
- ○ Before the usual or expected time *(adverb)*
- ○ Accordant with usage, custom, or habit *(adjective)*
- ○ A very poisonous snake found in Asia and Africa *(noun)*
- ○ A thick, flat piece of meat and especially beef *(noun)*
- ○ Having a flavor that is the opposite of sweet *(adjective)*
- ○ To hit something in a very forceful way *(verb)*
- ○ An organization that provides instruction *(noun)*
- ○ A document bearing record of graduation *(noun)*
- ○ To carefully look for someone or something *(verb)*
- ○ A vehicle that has a single wheel *(noun)*

28 | DIFFICULTY: ●○○○○○○○○○
COMPLETION: ☐ TIME: ______

SYNONYM FINDER

Find and circle the six pairs of SYNONYMS, one on each side, in the letter grids below.

A	N	I	C	E	F
C	B	N	D	T	N
B	P	H	S	G	I
T	H	A	O	B	A
X	O	D	O	R	L
B	C	A	S	T	P

=

E	G	S	G	R	B
N	D	M	A	J	F
I	K	E	R	M	E
F	L	L	B	T	W
C	F	L	A	C	G
N	T	H	R	O	W

○○○○○○

29 | DIFFICULTY: ●○○○○○○○○○
COMPLETION: ☐ TIME: ______

ANTONYM FINDER

Find and circle the six pairs of ANTONYMS, one on each side, in the letter grids below.

Q	R	E	N	D	F
A	D	S	L	M	L
K	C	E	O	I	H
R	I	U	A	F	J
Y	G	F	T	C	T
T	A	L	L	E	B

L	J	D	G	B	T
L	S	H	E	R	G
U	C	T	O	N	N
D	K	H	I	I	Y
F	S	W	O	F	N
B	J	J	P	D	F

○○○○○○

30 | DIFFICULTY: ●○○○○○○○○○○
COMPLETION: ☐ TIME: ______

DICTIONARY WORD WINDER

Use the clues below to help you find the answers word-winding their way through the grid. Each answer will connect one side of the grid to the other—left to right, top to bottom, right to left, and bottom to top.

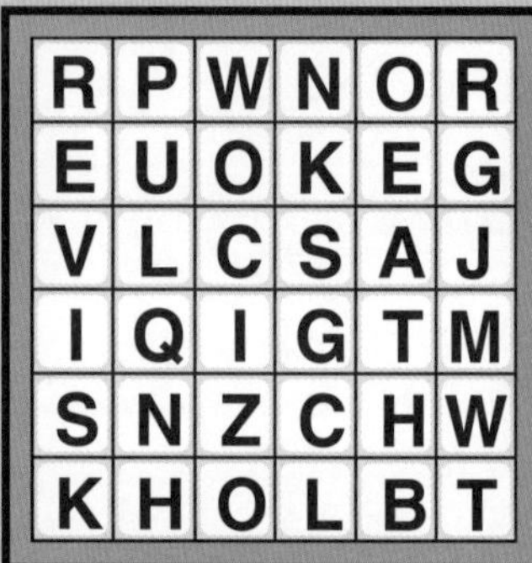

R	P	W	N	O	R
E	U	O	K	E	G
V	L	C	S	A	J
I	Q	I	G	T	M
S	N	Z	C	H	W
K	H	O	L	B	T

→ A soldier in the past who had a high social rank and who fought while riding a horse and usually wearing armor ______

↓ To make (something) smooth and shiny by rubbing it ______

← To save (someone or something) from danger or harm ______

↑ A flat shape that has eight sides and eight angles ______

31 | DIFFICULTY: ●○○○○○○○○○ COMPLETION: ☐ TIME: ______

ANTONYM UNSCRAMBLE

Unscramble the letters below to form pairs of ANTONYMS. Note: Some words can be unscrambled more than one way!

E V O L ≠ T L A H O E

C L M A ≠ T H C C I E

S R E I ≠ N L E E I D C

Z Y A L ≠ V I L L Y E

L E L W ≠ L I L

A A C L U S ≠ R A F L O M

D L O ≠ G O N Y U

32 | DIFFICULTY: ● ○ ○ ○ ○ ○ ○ ○ ○ ○ ○
COMPLETION: ☐ TIME: ______

MAKE THE CONNECTION

Fill in the boxes with common two-word phrases with the help of the clues below. The last word in each pair will be the first word in the following pair.

1 A hole-in-one, for example
2 Basketball timepiece
3 Show up for work
4 Enamored
5 Bit of fat at the waistline
6 Package warning: "____ ____ care"
7 Coffee option
8 Container for sweetener

33 | DIFFICULTY: ●○○○○○○○○○
COMPLETION: ☐ TIME: ________

CROSS'D WORDS UNSCRAMBLE

Unscramble the letters in each clue to fill in the puzzle grid below.

ACROSS

1 CUSBR *(one-syllable word)*
3 OCNBA *(two-syllable word)*
5 SEEMOWA *(two-syllable word)*
7 KNHCU *(one-syllable word)*
8 UYDMD *(two-syllable word)*
9 COITP *(two-syllable word)*
11 ARCLO *(two-syllable word)*
13 SOLLYCE *(two-syllable word)*
14 ONNLY *(two-syllable word)*
15 YSYLH *(two-syllable word)*

DOWN

1 OINCS *(two-syllable word)*
2 RAKBE *(one-syllable word)*
3 OMLBO *(one-syllable word)*
4 ELYNW *(two-syllable word)*
5 TQIACAU *(three-syllable word)*
6 REEDYLL *(three-syllable word)*
9 INOON *(two-syllable word)*
10 LWONC *(one-syllable word)*
11 SHSCE *(one-syllable word)*
12 YANLK *(two-syllable word)*

34 | DIFFICULTY: ●●○○○○○○○○
COMPLETION: ☐ TIME: ______

SYNONYM FINDER

Find and circle the seven pairs of SYNONYMS divided between the letter grids below.

P	P	R	U	S	T	I	C
P	R	K	E	T	C	M	N
D	O	E	E	M	L	H	D
N	C	I	S	L	O	L	P
G	U	O	A	E	E	T	F
Q	R	C	B	I	R	J	E
W	E	V	H	Z	F	V	C
R	L	S	W	D	W	Y	E

=

K	B	P	N	G	L	C	N
N	A	Q	L	A	D	I	R
I	F	C	R	A	A	K	N
H	M	U	Q	T	C	E	J
T	R	A	N	U	I	I	G
E	C	I	P	L	I	A	D
B	A	L	A	H	B	R	T
M	D	E	F	E	N	D	E

○○○○○○○

35 | DIFFICULTY: ●●○○○○○○○○
COMPLETION: ☐ TIME: ________

MISSING DEFINITIONS FINDER

Using the clues below, find and circle the words concealed in the letter grid.

T	A	S	T	E	A	S	I	L	Y
X	T	H	I	N	K	Q	Z	A	V
W	Z	G	R	E	A	T	E	R	X
T	E	C	H	N	O	L	O	G	Y
R	A	I	N	B	I	T	T	E	R
I	Z	D	E	C	I	S	I	O	N
A	J	V	H	E	A	R	D	K	B
L	A	N	G	U	A	G	E	Z	W

ac·rid *adjective* \ˈa-krəd\
________ and unpleasant in ________ or smell

clar·i·ty *noun* \ˈkler-ə-tē, ˈkla-rə-\
the quality of being ________ seen or ________

del·uge *noun* \ˈdel-ˌyüj, -ˌyüzh; ÷də-ˈlüj, ˈdā-ˌlüj\
a ________ amount of ________ that suddenly falls in an area

ex·ag·ger·ate *verb* \ig-ˈza-jə-ˌrāt\
to ________ of or describe something as larger or ________ than it really is

prim·i·tive *adjective* \ˈpri-mə-tiv\
not having a written ________, advanced ________, etc.

ver·dict *noun* \ˈvər-(ˌ)dikt\
law : the ________ made by a jury in a ________

36 | DIFFICULTY: ●○○○○○○○○○ COMPLETION: ☐ TIME: ______

SYNONYM FINDER

Find and circle the six pairs of SYNONYMS, one on each side, in the letter grids below.

G	L	U	M	E	T
C	E	A	S	E	L
Y	J	U	P	W	A
I	B	E	A	T	E
A	L	D	P	M	H
C	P	L	Z	G	B

=

D	S	I	C	K	S
P	A	F	K	Y	T
O	C	M	D	N	R
T	H	O	A	D	I
S	O	M	G	G	K
M	C	U	R	E	E

○○○○○○

37 | DIFFICULTY: ●○○○○○○○○○ COMPLETION: ☐ TIME: ______

MIXED-UP DEFINITION

Unscramble the letters below to reveal the definition of the given word.

hos·pi·ta·ble *adjective* \hä-ˈspi-tə-bəl, ˈhäs-(ˌ)pi-\
rnoeesgu dan nilfeydr ot ussgte ro riiossvt

☐☐☐☐☐☐☐☐

☐☐☐

☐☐☐☐☐☐☐☐

☐☐ ☐☐☐☐☐☐

☐☐ ☐☐☐☐☐☐☐☐

38 | DIFFICULTY: ●○○○○○○○○○
COMPLETION: ☐ TIME: ______

WORD WINDER

Use the clue to help you find the answers word-winding their way through the grid. Each answer will connect the top of the grid to the bottom.

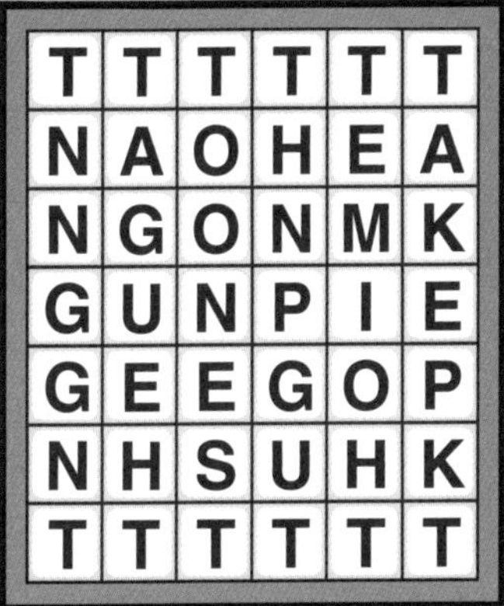

T	T	T	T	T	T
N	A	O	H	E	A
N	G	O	N	M	K
G	U	N	P	I	E
G	E	E	G	O	P
N	H	S	U	H	K
T	T	T	T	T	T

Find five words starting and ending with "T" word-winding their way from top to bottom.

______

______

______

______

______

39 | DIFFICULTY: ●●○○○○○○○○
COMPLETION: ☐ TIME: ________

DICTIONARY UNSCRAMBLE

Unscramble the letters below to form words that match the Merriam-Webster definitions.

adjective
Feeling or expressing great joy

AJIULTBN= ☐☐☐☐☐☐☐☐

pronoun
A person who is not known, named, or specified

MOODBEYS= ☐☐☐☐☐☐☐☐

noun
A conversation between two or more people

IGLOUDEA= ☐☐☐☐☐☐☐☐

adjective Feeling or showing strong and energetic support for a person or cause

UZOSALE= ☐☐☐☐☐☐☐

intransitive verb
To move or be shaped like waves

ADLUUNET= ☐☐☐☐☐☐☐☐

noun
A friendly relationship

PROTARP= ☐☐☐☐☐☐☐

40 | DIFFICULTY: ●●○○○○○○○○
COMPLETION: ☐ TIME: ______

SYNONYM UNSCRAMBLE

Unscramble the letters below to form pairs of SYNONYMS. Watch out—some words can be unscrambled more than one way!

T G E = R A Q C I E U

H I T A F = F E E L B I

C R E E B A M = U G H

W E N = D R O N M E

R Y D = D R A I

U V R I P O S E = I R R P O

A R F = N D A T T S I

41 | DIFFICULTY: ●○○○○○○○○○
COMPLETION: ☐ TIME: ______

SYLLABARY

Link word segments together in the grid below to create words, and enter them in the blanks.

NAL	I	LY	RO	NI
I	EAS	TRI	A	MAC
RIG	O	AN	TANT	AP
AN	IM	POR	GLE	PRE
Y	BOD	Y	ATE	CI

Three-Syllable Noun: _ _ _ _ _ G _ _

Four-Syllable Adjective: _ _ _ _ I _ _ _

Four-Syllable Pronoun: _ _ _ B _ _ _

Four-Syllable Verb: _ _ _ _ _ _ _ A _ _

Three-Syllable Adverb: _ A _ _ _ _

Four-Syllable Noun: _ _ C _ _ _ _ _

Three-Syllable Adjective: _ _ _ _ _ _ A _ _

42 | DIFFICULTY: ●●○○○○○○○○
COMPLETION: ☐ TIME: ______

MAKE THE CONNECTION

Fill in the boxes with common two-word phrases with the help of the clues below. The last word in each pair will be the first word in the following pair.

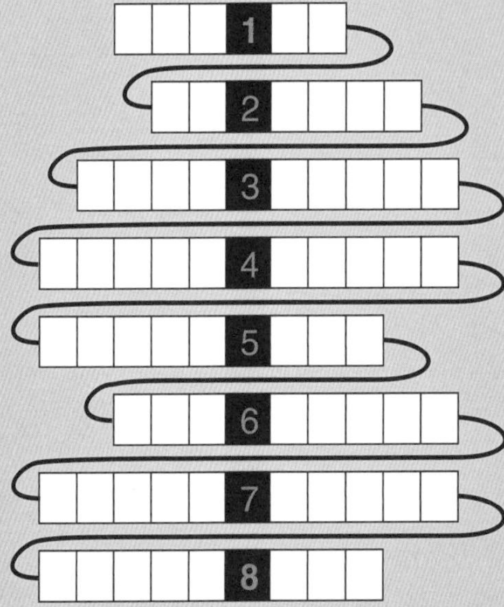

1 Release
2 Head back to your house
3 Location for a catcher and an umpire
4 Window material
5 *Columbo* star Peter Falk had one
6 Hazel or blue, for example
7 Carriers of the flag
8 Canine sentry

43 | DIFFICULTY: ●●○○○○○○○○
COMPLETION: ☐ TIME: ______

PRISM WORD FINDER

Using the color-coded clues below, find and circle the words in the letter grid.

G	W	L	B	L	A	C	K	N	B	D
V	R	J	E	S	N	O	W	Y	R	G
L	Q	A	H	X	F	B	Z	P	E	R
S	A	K	V	J	I	E	G	N	E	E
T	G	W	B	I	U	C	L	F	Z	I
O	N	B	F	L	T	A	A	L	Y	V
R	I	E	B	U	G	Y	E	L	L	A
M	V	I	K	E	L	R	K	E	N	E
Y	R	G	L	W	U	N	B	J	L	H
R	A	E	V	A	I	A	Q	P	H	B
F	C	X	L	P	L	B	R	O	W	N

Find five words that start and end with "L" starting with an orange letter ○○○○○

Find five one-syllable colors starting with a blue letter ○○○○○

Find three seven-letter words with "V" in the middle starting with a purple letter ○○○

Find three weather-related adjectives starting with a red letter ○○○

44 | DIFFICULTY: ●○○○○○○○○○
COMPLETION: ☐ TIME: ______

PRISM CROSS'D WORDS

Use the color-coded clues below to find words that fit in the like-colored portions of the puzzle grid below.

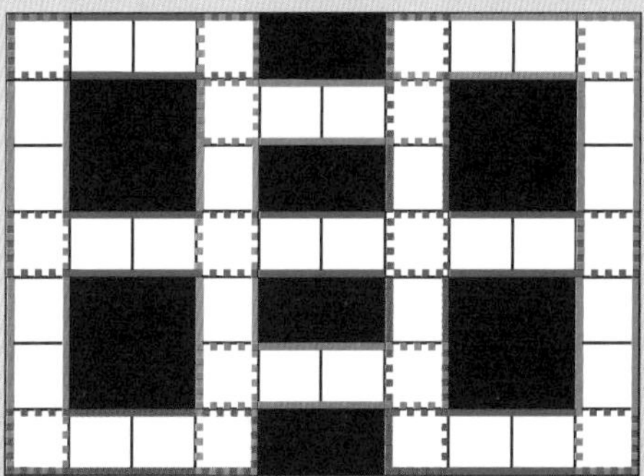

- ○ A small raised area (1-syllable noun)
- ○ A boggy area (1-syllable noun)
- ○ Coin-operated cleaning center (3-syllable noun)

- ○ Having a greasy quality (2-syllable adjective)
- ○ Courtroom officer (2-syllable noun)

- ○ Frozen precipitation (1-syllable noun)
- ○ A ghost (2-syllable noun)

- ○ A word meaning the same thing (3-syllable noun)
- ○ Land for growing crops (1-syllable noun)

- ○ Atmospheric conditions (2-syllable noun)
- ○ Having a divine quality (2-syllable adjective)

45 | DIFFICULTY: ●●○○○○○○○○
COMPLETION: ☐ TIME: ______

DEFINITION FINDER

Using the clues below, find and circle the words concealed in the letter grid.

- ○ A hard covering that protects something *(noun)*
- ○ A large number of things close together *(noun)*
- ○ Before any other in time, order, or importance *(adjective)*
- ○ A usually miniature representation of something *(noun)*
- ○ One of the hard white objects inside the mouth *(noun)*
- ○ Suitable or safe to eat *(adjective)*
- ○ To force (a liquid) into something *(verb)*
- ○ The quality of being physically attractive *(noun)*
- ○ To form by incision (as on wood or metal) *(verb)*
- ○ The bags a person carries when traveling *(noun)*
- ○ A desire to be successful, powerful, or famous *(noun)*

46 | DIFFICULTY: ●○○○○○○○○○ COMPLETION: ☐ TIME: ______

ANTONYM FINDER

Find and circle the six pairs of ANTONYMS, one on each side, in the letter grids below.

Q	H	I	G	H	N
L	C	R	H	C	N
M	D	O	U	B	T
V	O	F	A	I	R
J	H	V	P	X	K
L	I	V	E	M	C

X	B	U	L	L	Y
H	A	L	T	H	D
M	D	K	T	L	F
R	A	I	N	Y	W
Q	A	Z	E	O	H
F	G	M	L	R	J

○○○○○○

47 | DIFFICULTY: ●○○○○○○○○○ COMPLETION: ☐ TIME: ______

SYNONYM FINDER

Find and circle the six pairs of SYNONYMS, one on each side, in the letter grids below.

H	F	C	M	P	L
P	P	A	G	T	O
A	T	A	S	D	O
R	G	U	N	T	C
T	O	E	P	T	R
N	M	L	D	F	G

H	O	D	G	T	T
C	P	L	C	D	E
Z	A	I	D	R	E
F	V	L	A	N	L
E	R	N	M	C	F
C	S	G	A	S	P

○○○○○○

48 | DIFFICULTY: ●●○○○○○○○○ COMPLETION: ☐ TIME: ______

DICTIONARY WORD WINDER

Use the clues below to help you find the answers word-winding their way through the grid. Each answer will connect one side of the grid to the other—left to right, top to bottom, right to left, and bottom to top.

C	E	A	N	E	T
W	D	V	K	V	B
T	M	C	O	G	R
I	I	Q	O	Y	L
N	R	H	P	R	H
V	E	E	G	J	X

→ A piece of paper that allows you to see a show, participate in an event, travel on a vehicle, etc. ______

↓ To feel respect or approval for (someone or something) ______

← A punctuation mark that is used to connect words or parts of words ______

↑ A long, narrow cut or low area in a surface ______

49 | DIFFICULTY: ● ○ ○ ○ ○ ○ ○ ○ ○ ○
COMPLETION: ☐ TIME: ______

CROSS'D WORD CONNECTIONS

The crosswords below share common letters as indicated by the colored boxes. Use the clues to solve the puzzles.

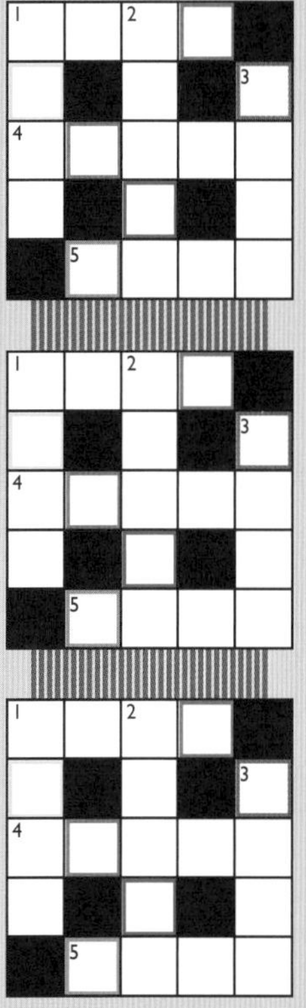

ACROSS
1 A small storage building
4 An idea or set of beliefs that guides the actions of a person or group
5 A tiny particle

DOWN
1 Not well
2 A planned occasion or activity
3 To make a deep and loud sound

ACROSS
1 To discover (something or someone)
4 A suspension of fighting
5 Poses a question

DOWN
1 Is the right size and shape for
2 People, places, or things
3 Makes an impassioned plea

ACROSS
1 Expressed in words
4 To complain about something
5 Gets older

DOWN
1 A posted command, warning, or direction
2 Creamy cake topping
3 Makes a wager

50 | DIFFICULTY: ●●○○○○○○○○
COMPLETION: ☐ TIME: _______

ANTONYM FINDER

Find and circle the seven pairs of ANTONYMS divided between the letter grids below.

T	H	X	P	F	J	K	D
N	O	C	Q	H	D	E	C
A	M	Z	J	L	E	I	K
L	E	J	E	C	O	J	I
I	L	I	C	R	M	G	N
G	Y	U	E	Z	X	W	D
I	S	H	J	K	D	Q	L
V	S	T	I	N	G	Y	E

L	W	T	I	M	I	D	H
A	Q	S	T	K	W	R	E
R	R	U	I	G	L	Z	E
E	E	A	E	B	P	D	D
B	S	V	F	N	M	N	L
I	I	E	R	Z	C	Q	E
L	S	Y	O	D	X	H	S
M	T	N	F	H	J	V	S

○○○○○○○

51 | DIFFICULTY: ●●○○○○○○○○ COMPLETION: ☐ TIME: ______

WORD WINDER

Use the clue to help you find the answers word-winding their way through the grid. Each answer will connect the top of the grid to the bottom.

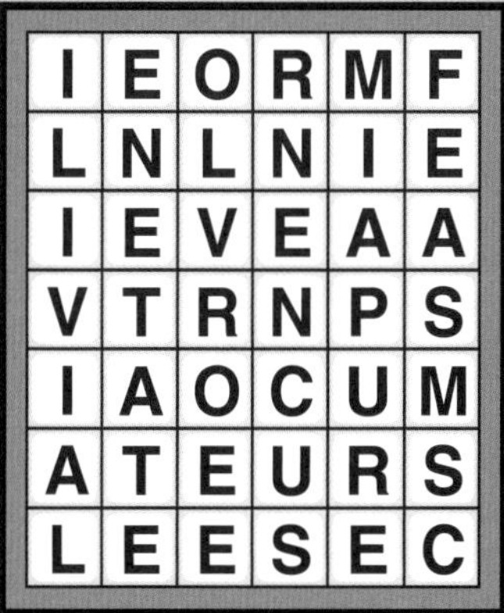

Find five words containing four vowels word-winding their way from top to bottom.

______

______

______

______

______

52 | DIFFICULTY: ●●○○○○○○○○
COMPLETION: ☐ TIME: ______

ANTONYM UNSCRAMBLE

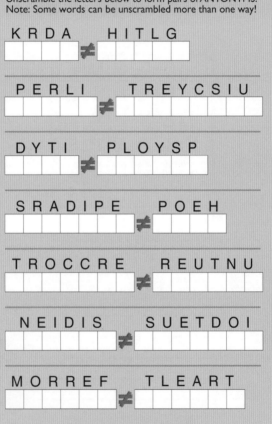

Unscramble the letters below to form pairs of ANTONYMS. Note: Some words can be unscrambled more than one way!

K R D A ≠ H I T L G

P E R L I ≠ T R E Y C S I U

D Y T I ≠ P L O Y S P

S R A D I P E ≠ P O E H

T R O C C R E ≠ R E U T N U

N E I D I S ≠ S U E T D O I

M O R R E F ≠ T L E A R T

53 | DIFFICULTY: ●●○○○○○○○○
COMPLETION: ☐ TIME: ______

DICTIONARY UNSCRAMBLE

Unscramble the letters below to form words that match the Merriam-Webster definitions.

noun
An empty space in which there is no air or other gas

UCAMVU= ☐☐☐☐☐☐

adjective
Known or recognized by very many people

SAMUFO= ☐☐☐☐☐☐

adverb
Marked by intensity or volume of sound

DULLOY= ☐☐☐☐☐☐

adjective
Of or relating to the present time

DRONEM= ☐☐☐☐☐☐

transitive verb To cause to move with quick little jerks or oscillating motions

GIGJEL= ☐☐☐☐☐☐

adverb
Very nearly but not exactly or entirely

SLATMO= ☐☐☐☐☐☐

54 | DIFFICULTY: ●●○○○○○○○○ COMPLETION: ☐ TIME: ______

ANTONYM FINDER

Find and circle the six pairs of ANTONYMS, one on each side, in the letter grids below.

D	F	U	L	L	P
M	X	C	H	F	G
L	M	E	R	I	T
F	O	A	Q	N	R
B	E	U	P	D	A
N	L	N	D	J	P

D	W	L	M	H	R
W	Q	J	O	A	Y
H	P	U	F	S	L
O	X	V	I	C	E
L	K	F	Z	E	G
E	M	P	T	Y	T

○○○○○○

55 | DIFFICULTY: ●●●○○○○○○○ COMPLETION: ☐ TIME: ______

MIXED-UP DEFINITION

Unscramble the letters below to reveal the definition of the given word.

ca·pri·cious *adjective* \kə-ˈpri-shəs, -ˈprē-\
efnot higgcnna dludysne ni omdo ro veibarho

☐☐☐☐☐

☐☐☐☐☐☐☐☐

☐☐☐☐☐☐☐☐

☐☐ ☐☐☐☐

☐☐ ☐☐☐☐☐☐☐☐

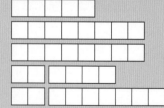

56 | DIFFICULTY: ●●●○○○○○○○
COMPLETION: ☐ TIME: ______

SYNONYM UNSCRAMBLE

Unscramble the letters below to form pairs of SYNONYMS. Watch out—some words can be unscrambled more than one way!

I D H E = N A C C O L E

C L E E T = K P C I

S Q T U E = K T E R

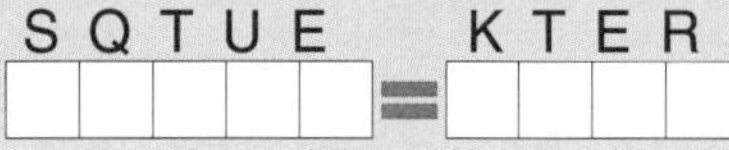

A Y E S = S P E L M I

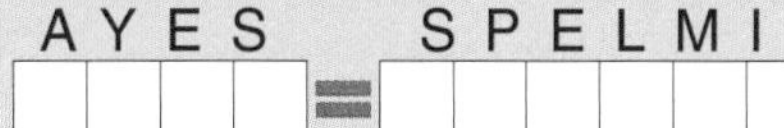

E R A E G = S C E T O N N

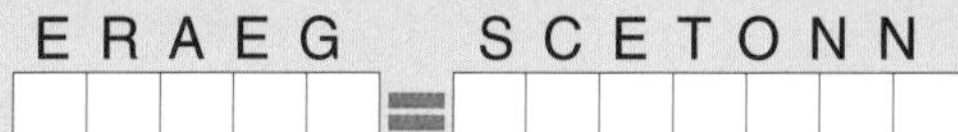

M A E S = C L E N I T I A D

T A C = F R E O P M R

57 | DIFFICULTY: ●●●○○○○○○○
COMPLETION: ☐ TIME: ________

MISSING DEFINITIONS FINDER

Using the clues below, find and circle the words concealed in the letter grid.

D	E	Z	D	G	R	O	U	P	H
E	R	P	I	N	X	J	N	T	A
G	U	R	S	I	G	S	O	H	P
N	T	E	A	V	R	L	I	G	P
A	U	V	G	A	E	O	N	I	E
R	F	E	R	E	A	W	I	M	N
R	X	N	E	L	T	J	P	Z	E
A	T	T	E	N	T	I	O	N	D

chro·no·log·i·cal *adjective* \ˌkrä-nə-ˈlä-ji-kəl, ˌkrō-\
________ in the order that things ________ or came to be

con·spic·u·ous *adjective* \kən-ˈspi-kyə-wəs, -kyü-əs\
attracting ________ by being ________ or impressive

dis·sent *intransitive verb* \di-ˈsent\
to publicly ________ with an official ________

ex·clude *transitive verb* \iks-ˈklüd\
to ________ (someone) from doing something or being a part of a ________

lin·ger *verb* \ˈliŋ-gər\
to be ________ in ________ or in quitting something

pre·dict *verb* \pri-ˈdikt\
to say that (something) will or ________ happen in the ________

58 | DIFFICULTY: ●●○○○○○○○○
COMPLETION: ☐ TIME: ______

PRISM CROSS'D WORDS

Use the color-coded clues below to find words that fit in the like-colored portions of the puzzle grid below.

- Done or happening late (2-syllable adjective)
- Too intense or powerful (1-syllable adjective)
- Patronizing or superior (4-syllable adjective)

- The business of buying and selling (1-syllable noun)
- A short-handled ax (2-syllable noun)

- Quality of being fair and truthful (3-syllable noun)
- An object that looks like a coin (2-syllable noun)

- Foolish from drinking (2-syllable adjective)
- A thing of little value (2-syllable noun)

- To command to go or come (2-syllable verb)
- Behaving badly (2-syllable adjective)

59 | DIFFICULTY: ●●●○○○○○○○
COMPLETION: ☐ TIME: ______

WORD WINDER

Use the clue to help you find the answers word-winding their way through the grid. Each answer will connect the top of the grid to the bottom.

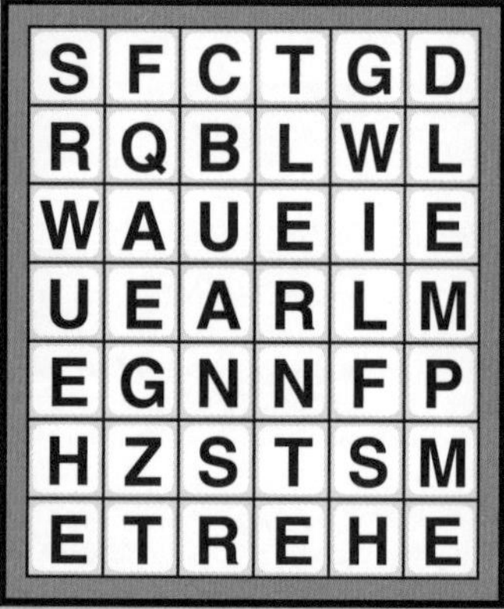

Find five one-syllable words word-winding their way from top to bottom.

60

DIFFICULTY: ●●○○○○○○○○
COMPLETION: ☐ TIME: ________

CROSS'D WORDS UNSCRAMBLE

Unscramble the letters in each clue to fill in the puzzle grid below.

ACROSS

1 ARGWE *(two-syllable word)*
3 VHESA *(one-syllable word)*
5 NECQORU *(two-syllable word)*
7 AHRET *(one-syllable word)*
8 KPYIC *(two-syllable word)*
9 MICCO *(two-syllable word)*
11 OBOKR *(one-syllable word)*
13 HECCNIK *(two-syllable word)*
14 FLUBF *(one-syllable word)*
15 AIRLV *(two-syllable word)*

DOWN

1 SHEWO *(one-syllable word)*
2 CRAHN *(one-syllable word)*
3 TUPSM *(one-syllable word)*
4 PYMET *(two-syllable word)*
5 ICCREAM *(three-syllable word)*
6 CROACNO *(two-syllable word)*
9 MICBL *(one-syllable word)*
10 FICEH *(one-syllable word)*
11 KRABE *(two-syllable word)*
12 ENKLE *(one-syllable word)*

61 | DIFFICULTY: ●●○○○○○○○○
COMPLETION: ☐ TIME: ______

MAKE THE CONNECTION

Fill in the boxes with common two-word phrases with the help of the clues below. The last word in each pair will be the first word in the following pair.

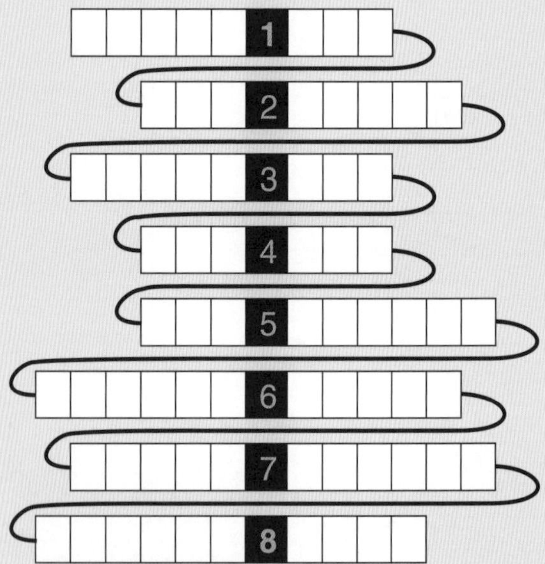

1 Most important, principally
2 "It's safe now" signal
3 It's sunny and bright
4 Profession
5 Reason to read the want ads
6 Group looking for a missing person
7 Overly social person
8 Political satire by George Orwell

62 | DIFFICULTY: ●●○○○○○○○○
COMPLETION: ☐ TIME: ______

SYLLABARY

Link word segments together in the grid below to create words, and enter them in the blanks.

A	OR	GAN	TER	DAY
MUS	ING	IZE	YES	ER
VI	SION	CAU	LI	FLOW
E	GEN	ER	SI	BLE
TEL	IM	POS	AL	LY

Four-Syllable Adjective: _ _ P _ _ _ _ _ _ _

Three-Syllable Adjective: _ _ _ S _ _ _

Four-Syllable Noun: _ _ _ L _ _ _ _ _ _ _

Four-Syllable Adverb: _ _ N _ _ _ _ _ _

Four-Syllable Noun: _ _ _ _ V _ _ _ _ _

Three-Syllable Verb: _ _ _ _ _ _ Z _

Three-Syllable Noun: _ _ S _ _ _ _ _ _

63 | DIFFICULTY: ●●○○○○○○○○
COMPLETION: ☐ TIME: ______

DICTIONARY WORD WINDER

Use the clues below to help you find the answers word-winding their way through the grid. Each answer will connect one side of the grid to the other—left to right, top to bottom, right to left, and bottom to top.

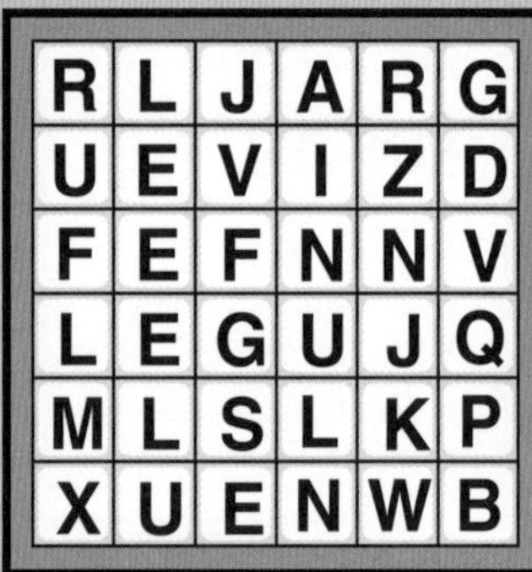

R	L	J	A	R	G
U	E	V	I	Z	D
F	E	F	N	N	V
L	E	G	U	J	Q
M	L	S	L	K	P
X	U	E	N	W	B

→ To return (money) in restitution, repayment, or balancing of accounts ______

↓ A short song that is easy to remember and that is used to help sell a product on television or radio ______

← Loose rounded fragments of rock ______

↑ Helping to do or achieve something ______

64 | DIFFICULTY: ●●○○○○○○○○
COMPLETION: ☐ TIME: ________

ANTONYM FINDER

Find and circle the six pairs of ANTONYMS, one on each side, in the letter grids below.

R	Q	M	B	H	S
O	X	U	J	P	H
O	J	D	I	A	O
P	Z	D	X	E	R
C	K	Y	D	R	T
T	A	M	E	N	H

≠

N	O	I	S	Y	R
W	C	N	X	A	W
X	I	L	E	W	O
H	J	L	O	Q	S
Z	C	F	D	N	Z
R	I	C	H	K	G

○○○○○○

65 | DIFFICULTY: ●●○○○○○○○○
COMPLETION: ☐ TIME: ________

MIXED-UP DEFINITION

Unscramble the letters below to reveal the definition of the given word.

fur·tive *adjective* \ˈfər-tiv\
node ni a eutqi nda treecs awy ot iadvo negbi tniedoc

☐☐☐☐ ☐☐ ☐ ☐☐☐☐☐
☐☐☐ ☐☐☐☐☐☐
☐☐☐ ☐☐ ☐☐☐☐☐
☐☐☐☐☐
☐☐☐☐☐☐☐

66 | DIFFICULTY: ●●○○○○○○○○
COMPLETION: ☐ TIME: ______

DICTIONARY CROSS'D WORDS

Fill in the puzzle using the Merriam-Webster definition clues below.

Across

1 To burn slightly or partly (1-syllable verb)

3 To bite on repeatedly with the teeth (1-syllable verb)

5 Sound that is a copy of another sound (2-syllable noun)

6 To meet at a particular time and place (3-syllable verb)

7 Expanse of grass that is kept mowed (1-syllable noun)

8 Obscured or made dim or cloudy (2-syllable adjective)

9 Trained to obey people (1-syllable adjective)

Down

1 To feel or show great love for (2-syllable verb)

2 Quickly and easily (3-syllable adverb)

3 An establishment of nuns (2-syllable noun)

4 To make a shrill clear sound (2-syllable verb)

67 | DIFFICULTY: ●●○○○○○○○○
COMPLETION: ☐ TIME: ______

DEFINITION FINDER

Using the clues below, find and circle the words concealed in the letter grid.

R	E	L	A	X	G	J	Q	W
J	T	D	A	I	R	Y	K	D
N	I	S	O	L	A	T	E	N
O	U	X	B	X	F	C	N	A
R	R	Z	M	J	F	E	N	L
M	F	Q	U	Z	I	J	E	S
A	X	V	J	K	T	B	L	I
L	E	G	A	L	I	O	X	Q

- ○ The part of a plant that has the seeds in it *(noun)*
- ○ Allowed by the law or by the rules in a game *(adjective)*
- ○ To relieve from nervous tension *(verb)*
- ○ A farm that produces milk *(noun)*
- ○ A tract of land surrounded by water *(noun)*
- ○ Usual or ordinary : not strange *(adjective)*
- ○ To set apart from others *(verb)*
- ○ Unauthorized writing or drawing on a surface *(noun)*
- ○ Very large for its kind *(adjective)*
- ○ A shelter for a dog or cat *(noun)*
- ○ To disagree with something or oppose something *(verb)*

68 | DIFFICULTY: ●●●●●●●●●●●
COMPLETION: ☐ TIME: ______

DICTIONARY CROSS'D WORDS

Fill in the puzzle using the Merriam-Webster definition clues below.

Across

1 A very small piece of food (1-syllable noun)
3 To hold tightly with your hands (1-syllable verb)
5 To regard with extreme repugnance (2-syllable verb)
6 To get a wrong idea of or about (4-syllable verb)
7 More than is reasonable (2-syllable adjective)
8 To have or end with the same sounds (1-syllable verb)
9 Rough or noisy (2-syllable adjective)

Down

1 A small space inside something (2-syllable noun)
2 Characterized by flamboyance (2-syllable adjective)
3 A plant that grows along the ground (2-syllable noun)
4 A highly talented child or youth (3-syllable noun)

69 | DIFFICULTY: ●●●○○○○○○○
COMPLETION: ☐ TIME: ______

PRISM CROSS'D WORDS

Use the color-coded clues below to find words that fit in the like-colored portions of the puzzle grid below.

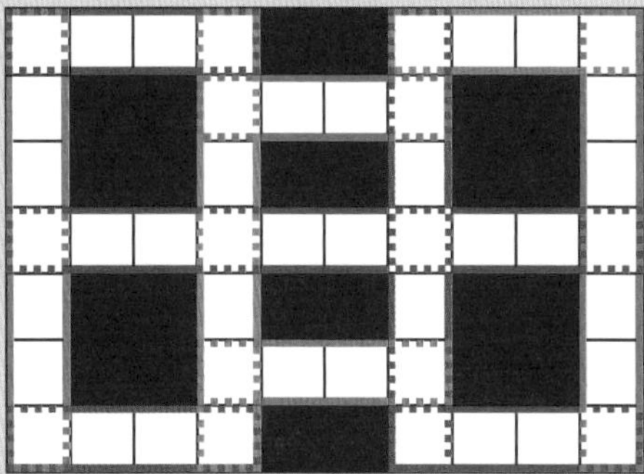

- A long narrow mark (1-syllable noun)
- Having a lot of money (1-syllable adjective)
- Helpful and friendly (3-syllable adjective)

- A multicolored array (2-syllable noun)
- Determine relative rank (1-syllable verb)

- Looking thin and sleepless (2-syllable adjective)
- Tool for making hair neat (1-syllable noun)

- Movement of air (1-syllable noun)
- High-ranking military officer (2-syllable noun)

- Two-wheeled vehicle (3-syllable noun)
- Singing voice lower than soprano (2-syllable noun)

70 | DIFFICULTY: ●●○○○○○○○○ COMPLETION: ☐ TIME: ______

SYNONYM UNSCRAMBLE

Unscramble the letters below to form pairs of SYNONYMS. Watch out—some words can be unscrambled more than one way!

L O G A = I M A

I S N Y H = T G R I B H

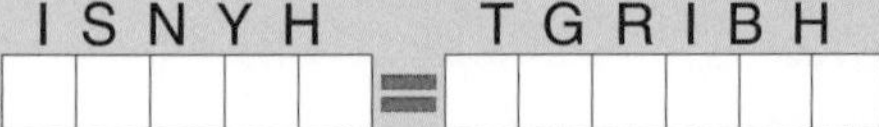

D R E W N A = A M O R

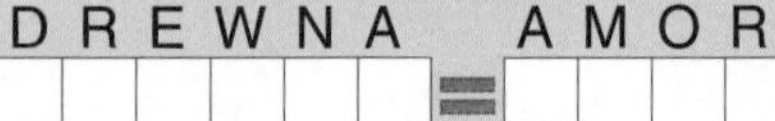

W A L F = U T L F A

B E A D I = L O O W L F

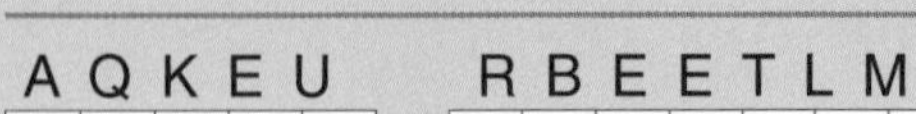

A Q K E U = R B E E T L M

S L E F A = T E N U U R

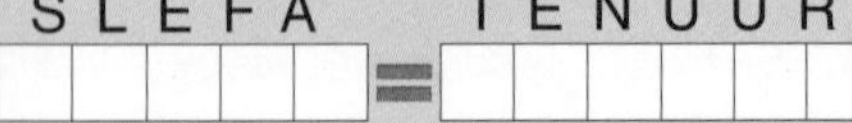

71 | DIFFICULTY: ●●●○○○○○○○ COMPLETION: ☐ TIME: ______

ANTONYM FINDER

Find and circle the six pairs of ANTONYMS, one on each side, in the letter grids below.

T	R	Z	V	J	L
S	O	F	C	U	H
E	L	K	O	T	C
B	A	F	F	L	E
G	V	S	I	C	K
K	E	N	T	R	Y

≠

T	F	E	X	I	T
S	T	R	O	N	G
R	B	A	A	N	D
O	H	E	A	C	F
W	L	F	P	I	Q
C	G	T	R	M	D

○○○○○○

72 | DIFFICULTY: ●●●○○○○○○○ COMPLETION: ☐ TIME: ______

MIXED-UP DEFINITION

Unscramble the letters below to reveal the definition of the given word.

du·bi·ous *adjective* \ˈdü-bē-əs\

taunlibqeeos ro tesscup sa ot rute trunea ro taiqylu

73 | DIFFICULTY: ●●●○○○○○○○ COMPLETION: ☐ TIME: ______

DICTIONARY UNSCRAMBLE

Unscramble the letters below to form words that match the Merriam-Webster definitions.

adjective
Being without content or occupant

TACAVN= ☐☐☐☐☐☐

noun
A very hard usually colorless stone

MIDDANO= ☐☐☐☐☐☐☐

adverb
At an earlier time

OBREEF= ☐☐☐☐☐☐

noun
A food that is made when bacteria is added to milk

GROYTU= ☐☐☐☐☐☐

adjective
Small from one side to the other side

WONRAR= ☐☐☐☐☐☐

intransitive verb To lose clear vision especially from looking at bright light

ZLAZED= ☐☐☐☐☐☐

74 | DIFFICULTY: ●●○○○○○○○○
COMPLETION: ☐ TIME: ______

PRISM WORD FINDER

Using the color-coded clues below, find and circle the words in the letter grid.

C	O	N	J	U	N	C	T	I	O	N
J	T	I	G	H	T	W	E	M	L	S
C	S	P	S	H	X	V	N	L	R	U
A	R	O	Q	O	L	B	U	Z	M	O
K	P	V	F	O	O	L	H	B	Q	I
P	K	P	V	T	D	T	R	R	T	C
N	A	E	E	I	E	E	H	N	E	A
U	R	C	V	A	V	N	U	E	V	V
O	H	I	I	D	S	A	C	J	L	I
N	V	T	A	F	T	E	M	K	A	V
T	A	I	N	T	Y	S	A	V	V	Y

Find five antonyms for "excite" starting with an orange letter ○○○○○

Find five words with two "V's" starting with a blue letter ○○○○○

Find three parts of speech starting with a purple letter ○○○

Find three five-letter words that start and end with "T" starting with a red letter ○○○

75 | DIFFICULTY: ●●○○○○○○○○
COMPLETION: ☐ TIME: ______

WORD WINDER

Use the clue to help you find the answers word-winding their way through the grid. Each answer will connect the top of the grid to the bottom.

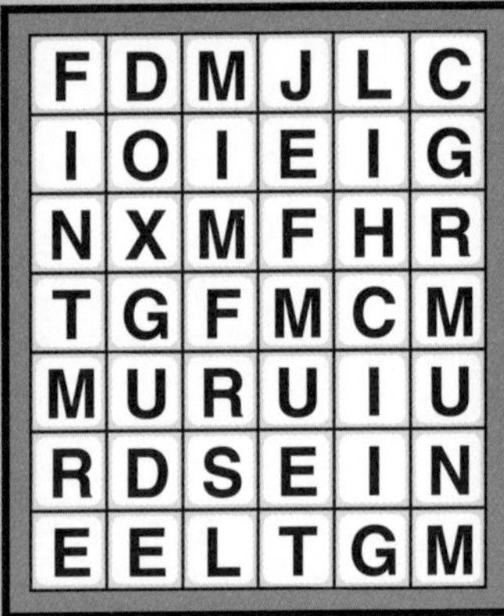

F	D	M	J	L	C
I	O	I	E	I	G
N	X	M	F	H	R
T	G	F	M	C	M
M	U	R	U	I	U
R	D	S	E	I	N
E	E	L	T	G	M

Find five two-syllable words word-winding their way from top to bottom.

76 | DIFFICULTY: ●●○○○○○○○○ COMPLETION: ☐ TIME: ______

MAKE THE CONNECTION

Fill in the boxes with common two-word phrases with the help of the clues below. The last word in each pair will be the first word in the following pair.

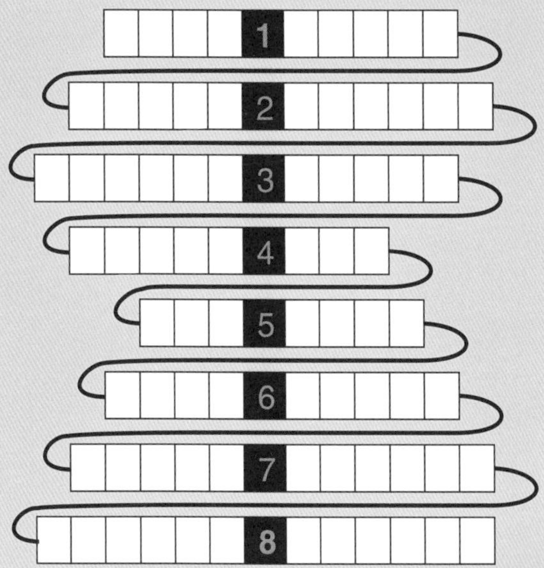

1 Follow
2 When to have dessert
3 Where to eat supper
4 Furniture support
5 Femur, for one
6 Type of porcelain
7 Mongolia has one
8 Breed of canine

77 | DIFFICULTY: ●●●○○○○○○○
COMPLETION: ☐ TIME: ______

SYNONYM FINDER

Find and circle the seven pairs of SYNONYMS divided between the letter grids below.

W	X	T	Q	F	C	L	Y
Y	S	J	A	K	P	R	B
P	P	K	W	W	A	M	E
P	A	R	E	L	D	S	F
A	R	J	A	P	I	R	M
H	K	S	T	V	T	N	Y
N	L	B	E	H	D	I	Z
U	E	R	I	G	H	T	C

=

○ ○ ○ ○ ○ ○ ○

78 | DIFFICULTY: ●●●○○○○○○○
COMPLETION: ☐ TIME: ______

ANTONYM UNSCRAMBLE

Unscramble the letters below to form pairs of ANTONYMS. Note: Some words can be unscrambled more than one way!

W N E ≠ D U S E

T R H I G ≠ N R G W O

D E R G N A ≠ T A Y F S E

D H I E ≠ L E E R A V

V I G E ≠ K A T E

L T E E N G ≠ S C E O R A

C E E P A ≠ F E R R W A A

79 | DIFFICULTY: ●●○○○○○○○○ COMPLETION: ☐ TIME: ______

SYNONYM FINDER

Find and circle the six pairs of SYNONYMS, one on each side, in the letter grids below.

B	S	N	A	R	E
R	A	H	B	V	T
A	P	N	I	S	P
E	F	T	I	E	C
F	C	O	E	S	M
A	M	K	D	B	H

=

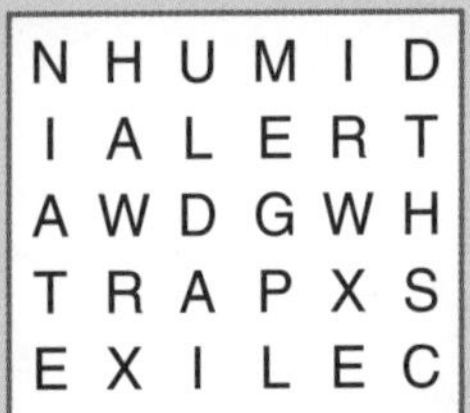

N	H	U	M	I	D
I	A	L	E	R	T
A	W	D	G	W	H
T	R	A	P	X	S
E	X	I	L	E	C
R	D	R	E	A	D

○○○○○○

80 | DIFFICULTY: ●●○○○○○○○○ COMPLETION: ☐ TIME: ______

ANTONYM FINDER

Find and circle the six pairs of ANTONYMS, one on each side, in the letter grids below.

P	H	E	A	T	T
F	R	X	C	S	G
E	Q	O	I	W	I
I	F	O	F	Y	V
R	M	B	N	I	E
G	A	D	M	I	T

A	B	G	S	N	W
Q	R	S	J	Y	F
C	O	I	N	O	E
L	O	E	D	K	Y
Y	D	L	A	Z	M
J	H	T	D	C	T

○○○○○○

81 | DIFFICULTY: ●●○○○○○○○○ COMPLETION: ☐ TIME: ______

CROSS'D WORD CONNECTIONS

The crosswords below share common letters as indicated by the colored boxes. Use the clues to solve the puzzles.

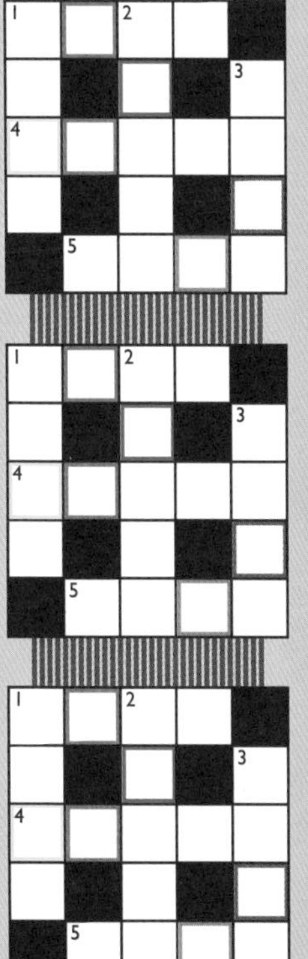

ACROSS
1 Traveled on a horse or bicycle
4 Lacking motion or activity
5 A device for catching animals

DOWN
1 Thorned flower
2 Having less moisture
3 To cause (something) to turn or turn over quickly

ACROSS
1 A large mass of stone
4 To bring to a standstill
5 To strike sharply with the open hand

DOWN
1 Possibility of loss or injury
2 To move on hands and knees
3 A short, crisp sound, as of a radar

ACROSS
1 To treat with contempt or ridicule
4 A male bovine animal
5 Expectorated

DOWN
1 A fine spray
2 To go or seem to go very slowly
3 Unyielding courage in the face of hardship or danger

82 | DIFFICULTY: ●●○○○○○○○○
COMPLETION: ☐ TIME: ______

SYLLABARY

Link word segments together in the grid below to create words, and enter them in the blanks.

AN	BAR	LY	IC	CLAR
UE	I	BAR	LITE	I
TIN	CON	TAR	FY	PO
BEL	E	ER	ENT	TION
VEG	LIG	COM	BI	NA

Four-Syllable Noun ☐☐☐☐☐N☐☐☐☐☐

Three-Syllable Adjective ☐☐☐B☐☐☐☐

Three-Syllable Verb ☐L☐☐☐☐☐

Five-Syllable Noun ☐☐☐☐☐☐☐☐☐N

Four-Syllable Adjective ☐☐☐☐☐G☐☐☐☐☐

Three-Syllable Adverb ☐☐☐☐T☐☐☐

Three-Syllable Verb ☐☐☐☐☐☐U☐

83 | DIFFICULTY: ●●●○○○○○○○ COMPLETION: ☐ TIME: ______

DICTIONARY CROSS'D WORDS

Fill in the puzzle using the Merriam-Webster definition clues below.

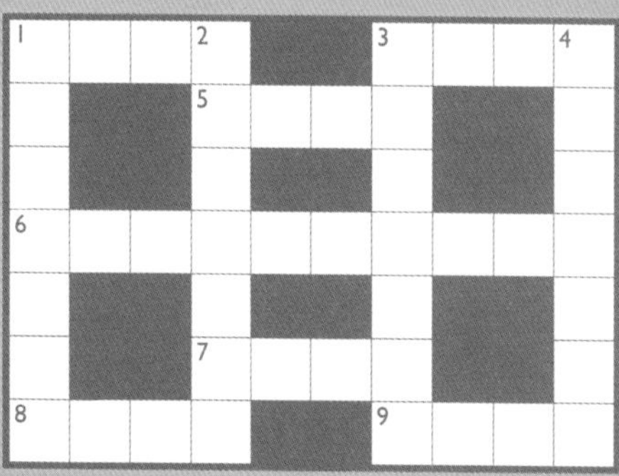

Across
1 Having or showing a gentle nature (1-syllable adjective)
3 To clean with water and usually soap (1-syllable verb)
5 To delineate or impress clearly (1-syllable verb)
6 Suppressing speech or writing (3-syllable noun)
7 Ornamental openwork fabric (1-syllable noun)
8 A nation's ships of war (2-syllable noun)
9 Deep red stone that is used in jewelry (2-syllable noun)

Down
1 Room in which food is cooked (2-syllable noun)
2 Having parts that are close together (2-syllable adverb)
3 To speak very softly or quietly (2-syllable verb)
4 In a very willing way (3-syllable adverb)

84 | DIFFICULTY: ●●○○○○○○○○
COMPLETION: ☐ TIME: ______

DICTIONARY WORD WINDER

Use the clues below to help you find the answers word-winding their way through the grid. Each answer will connect one side of the grid to the other—left to right, top to bottom, right to left, and bottom to top.

W	K	N	N	E	C
T	I	E	L	O	E
N	C	R	K	V	F
X	D	P	O	C	W
B	M	O	Z	V	I
I	H	Q	W	J	P

→ To enhance in value or quality ______

↓ An opening in a wall, door, etc., that usually contains a sheet of glass ______

← To join with or become joined to something else ______

↑ A food preserved in a brine or vinegar solution ______

85 | DIFFICULTY: ●●●○○○○○○○
COMPLETION: ☐ TIME: ______

SYNONYM UNSCRAMBLE

Unscramble the letters below to form pairs of SYNONYMS. Watch out—some words can be unscrambled more than one way!

KAS = RIQINEU

IXM = BRECALMS

SREELAV = MYNA

IDE = SPIHER

GAIEM = TRIPUCE

CLOEDI = TEENGL

ERRA = EUUINQ

86 | DIFFICULTY: ●●●●○○○○○○ COMPLETION: ☐ TIME: ______

CROSS'D WORDS UNSCRAMBLE

Unscramble the letters in each clue to fill in the puzzle grid below.

ACROSS

1 ELPLS *(one-syllable word)*
3 LIQTU *(one-syllable word)*
5 IWHERAY *(two-syllable word)*
7 TLAFA *(two-syllable word)*
8 COKKN *(one-syllable word)*
9 HACNI *(two-syllable word)*
11 PSOEC *(two-syllable word)*
13 LEEGRAY *(three-syllable word)*
14 KLEFA *(one-syllable word)*
15 ELIDY *(one-syllable word)*

DOWN

1 HELFS *(one-syllable word)*
2 AOYLL *(two-syllable word)*
3 RUKQI *(one-syllable word)*
4 KURTN *(one-syllable word)*
5 TILEHON *(two-syllable word)*
6 COOLYEG *(three-syllable word)*
9 FLICF *(one-syllable word)*
10 GAAEL *(two-syllable word)*
11 ROYSR *(one-syllable word)*
12 BEEMD *(two-syllable word)*

87 | DIFFICULTY: ●●○○○○○○○○
COMPLETION: ☐ TIME: ______

DEFINITION FINDER

Using the clues below, find and circle the words concealed in the letter grid.

- ○ A musical instrument like a small guitar *(noun)*
- ○ Very useful or helpful *(adjective)*
- ○ A usually sharp blade attached to a handle *(noun)*
- ○ A bed cover with stitched designs *(noun)*
- ○ Not divided or cut into parts or pieces *(adjective)*
- ○ A light meal eaten in the middle of the day *(noun)*
- ○ To fail to remember to bring or take (something) *(verb)*
- ○ Equally distant from the ends or sides *(adjective)*
- ○ To make as small as possible *(verb)*
- ○ Calling for immediate attention *(adjective)*
- ○ To make a statement about someone or something *(verb)*

88 | DIFFICULTY: ●●●○○○○○○○
COMPLETION: ☐ TIME: ______

MISSING DEFINITIONS FINDER

Using the clues below, find and circle the words concealed in the letter grid.

J	E	B	E	L	I	E	F	W	Y
K	D	X	G	O	O	D	K	Q	V
S	G	Z	N	B	W	O	R	D	A
U	E	V	A	D	E	S	I	R	E
O	C	A	R	R	Y	X	Q	Z	H
M	Y	S	T	E	R	I	O	U	S
A	W	X	S	Z	V	R	O	A	D
F	J	U	S	U	A	L	Z	K	V

am·bi·tion *noun* \am-ˈbi-shən\
a ______ to be successful, powerful, or ______

burden *transitive verb* \ˈbər-dən\
to make (someone) hold or ______ something ______

ee·rie *adjective* \ˈir-ē\
______ and ______

lit·er·al *adjective* \ˈli-t(ə-)rəl\
involving the ordinary or ______ meaning of a ______

op·ti·mism *noun* \ˈäp-tə-ˌmi-zəm\
a feeling or ______ that ______ things will happen in the future

verge *noun* \ˈvərj\
an area along the ______ of a ______, path, etc.

89 | DIFFICULTY: ●●○○○○○○○○
COMPLETION: ☐ TIME: ______

ANTONYM FINDER

Find and circle the seven pairs of ANTONYMS divided between the letter grids below.

A	P	M	H	T	E	Y	X
Q	M	Z	P	C	R	K	A
C	G	A	U	E	C	P	C
N	D	D	T	A	N	Y	T
A	E	S	S	E	N	W	U
R	A	N	X	E	U	D	A
M	A	K	D	F	P	R	L
R	N	O	R	M	A	L	T

A	F	F	I	R	M	E	E
T	R	Z	J	X	R	S	S
P	W	E	Q	K	A	L	T
E	X	R	S	E	Z	A	R
D	F	E	R	T	Q	F	A
A	D	C	Z	J	O	X	N
R	N	X	G	Z	C	R	G
I	F	A	I	L	U	R	E

90 | DIFFICULTY: ●●●○○○○○○○
COMPLETION: ☐ TIME: ______

DICTIONARY UNSCRAMBLE

Unscramble the letters below to form words that match the Merriam-Webster definitions.

adverb
Happening at the end of a process

LIYFALN= ☐☐☐☐☐☐☐

adjective
Dull and uninteresting

GROIBN= ☐☐☐☐☐☐

noun A place in which literary, musical, or reference materials are kept

BARRILY= ☐☐☐☐☐☐☐

transitive verb
To think about or consider (something) carefully

PRDONE= ☐☐☐☐☐☐

intransitive verb
To take a quick look at something

CLEANG= ☐☐☐☐☐☐

adjective
Free from fraud or deception

SNOTHE= ☐☐☐☐☐☐

91 | DIFFICULTY: ●●●○○○○○○○
COMPLETION: ☐ TIME: ______

WORD WINDER

Use the clue to help you find the answers word-winding their way through the grid. Each answer will connect the top of the grid to the bottom.

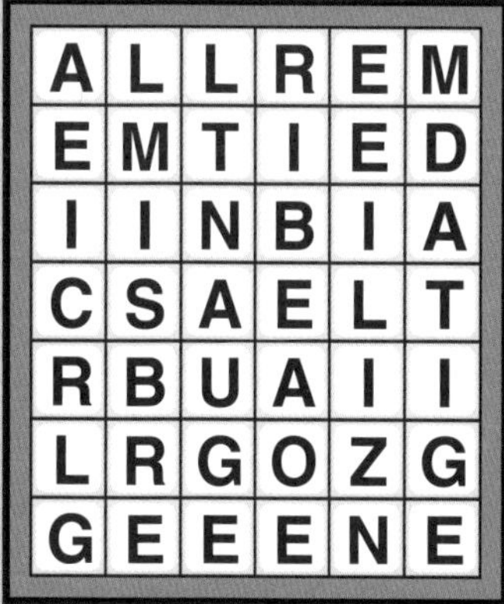

A	L	L	R	E	M
E	M	T	I	E	D
I	I	N	B	I	A
C	S	A	E	L	T
R	B	U	A	I	I
L	R	G	O	Z	G
G	E	E	E	N	E

Find five words with four vowels word-winding their way from top to bottom.

92 | DIFFICULTY: ●●○○○○○○○○ COMPLETION: ☐ TIME: ______

MIXED-UP DEFINITION

Unscramble the letters below to reveal the definition of the given word.

an·tag·o·nize *transitive verb* \an-ˈta-gə-ˌnīz\
ot saecu ot lefe slothie ro garyn : ot rarttiei ro stupe

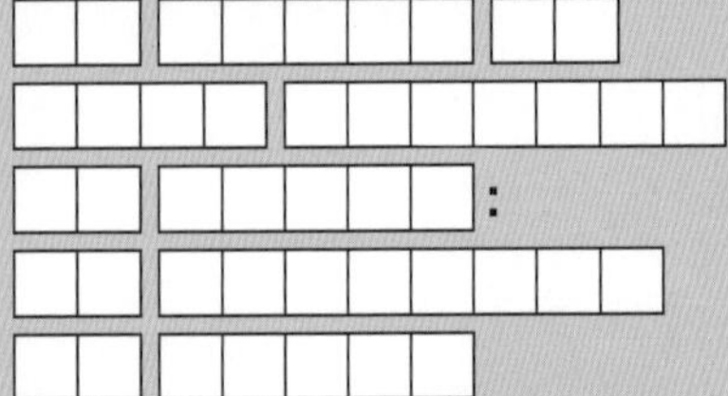

93 | DIFFICULTY: ●●○○○○○○○○ COMPLETION: ☐ TIME: ______

SYNONYM FINDER

Find and circle the six pairs of SYNONYMS, one on each side, in the letter grids below.

E	J	O	I	N	T
S	P	M	K	I	N
I	D	I	U	Q	A
A	P	Q	L	N	M
R	C	T	C	E	E
A	B	L	A	N	K

=

E	V	P	S	D	E
L	R	N	T	I	T
T	K	E	A	O	I
I	P	D	C	V	N
T	V	M	K	T	U
P	A	R	D	O	N

○○○○○○

94 | DIFFICULTY: ●●○○○○○○○○
COMPLETION: ☐ TIME: ______

SYLLABARY

Link word segments together in the grid below to create words, and enter them in the blanks.

COM	PET	BEN	E	DO
EN	ATE	I	FIT	CA
ER	ER	TIVE	AV	O
FRIG	GY	BLY	I	DEN
RE	TER	RI	CAL	TI

Three-Syllable Noun: _ _ _ R _ _

Four-Syllable Adjective: _ _ _ _ _ I _ _ _

Three-Syllable Verb: _ E _ _ _ _ _

Four-Syllable Adjective: _ _ _ _ _ _ _ _ _ V _

Four-Syllable Noun: _ _ _ _ _ D _

Three-Syllable Adverb: _ _ _ _ I _ _ _

Four-Syllable Verb: _ _ _ R _ _ _ _ _ _ _

95 | DIFFICULTY: ●●○○○○○○○○
COMPLETION: ☐ TIME: ______

MAKE THE CONNECTION

Fill in the boxes with common two-word phrases with the help of the clues below. The last word in each pair will be the first word in the following pair.

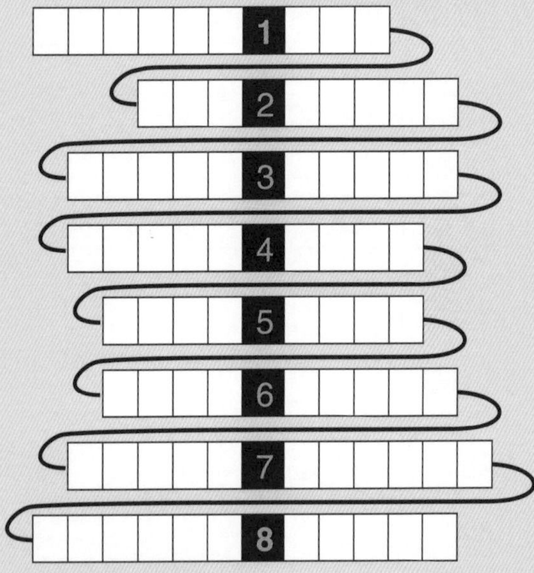

1 Prius, for example
2 Auto theft deterrent
3 Bedside timepiece
4 Place for numbers and hands
5 Jack, queen, or king
6 Place to play bridge
7 Fast-paced sport
8 Court competition

96 | DIFFICULTY: ●●●○○○○○○○
COMPLETION: ☐ TIME: ______

ANTONYM UNSCRAMBLE

Unscramble the letters below to form pairs of ANTONYMS. Note: Some words can be unscrambled more than one way!

L W A O L ≠ T E E P V N R

U C E E D L X ≠ M A T I D

G R S O T N ≠ E L B E F E

D R U E E N ≠ S N I R G E

D R U E ≠ L E P I O T

T I C X E E ≠ S T O E H O

F R O C M I N ≠ L A C C N E

97 | DIFFICULTY: ●●●○○○○○○○ COMPLETION: ☐ TIME: ______

SYNONYM FINDER

Find and circle the six pairs of SYNONYMS, one on each side, in the letter grids below.

E	N	D	E	D	Y
D	A	G	K	D	R
I	C	L	E	E	P
S	Y	M	T	D	S
E	E	T	F	E	M
R	U	G	H	N	R

=

N	C	U	R	E	T
S	I	W	D	L	F
E	P	M	L	W	I
N	B	E	B	C	H
O	W	M	A	L	S
D	K	B	N	K	E

○○○○○○

98 | DIFFICULTY: ●●●●○○○○○○ COMPLETION: ☐ TIME: ______

ANTONYM FINDER

Find and circle the six pairs of ANTONYMS, one on each side, in the letter grids below.

D	L	W	B	N	F
I	F	O	A	G	D
A	M	E	F	Z	E
M	L	P	A	T	N
C	Y	N	E	R	Y
A	D	D	C	L	W

D	R	Y	C	T	A
I	O	E	M	N	D
R	L	R	A	W	M
T	A	D	O	C	I
Y	V	L	W	B	T
L	E	S	S	E	N

○○○○○○

99 | DIFFICULTY: ●●●●○○○○○○
COMPLETION: ☐ TIME: ______

SYNONYM UNSCRAMBLE

Unscramble the letters below to form pairs of SYNONYMS. Watch out—some words can be unscrambled more than one way!

S W I H = R E E S I D

T H A I B = S M U C T O

T M A P E T T = Y R T

D I P E E M = P R A E M H

U T R E O = O S C R E U

P A E H N P = C R U O C

S N L O M E = O R U E I S S

100 | DIFFICULTY: ●●●●○○○○○○
COMPLETION: ☐ TIME: ______

DEFINITION FINDER

Using the clues below, find and circle the words concealed in the letter grid.

- ○ A person not yet of age *(noun)*
- ○ Happening or coming at the end *(adjective)*
- ○ To make an official decision about *(verb)*
- ○ To discover or notice the presence of *(verb)*
- ○ To find how heavy (someone or something) is *(verb)*
- ○ A period of dryness especially when prolonged *(noun)*
- ○ Causing a feeling of happiness *(adjective)*
- ○ To go stealthily or furtively *(verb)*
- ○ Able to speak a language easily and very well *(adjective)*
- ○ A figure that is made from stone, metal, etc. *(noun)*
- ○ Something beyond understanding *(noun)*

101 | DIFFICULTY: ●●●○○○○○○○ COMPLETION: ☐ TIME: ______

CROSS'D WORDS UNSCRAMBLE

Unscramble the letters in each clue to fill in the puzzle grid below.

ACROSS

1 PATLE *(one-syllable word)*
3 TREVO *(two-syllable word)*
5 RUFLACE *(two-syllable word)*
7 NUHHC *(one-syllable word)*
8 ABIRD *(two-syllable word)*
9 ELWEH *(one-syllable word)*
11 ZCRYA *(two-syllable word)*
13 GLITTYH *(two-syllable word)*
14 BATHI *(two-syllable word)*
15 THARE *(one-syllable word)*

DOWN

1 CRPHE *(one-syllable word)*
2 OHTRC *(one-syllable word)*
3 FROFE *(two-syllable word)*
4 TRHDI *(one-syllable word)*
5 ETTONCX *(two-syllable word)*
6 BLIRRYA *(three-syllable word)*
9 THAWC *(one-syllable word)*
10 TGILH *(one-syllable word)*
11 THACC *(one-syllable word)*
12 CHATY *(one-syllable word)*

102 | DIFFICULTY: ●●●○○○○○○○
COMPLETION: ☐ TIME: ______

PRISM CROSS'D WORDS

Use the color-coded clues below to find words that fit in the like-colored portions of the puzzle grid below.

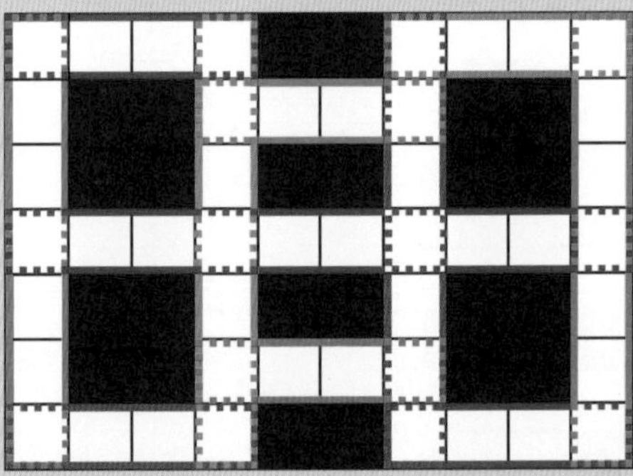

- Defensive football player (3-syllable noun)
- Collapsible fabric shelter (1-syllable noun)
- Bluish-white metal (1-syllable noun)

- Having a small cross section (1-syllable adjective)
- Showing energetic support for a cause (2-syllable adjective)

- Action that causes suffering (3-syllable noun)
- Push with a finger (1-syllable verb)

- One part in a hundred (2-syllable noun)
- Move slowly back and forth (1-syllable verb)

- Remove by pulling or cutting out (2-syllable verb)
- Pronged gardening implement (1-syllable noun)

103 | DIFFICULTY: ●●○○○○○○○○
COMPLETION: ☐ TIME: ______

CROSS'D WORD CONNECTIONS

The crosswords below share common letters as indicated by the colored boxes. Use the clues to solve the puzzles.

ACROSS
1 Habitually clean and orderly
4 A limbless scaled reptile
5 A particular smell

DOWN
1 The front end or part of something
2 Something that is given to someone or something for being excellent
3 The time in which a planet completes a revolution about the sun

ACROSS
1 A large, disordered pile of things
4 A contrivance often consisting of a noose for entangling birds or mammals
5 To leave out or leave unmentioned

DOWN
1 A flexible tube for conveying fluids
2 A warning of danger
3 A place for sitting

ACROSS
1 To kiss (someone) lightly and quickly
4 To join together to achieve something
5 To cause (something) to no longer be covered, sealed, or blocked

DOWN
1 To dispense from a container
2 To make a short high-pitched sound
3 Characterized by petty selfishness or malice

104 | DIFFICULTY: ●●●●○○○○○○ COMPLETION: ☐ TIME: ______

COLOR WORD CHAINS

Using the clues and letters below, make word paths between like colors to fill the board.

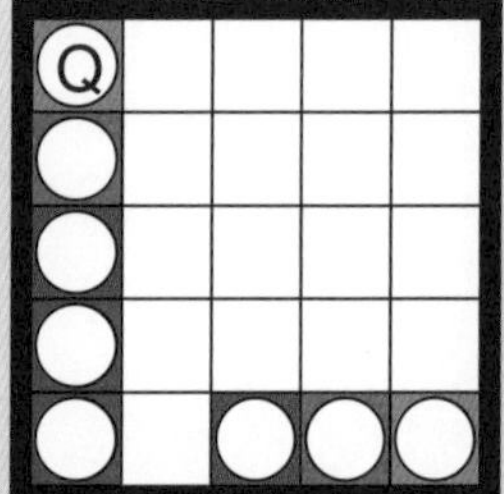

- At three-month intervals
- Gas for cooking or heating
- To stop feeling nervous or worried
- A way out of a place

A	A	A	E	E	E
E	I	L	L	N	O
P	P	R	R	R	R
T	T	U	X	X	Y

105 | DIFFICULTY: ●●●○○○○○○○ COMPLETION: ☐ TIME: ______

SYNONYM FINDER

Find and circle the six pairs of SYNONYMS, one on each side, in the letter grids below.

S	U	L	L	E	N
D	I	D	V	T	Y
R	F	M	S	P	L
I	H	A	P	A	G
E	V	A	E	L	P
W	H	R	W	C	E

=

P	G	C	M	G	L
L	H	L	H	A	D
A	D	P	U	D	A
I	L	T	G	M	L
N	C	H	E	W	G
A	E	E	R	I	E

○ ○ ○ ○ ○ ○

106 | DIFFICULTY: ●●○○○○○○○○
COMPLETION: ☐ TIME: ______

DICTIONARY WORD WINDER

Use the clues below to help you find the answers word-winding their way through the grid. Each answer will connect one side of the grid to the other—left to right, top to bottom, right to left, and bottom to top.

H	V	Q	Y	L	E
K	O	E	D	R	Z
N	E	L	O	T	P
J	F	B	L	E	C
E	L	O	B	A	H
L	W	G	H	F	V

→ One of the two long, thin sticks that are used in knitting and that are pointed at one end ______

↓ Having nothing inside : not solid ______

← A small, round stone, especially one that has been made smooth by the movement of water ______

↑ A building or group of buildings where products are made ______

107 | DIFFICULTY: ●●●○○○○○○○
COMPLETION: ☐ TIME: ______

MISSING DEFINITIONS FINDER

Using the clues below, find and circle the words concealed in the letter grid.

C	I	H	I	D	D	E	N	X	T
H	N	N	D	E	T	A	I	L	I
A	E	D	D	L	I	V	E	S	M
N	T	O	Z	I	J	Q	Z	W	E
G	F	N	V	K	R	V	X	A	E
E	O	E	X	V	W	E	K	I	V
X	V	H	A	N	D	S	C	T	O
B	P	L	A	C	E	J	Z	T	M

abode *noun* \ə-ˈbōd\
the ______ where someone ______

con·stant *adjective* \ˈkän(t)-stənt\
happening all the ______ or very ______ over a period of time

influence *transitive verb* \ˈin-ˌflü-ən(t)s\
to affect or ______ (someone or something) in an ______ but usually important way

lurk *intransitive verb* \ˈlərk\
to ______ in a secret or ______ place

ma·nip·u·late *transitive verb* \mə-ˈni-pyə-ˌlāt\
to ______ or control (something) with your ______ or by using a machine

rig·or·ous *adjective* \ˈri-g(ə-)rəs\
______ with a lot of attention to ______

108 | DIFFICULTY: ●●●○○○○○○○
COMPLETION: ☐ TIME: ______

PRISM WORD FINDER

Using the color-coded clues below, find and circle the words in the letter grid.

B	R	G	W	B	E	G	G	I	N	G
S	O	T	L	A	G	H	U	S	K	Y
W	R	X	Y	Z	I	P	F	Y	H	L
B	A	J	E	P	M	T	R	K	B	T
E	N	G	P	R	I	A	I	R	Q	G
V	G	Z	G	E	N	C	A	N	J	N
R	E	H	S	I	H	L	A	M	G	I
E	C	N	D	C	U	H	B	L	N	T
N	E	R	T	G	M	I	N	C	E	T
T	O	A	E	C	O	M	M	O	N	E
S	C	R	A	V	E	R	A	G	E	B

Find six five-letter one-syllable words starting with an orange letter ○○○○○○

Find five synonyms for "normal" starting with a blue letter ○○○○○

Find three verbs ending in "ING" starting with a purple letter ○○○

Find two five-letter dog breeds starting with a red letter ○○

109 | DIFFICULTY: ●●●○○○○○○○
COMPLETION: ☐ TIME: ______

WORD WINDER

Use the clue to help you find the answers word-winding their way through the grid. Each answer will connect the top of the grid to the bottom.

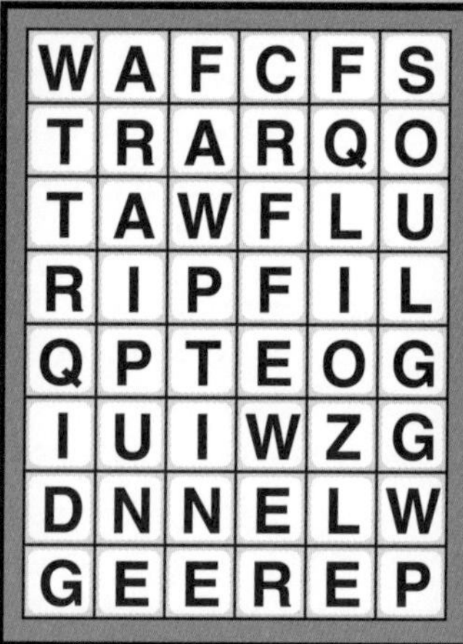

Find five words containing double consonants word-winding their way from top to bottom.

110 | DIFFICULTY: ●●●○○○○○○○ COMPLETION: ☐ TIME: ______

CROSS'D WORD CONNECTIONS

The crosswords below share common letters as indicated by the colored boxes. Use the clues to solve the puzzles.

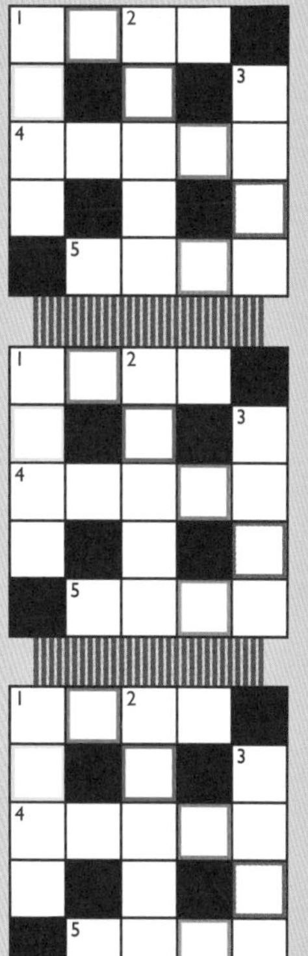

ACROSS
1 A small restaurant where you can get simple meals and drinks
4 To put in a secret or hidden place
5 Sad or unhappy

DOWN
1 The price of something
2 To move or swing your arms or legs in a wild and uncontrolled way
3 Archaic form of "you"

ACROSS
1 To make chopping strokes or blows
4 A way of seeming or looking that is not true or real
5 To touch along an edge

DOWN
1 Male pigs
2 To go upward with gradual or continuous progress
3 To come together in order to talk

ACROSS
1 After all others
4 Fat in a way that is unhealthy
5 To make senseless, groggy, or dizzy by or as if by a blow

DOWN
1 A circular airplane maneuver
2 Frozen or partly frozen rain
3 Having a fine edge or point

111 | DIFFICULTY: ●●●○○○○○○○
COMPLETION: ☐ TIME: ______

MAKE THE CONNECTION

Fill in the boxes with common two-word phrases with the help of the clues below. The last word in each pair will be the first word in the following pair.

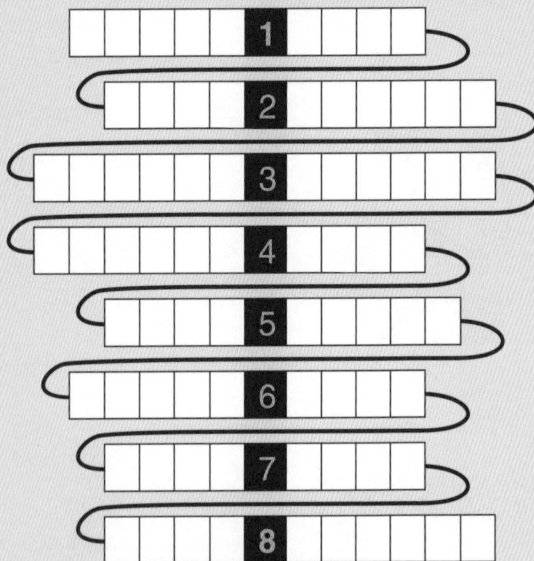

1 Grows in an orchard
2 Limb
3 Local division of a business
4 Type of commercial complex
5 Space for a plastic hotel
6 Football action
7 Take it easy
8 Less prominent road

112 | DIFFICULTY: ●●●●○○○○○○
COMPLETION: ☐ TIME: ______

SYNONYM UNSCRAMBLE

Unscramble the letters below to form pairs of SYNONYMS. Watch out—some words can be unscrambled more than one way!

K C H A = H P O C

N O P Y H = A E K F

D A Y H N = S L U U F E

D L U A = S P E I A R

L O J Y L = R M R Y E

O S H E C O = C L E E S T

A D R E T = T R A B R E

113 | DIFFICULTY: ●●●●●○○○○○
COMPLETION: ☐ TIME: ______

SYLLABARY

Link word segments together in the grid below to create words, and enter them in the blanks.

DE	LAR	ER	TOR	AN
I	LIV	LA	AS	GRI
SIM	CAL	CU	TROL	LY
NEC	EL	E	O	TOR
ES	SAR	Y	VA	GY

Four-Syllable Noun | | | | V | | | | |

Three-Syllable Adjective | | | | | L | | |

Four-Syllable Noun | | | | | | | | | | R |

Three-Syllable Adverb | | | G | | | | |

Four-Syllable Noun | | | | | | L | | | |

Three-Syllable Verb | | | | | V | | |

Four-Syllable Adjective | | | | E | | | | | |

114 | DIFFICULTY: ●●●○○○○○○○
COMPLETION: ☐ TIME: ______

DICTIONARY UNSCRAMBLE

Unscramble the letters below to form words that match the Merriam-Webster definitions.

adverb
Fast in moving or reacting

CLIQYUK= ☐☐☐☐☐☐☐

adjective
Showing good taste : graceful and attractive

GLEETAN= ☐☐☐☐☐☐☐

noun
Something spoken or written in reply to a question

SAWRNE= ☐☐☐☐☐☐

transitive verb
To gather in (a crop)

SHEVRAT= ☐☐☐☐☐☐☐

intransitive verb
To talk in an annoying way usually for a long time

MRAMYE= ☐☐☐☐☐☐

adjective
Very loving and gentle

DREETN= ☐☐☐☐☐☐

115 | DIFFICULTY: ●●●○○○○○○○
COMPLETION: ☐ TIME: ______

SYNONYM FINDER

Find and circle the seven pairs of SYNONYMS divided between the letter grids below.

A	B	D	I	C	A	T	E
T	D	G	L	M	D	T	Y
S	H	E	Q	K	U	T	E
C	F	R	P	L	I	T	W
O	Y	D	O	L	I	H	J
L	G	S	I	N	E	F	N
D	B	B	T	X	G	T	B
A	A	C	P	M	Z	C	E

=

C	W	C	F	R	N	P	Y
O	O	N	M	I	B	L	T
M	D	M	A	K	B	N	B
M	T	R	P	M	E	N	E
O	D	L	E	L	J	C	R
N	G	S	A	Q	E	R	A
Y	S	T	B	H	P	T	T
A	R	E	S	I	G	N	E

○○○○○○○

116 | DIFFICULTY: ●●●●○○○○○○
COMPLETION: ☐ TIME: ______

DICTIONARY CROSS'D WORDS

Fill in the puzzle using the Merriam-Webster definition clues below.

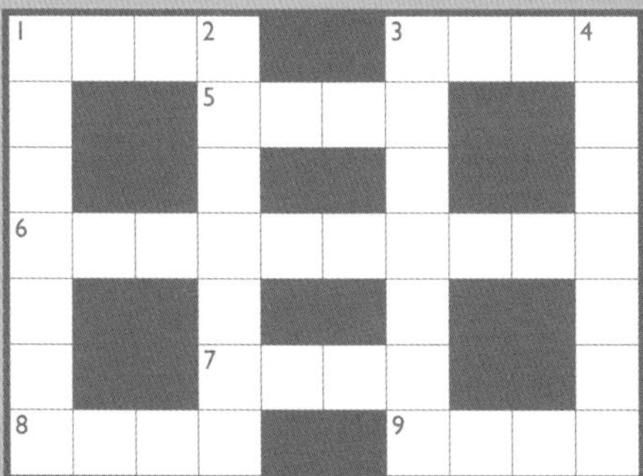

Across
1 To cease activity or operation (1-syllable verb)
3 Fruit that has red or purple skin (1-syllable noun)
5 Every one of two or more people (1-syllable adjective)
6 Reacting in a desired or positive way (3-syllable adjective)
7 Very great or large (2-syllable adjective)
8 To bend, especially repeatedly (1-syllable verb)
9 To take up residence (1-styllable verb)

Down
1 Chief law-enforcement officer in a county (2-syllable noun)
2 To confuse (someone) very much (2-syllable verb)
3 Science that deals with matter and energy (2-syllable noun)
4 Hating to spend money (3-syllable adjective)

117 | DIFFICULTY: ●●●○○○○○○○ COMPLETION: ☐ TIME: ______

SYNONYM FINDER

Find and circle the six pairs of SYNONYMS, one on each side, in the letter grids below.

R	E	V	E	A	L
K	R	D	Q	F	A
T	A	U	N	T	M
S	U	V	C	W	R
E	Q	N	G	M	O
R	S	I	C	K	N

=

○○○○○○

118 | DIFFICULTY: ●●●○○○○○○○ COMPLETION: ☐ TIME: ______

MIXED-UP DEFINITION

Unscramble the letters below to reveal the definition of the given word.

vo·ca·tion *noun* \vō-ˈkā-shən\

a rgosnt sreedi ot pnsde royu fiel igdno a tcranie idkn fo kwro

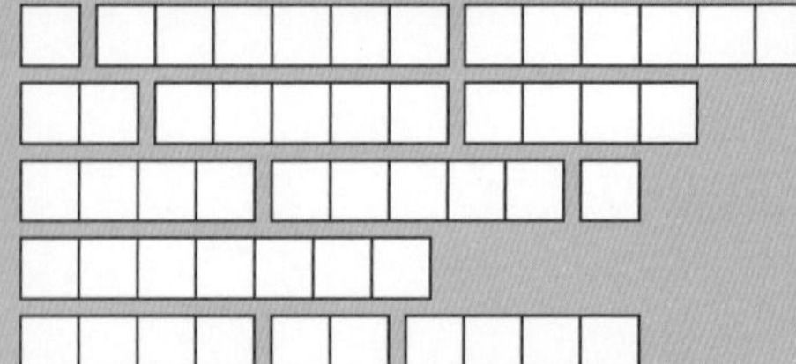

119 | DIFFICULTY: ●●●○○○○○○○
COMPLETION: ☐ TIME: ______

ANTONYM FINDER

Find and circle the seven pairs of ANTONYMS divided between the letter grids below.

C	O	L	L	E	C	T	E
D	D	X	P	J	R	M	R
I	N	E	Q	D	O	W	E
S	L	Z	R	C	Q	L	J
P	X	J	L	I	O	J	E
L	F	E	Q	H	D	X	C
A	W	Z	W	C	N	E	T
Y	N	E	U	T	R	A	L

Z	C	F	S	X	L	T	P
S	Q	O	D	H	I	Q	A
D	C	J	N	M	U	E	R
E	Z	A	R	C	T	N	T
S	Q	E	T	I	E	K	I
A	P	J	C	T	G	A	A
I	W	N	H	G	E	J	L
B	I	X	J	Q	H	R	X

○ ○ ○ ○ ○ ○ ○

120 | DIFFICULTY: ●●●●○○○○○○
COMPLETION: ☐ TIME: ______

ANTONYM UNSCRAMBLE

Unscramble the letters below to form pairs of ANTONYMS. Note: Some words can be unscrambled more than one way!

L O R M A ≠ K I D W C E

F S I F T ≠ B E E I F X L L

S N R W A Y C ≠ Y R N B W A

S T A N E B ≠ T R E E P N S

D E R R W A ≠ P L Y N E T A

R H I E ≠ I F R E

C L E E A D I T ≠ G R U H O

121 | DIFFICULTY: ●●●○○○○○○○
COMPLETION: ☐ TIME: ______

PRISM CROSS'D WORDS

Use the color-coded clues below to find words that fit in the like-colored portions of the puzzle grid below.

- ○ Shorten a word or name (4-syllable verb)
- ○ Feeling happy (1-syllable adjective)
- ○ Animal's den (1-syllable noun)

- ○ Shone brightly (1-syllable verb)
- ○ Section of space within a building (3-syllable noun)

- ○ Head cook (1-syllable noun)
- ○ Means of entry (2-syllable noun)

- ○ Distrustful of human nature (3-syllable adjective)
- ○ Declare untrue (2-syllable verb)

- ○ Perpetually (3-syllable adverb)
- ○ To follow an order (2-syllable verb)

122 | DIFFICULTY: ●●●○○○○○○○ COMPLETION: ☐ TIME: ______

CROSS'D WORDS UNSCRAMBLE

Unscramble the letters in each clue to fill in the puzzle grid below.

ACROSS

1 JIBUO *(two-syllable word)*
3 RETVO *(two-syllable word)*
5 BETIXIH *(three-syllable word)*
7 CORUC *(two-syllable word)*
8 SROTW *(one-syllable word)*
9 VUCER *(one-syllable word)*
11 EDFIL *(one-syllable word)*
13 NYTAYRN *(three-syllable word)*
14 EHRVO *(two-syllable word)*
15 TIHHC *(one-syllable word)*

DOWN

1 JABON *(two-syllable word)*
2 SRUEH *(two-syllable word)*
3 BWOOX *(two-syllable word)*
4 PETTM *(one-syllable word)*
5 PCEETXR *(two-syllable word)*
6 YESETRL *(two-syllable word)*
9 HOGCU *(one-syllable word)*
10 ORRRE *(two-syllable word)*
11 IHCFN *(one-syllable word)*
12 THIDC *(one-syllable word)*

123 | DIFFICULTY: ●●●●○○○○○○
COMPLETION: ☐ TIME: ______

CROSS'D WORD CONNECTIONS

The crosswords below share common letters as indicated by the colored boxes. Use the clues to solve the puzzles.

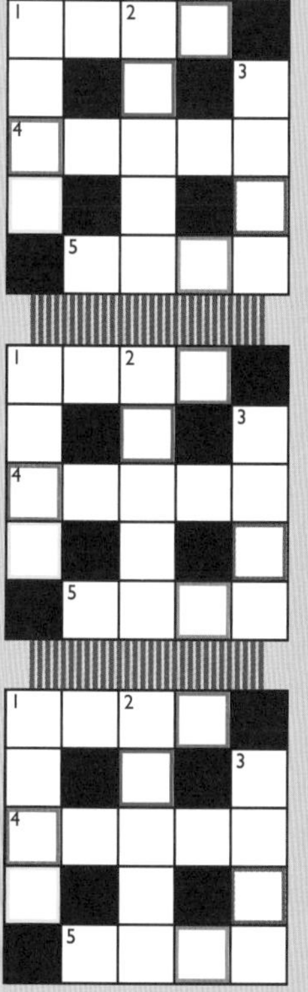

ACROSS
1 To cherish a desire with anticipation
4 To flow over the edge of a container
5 A pattern of lines that cross each other to form squares

DOWN
1 One that receives or entertains guests
2 Existing earlier in time
3 To walk heavily or slowly

ACROSS
1 One of the leaves of a publication
4 A piece of cloth that is used as a covering for the head or shoulders
5 To slide out of place

DOWN
1 A person who annoys other people
2 The object of an extended quest
3 To fail completely

ACROSS
1 The period from birth to death
4 A garment for the upper part of the body
5 To pass over or omit an item or step

DOWN
1 A simple series of words or numerals
2 Search for something that may be hidden in clothing
3 To hinder or prevent the passage of

124 | DIFFICULTY: ●●●○○○○○○○ COMPLETION: ☐ TIME: ______

WORD WINDER

Use the clue to help you find the answers word-winding their way through the grid. Each answer will connect the top of the grid to the bottom.

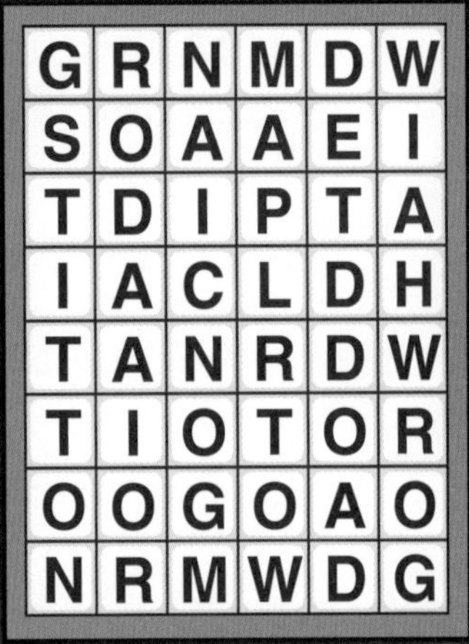

G	R	N	M	D	W
S	O	A	A	E	I
T	D	I	P	T	A
I	A	C	L	D	H
T	A	N	R	D	W
T	I	O	T	O	R
O	O	G	O	A	O
N	R	M	W	D	G

Find five words starting and ending with the same letter word-winding their way from top to bottom.

125 | DIFFICULTY: ●●●○○○○○○○
COMPLETION: ☐ TIME: ______

PRISM WORD FINDER

Using the color-coded clues below, find and circle the words in the letter grid.

H	S	B	U	R	S	T	W	G	H	T
T	B	E	R	K	H	F	T	L	J	E
G	N	W	V	S	Q	H	K	P	G	V
N	K	E	A	E	G	L	D	D	R	E
E	L	M	V	I	R	E	E	V	S	H
R	S	E	A	E	H	P	K	L	B	S
T	E	R	V	S	R	C	E	E	K	U
S	T	P	A	E	A	W	S	G	L	R
S	N	L	E	R	R	A	X	Q	B	C
H	P	G	C	E	E	V	W	P	N	L
S	T	H	R	A	S	H	E	D	J	G

Find four eight-letter one-syllable words starting with an orange letter ○○○○

Find four four-letter words starting and ending with "E" starting with a blue letter ○○○○

Find four five-letter synonyms for "break" starting with a purple letter ○○○○

Find three five-letter words with "V" in the middle that rhyme with "clever" starting with a red letter ○○○

126 | DIFFICULTY: ●●●○○○○○○○
COMPLETION: ☐ TIME: ______

DICTIONARY WORD WINDER

Use the clues below to help you find the answers word-winding their way through the grid. Each answer will connect one side of the grid to the other—left to right, top to bottom, right to left, and bottom to top.

→ A group of four singers or musicians who perform together ______

↓ Not having any extra substances or chemicals added ______

← Tending to talk a lot ______

↑ A garment for the upper body usually having a front opening, collar, lapels, sleeves, and pockets ______

127 | DIFFICULTY: ●●●●○○○○○○
COMPLETION: ☐ TIME: ______

SYNONYM FINDER

Find and circle the six pairs of SYNONYMS, one on each side, in the letter grids below.

R	I	D	L	Y	R
D	M	S	M	P	E
L	P	G	A	Z	D
I	L	D	I	N	N
U	Y	E	D	B	E
B	S	G	Z	Y	R

=

E	G	P	V	T	L
N	R	C	Y	A	N
A	T	E	M	K	H
E	W	R	C	E	E
M	O	H	W	T	L
N	G	I	V	E	P

○○○○○○

128 | DIFFICULTY: ●●●○○○○○○○
COMPLETION: ☐ TIME: ______

ANTONYM FINDER

Find and circle the six pairs of ANTONYMS, one on each side, in the letter grids below.

T	O	A	S	T	E
A	B	H	O	R	F
A	M	X	U	D	B
E	N	L	A	E	R
R	A	G	R	E	E
O	R	D	E	R	J

L	O	V	E	Z	E
L	X	J	W	N	S
I	R	E	P	E	L
H	Z	G	Q	T	A
C	H	A	O	S	F
D	I	F	F	E	R

○○○○○○

129 | DIFFICULTY: ●●●○○○○○○○
COMPLETION: ☐ TIME: ______

DEFINITION FINDER

Using the clues below, find and circle the words concealed in the letter grid.

E	S	C	A	P	E	V	X	Z
D	X	R	E	A	S	O	N	J
O	F	Q	Y	G	S	H	V	T
L	I	M	E	R	I	C	K	E
P	N	I	N	U	M	N	X	N
X	I	N	O	F	S	E	J	G
E	S	O	H	F	I	B	Z	A
Z	H	R	V	X	D	K	Q	M

○ A long seat for two or more persons *(noun)*
○ To burst violently as a result of internal pressure *(verb)*
○ A thick, sweet substance made by bees *(noun)*
○ To reach the end of (something) *(verb)*
○ Not very important or valuable *(adjective)*
○ To get away from a dangerous place or situation *(verb)*
○ A humorous rhyming poem of five lines *(noun)*
○ Rough or very serious in manner or speech *(adjective)*
○ A body having the property of attracting iron *(noun)*
○ A rational ground or motive *(noun)*
○ To send (someone) away *(verb)*

130 | DIFFICULTY: ●●●●○○○○○○
COMPLETION: ☐ TIME: ______

MAKE THE CONNECTION

Fill in the boxes with common two-word phrases with the help of the clues below. The last word in each pair will be the first word in the following pair.

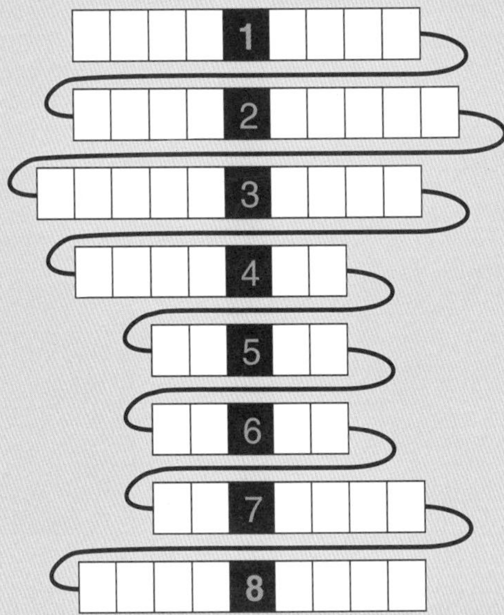

1 Einstein, to Albert
2 Honor a grandparent via a newborn
3 Time to head home or out with friends
4 Apply serious effort toward
5 Aware of the true nature of
6 Fast-food ordering option
7 Card game for two players
8 Nourishment for tank dwellers

131 | DIFFICULTY: ●●●●○○○○○○
COMPLETION: ☐ TIME: ______

WORD WINDER

Use the clue to help you find the answers word-winding their way through the grid. Each answer will connect the top of the grid to the bottom.

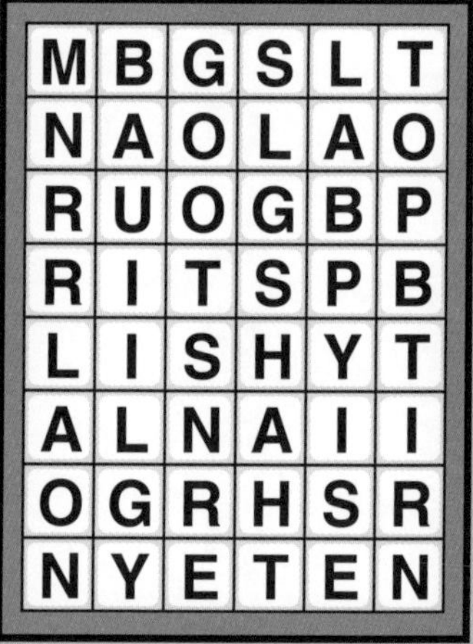

M B G S L T
N A O L A O
R U O G B P
R I T S P B
L I S H Y T
A L N A I I
O G R H S R
N Y E T E N

↓ Find five words with double consonants word-winding their way from top to bottom.

______

______

______

______

______

132 | DIFFICULTY: ●●●○○○○○○○
COMPLETION: ☐ TIME: ________

SYNONYM UNSCRAMBLE

Unscramble the letters below to form pairs of SYNONYMS. Watch out—some words can be unscrambled more than one way!

O M B = W C O D R

N W O = S P E S S S O

C R E E T F P = E L A I D

D O L = I C A T N N E

K R N A = E G E D E R

T I C E I N = G R E U

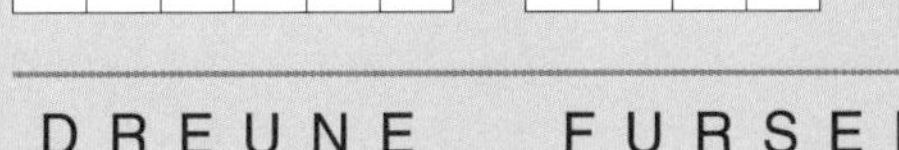

D R E U N E = F U R S E F

133 | DIFFICULTY: ●●●●○○○○○○
COMPLETION: ☐ TIME: ______

SYLLABARY

Link word segments together in the grid below to create words, and enter them in the blanks.

AD	O	RA	BLE	FUL
MEM	VEN	I	DEN	DER
O	AL	TURE	WON	TI
BE	READ	Y	DE	FY
DI	ENT	IN	PEN	DENT

Three-Syllable Noun: _ D _ _ _ _ _ _ _

Three-Syllable Adjective: _ _ _ _ E _ _ _ _

Four-Syllable Verb: _ D _ _ _ _ _ _

Four-Syllable Adjective: _ _ D _ _ _ _ _ _ _ _

Three-Syllable Adverb: _ _ _ _ _ D _

Four-Syllable Adjective: _ _ _ O _ _ _ _ _

Four-Syllable Adjective: _ _ _ _ _ _ N _

134 | DIFFICULTY: ●●●○○○○○○○
COMPLETION: ☐ TIME: ________

CROSS'D WORDS UNSCRAMBLE

Unscramble the letters in each clue to fill in the puzzle grid below.

ACROSS

1 GRSUH *(one-syllable word)*
3 CRATH *(one-syllable word)*
5 MANGAZI *(three-syllable word)*
7 EYATS *(one-syllable word)*
8 ZONDE *(two-syllable word)*
9 CEEPI *(one-syllable word)*
11 TANBO *(two-syllable word)*
13 JEERICO *(two-syllable word)*
14 FLYTO *(two-syllable word)*
15 OAKOZ *(two-syllable word)*

DOWN

1 HAYSD *(two-syllable word)*
2 ITGNA *(two-syllable word)*
3 LCDIH *(one-syllable word)*
4 LATNO *(two-syllable word)*
5 RTEAMAU *(three-syllable word)*
6 TZAGEET *(two-syllable word)*
9 LOWPR *(one-syllable word)*
10 JEYON *(two-syllable word)*
11 CRIKB *(one-syllable word)*
12 COANH *(two-syllable word)*

135 | DIFFICULTY: ●●●○○○○○○○ COMPLETION: ☐ TIME: ______

COLOR WORD CHAINS

Use the clues and letters below to make word paths between like colors to fill the board.

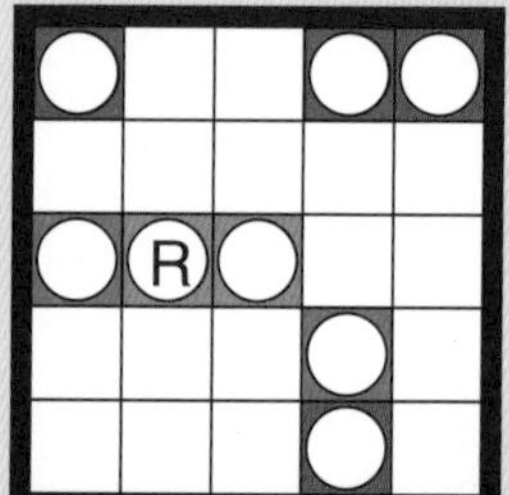

- Based on facts or reason
- To eat or drink something
- An official agreement made between countries
- To shed hair, feathers, etc.

A	A	A	C	E	E
I	L	L	M	M	N
N	O	O	O	R	S
T	T	T	T	U	Y

136 | DIFFICULTY: ●●●●●○○○○○ COMPLETION: ☐ TIME: ______

SYNONYM FINDER

Find and circle the six pairs of SYNONYMS, one on each side, in the letter grids below.

A	S	L	I	P	G
S	C	F	B	X	T
H	H	E	X	E	D
C	X	A	E	K	L
G	O	R	P	D	O
H	G	H	F	E	B

=

○○○○○○

137 | DIFFICULTY: ●●●○○○○○○○
COMPLETION: ☐ TIME: ______

ANTONYM UNSCRAMBLE

Unscramble the letters below to form pairs of ANTONYMS. Note: Some words can be unscrambled more than one way!

A L X ≠ F L A R U C E

S R F H E ≠ A S L E T

T A G Y H H U ≠ B U E M H L

C T C A P E ≠ F E E U R S

T R I P A M ≠ L O C C A N E

W L L U F A ≠ L G I L E L A

P I R I A M ≠ R I P E O M V

138 | DIFFICULTY: ●●●●○○○○○○ COMPLETION: ☐ TIME: ______

CROSS'D WORD CONNECTIONS

The crosswords below share common letters as indicated by the colored boxes. Use the clues to solve the puzzles.

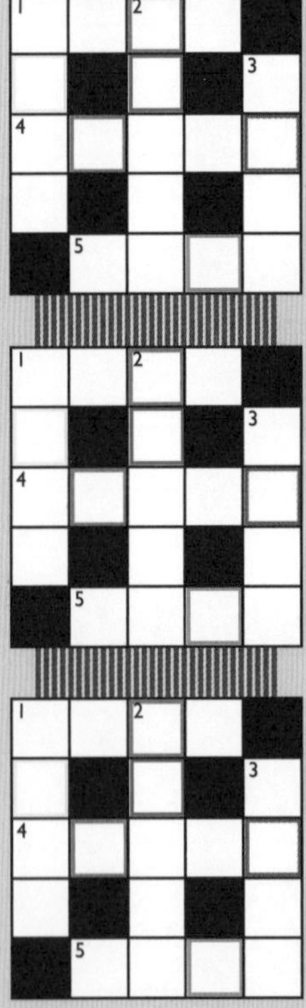

ACROSS
1 An emptied shell
4 To cut the hair, wool, etc., off (an animal)
5 To flood (the market) with goods so that supply exceeds demand

DOWN
1 Chopped meat mixed with potatoes and browned
2 To name the letters of in order
3 To become vexed or worried

ACROSS
1 Smaller in amount or number
4 A seat for one person that has a back and usually four legs
5 Fitting closely and often too tightly

DOWN
1 To not have enough of (something)
2 To produce young especially in large numbers
3 A pompous or boastful statement

ACROSS
1 Be compelled by physical necessity to
4 Of very thin or transparent texture
5 A substance that is used as a medicine

DOWN
1 A cover or partial cover for the face
2 A thrusting or throwing weapon with long shaft and sharp head or blade
3 A place (as on a ship) for temporary confinement of offenders

139 | DIFFICULTY: ●●●●○○○○○○
COMPLETION: ☐ TIME: ______

ANTONYM FINDER

Find and circle the seven pairs of ANTONYMS divided between the letter grids below.

H	E	X	T	E	N	D	X
C	T	G	P	K	L	R	M
A	Z	E	Q	R	A	B	Y
T	B	J	D	L	O	R	Z
E	W	S	U	I	O	V	D
D	Z	G	O	V	O	X	E
X	E	W	A	R	C	U	Y
R	Z	S	X	J	B	Z	S

D	R	E	F	U	T	E	G
X	I	L	Z	V	Q	N	E
E	Z	S	E	J	I	F	T
L	D	Q	P	S	N	K	I
P	X	J	U	E	S	P	N
M	Z	M	G	M	R	E	U
O	A	Z	X	Q	J	S	N
C	B	I	T	T	E	R	E

○○○○○○○

140 | DIFFICULTY: ●●●●○○○○○○
COMPLETION: ☐ TIME: ______

SYNONYM FINDER

Find and circle the seven pairs of SYNONYMS divided between the letter grids below.

E	D	A	I	N	T	Y	S
T	W	T	Q	D	R	L	S
A	F	P	R	O	A	K	E
M	C	J	V	U	G	R	L
I	N	A	Q	P	T	Y	H
T	S	E	T	W	L	H	T
L	N	D	M	N	H	C	U
U	N	I	N	E	P	T	R

=

C	A	N	D	O	R	Y	R
M	B	G	B	P	S	K	E
U	U	R	K	M	C	J	F
M	D	N	U	W	F	M	I
I	H	L	E	T	X	H	N
X	C	N	G	V	A	C	E
A	L	M	J	V	E	L	D
M	P	U	N	G	E	N	T

○ ○ ○ ○ ○ ○ ○

141 | DIFFICULTY: ●●●●○○○○○○
COMPLETION: ☐ TIME: ______

COLOR WORD CHAINS

Use the clues and letters below to make word paths between like colors to fill the board.

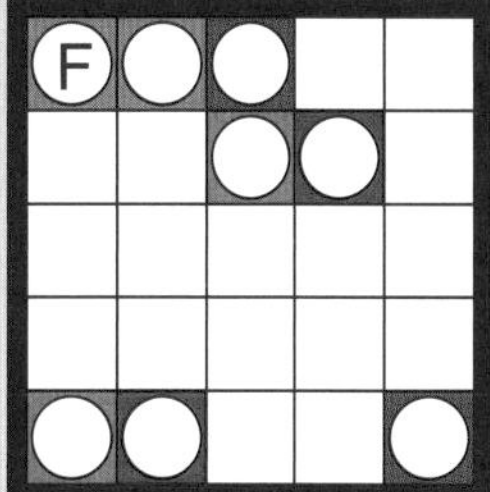

- A group of related people
- Careful use of money
- Reach a goal by hard work
- Trusted counselor or guide

A	A	C	E	E	E
F	H	H	I	I	I
L	M	M	N	O	R
R	T	T	T	V	Y

142 | DIFFICULTY: ●●●●○○○○○○
COMPLETION: ☐ TIME: ______

SYNONYM FINDER

Find and circle the six pairs of SYNONYMS, one on each side, in the letter grids below.

P	E	R	H	D	L
O	A	J	A	L	S
O	P	D	E	I	A
N	C	U	A	C	D
S	Q	R	Q	P	T
R	A	L	L	O	T

S	U	B	D	U	E
U	P	Y	E	L	E
I	N	V	E	B	C
T	I	P	O	L	D
G	X	R	F	U	M
E	P	Y	C	E	T

○○○○○○

143 | DIFFICULTY: ●●●●○○○○○○
COMPLETION: ☐ TIME: ______

DICTIONARY UNSCRAMBLE

Unscramble the letters below to form words that match the Merriam-Webster definitions.

noun
A group of related parts that move or work together

MESSTY= ☐☐☐☐☐☐

adverb
At all times

WAASLY= ☐☐☐☐☐☐

adjective
Liked or enjoyed by many people

RUPPALO= ☐☐☐☐☐☐☐

transitive verb
To greet hospitably and with courtesy

CLOWEEM= ☐☐☐☐☐☐☐

transitive verb
To start (a fire) burning

NLEKDI= ☐☐☐☐☐☐

adjective
Very different, strange, or unusual

TECOIX= ☐☐☐☐☐☐

144 | DIFFICULTY: ●●●●○○○○○○
COMPLETION: ☐ TIME: ______

MISSING DEFINITIONS FINDER

Using the clues below, find and circle the words concealed in the letter grid.

E	W	S	L	O	W	E	K	W	B
G	O	Z	T	X	L	F	O	R	M
N	R	J	N	B	S	P	A	C	E
A	T	V	U	O	W	N	I	N	G
H	H	O	O	A	C	T	I	O	N
C	R	Q	M	L	I	T	T	L	E
T	J	Z	A	X	L	A	R	G	E
L	V	E	A	S	I	L	Y	Z	Q

af·flu·ent *adjective* \ˈa-(ˌ)flü-ənt also a-ˈflü- or ə-\
having a large ______ of money and ______ many expensive things

con·ve·nient *adjective* \kən-ˈvēn-yənt\
allowing you to do something ______ or without ______

ex·panse *noun* \ik-ˈspan(t)s\
a ______ and usually flat open ______ or area

ham·per *transitive verb* \ˈham-pər\
to ______ movement, progress, or ______

pal·try *adjective* \ˈpȯl-trē\
having ______ meaning, importance, or ______

trans·form *verb* \tran(t)s-ˈfȯrm\
to ______ the outward ______ or appearance of (something)

145 | DIFFICULTY: ●●●●○○○○○○
COMPLETION: ☐ TIME: ______

PRISM WORD FINDER

Using the color-coded clues below, find and circle the words in the letter grid.

O	W	D	Q	B	Q	U	A	L	M	Z
Q	V	B	R	C	R	Y	K	L	L	H
J	U	E	L	A	T	O	A	C	O	R
P	U	I	R	I	F	C	O	R	O	A
T	K	B	L	S	I	T	J	K	S	L
D	R	A	I	T	E	T	E	D	E	U
Z	U	U	N	L	R	E	O	E	H	G
Q	J	E	S	A	E	O	C	P	T	E
K	D	J	U	T	L	E	M	L	O	R
I	N	Q	B	F	E	N	K	V	O	R
E	S	C	A	P	E	E	Q	T	T	I

Find five seven-letter words ending in "EE" starting with an orange letter ○○○○○

Find four nouns starting with a blue "Q" ○○○○

Find four five-letter words with double "O's" starting with a purple letter ○○○○

Find two four-syllable words starting with a red "I" ○○

146 | DIFFICULTY: ●●●●●○○○○○
COMPLETION: ☐ TIME: ________

DICTIONARY WORD WINDER

Use the clues below to help you find the answers word-winding their way through the grid. Each answer will connect one side of the grid to the other—left to right, top to bottom, right to left, and bottom to top.

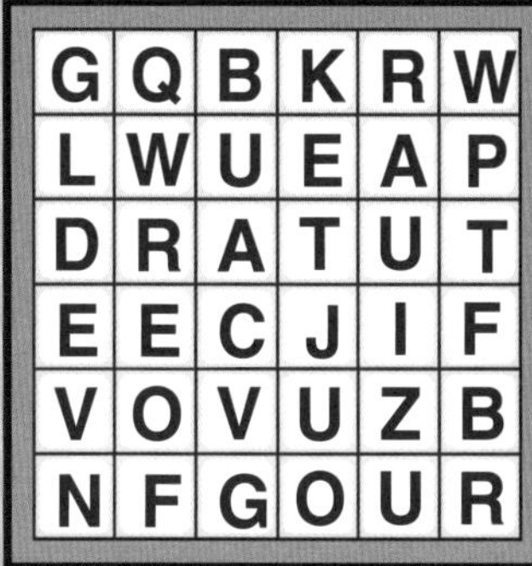

G	Q	B	K	R	W
L	W	U	E	A	P
D	R	A	T	U	T
E	E	C	J	I	F
V	O	V	U	Z	B
N	F	G	O	U	R

→ To eat up greedily or ravenously ________

↓ A radio signal that is broadcast to help guide ships, airplanes, etc. ________

← Existing or occurring at a later time ________

↑ A flat-bodied stringed instrument with a long fretted neck and usually six strings played with a pick or with the fingers ________

147 | DIFFICULTY: ●●●●○○○○○○
COMPLETION: ☐ TIME: ______

DICTIONARY CROSS'D WORDS

Fill in the puzzle using the Merriam-Webster definition clues below.

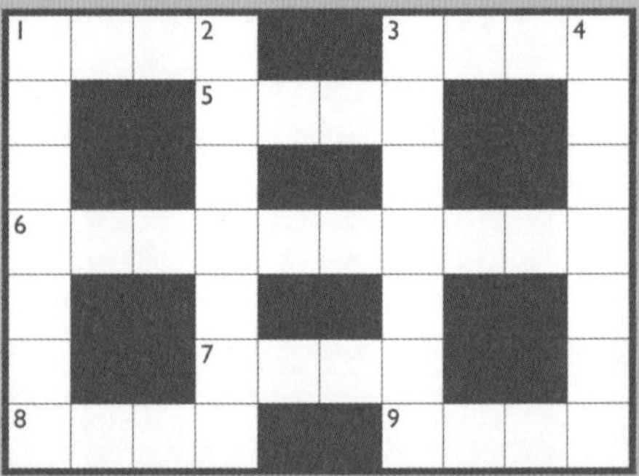

Across
1 The place where a bird lays its eggs (1-syllable noun)
3 Skilled cook who manages the kitchen (1-syllable noun)
5 Common basic monetary unit (2-syllable noun)
6 Meteorologist (3-syllable noun)
7 A sloping floor, walk, or roadway (1-syllable noun)
8 Joint that bends at the middle of the leg (1-syllable noun)
9 The rear part of an airplane (1-syllable noun)

Down
1 Interconnected group or association (2-syllable noun)
2 The way that something feels (2-syllable noun)
3 Morally debased (2-syllable adjective)
4 A soft cloth made of wool or cotton (2-syllable noun)

148 | DIFFICULTY: ●●●●○○○○○○
COMPLETION: ☐ TIME: ________

SYNONYM UNSCRAMBLE

Unscramble the letters below to form pairs of SYNONYMS. Watch out—some words can be unscrambled more than one way!

D D A   A S C E E N I R

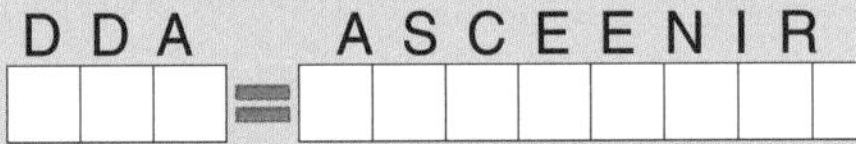

C R A H E   T I N T A A

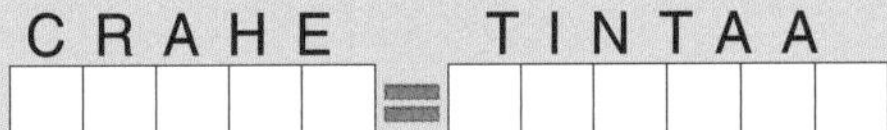

S O N T H E   S U J T

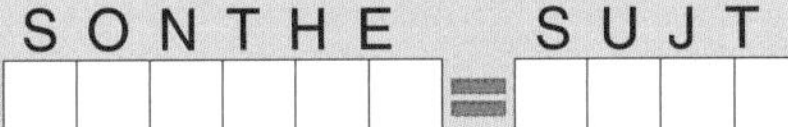

L F L A   P E T L O P

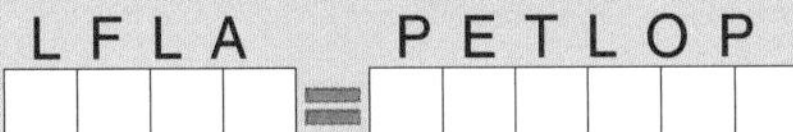

Y R A H D   G R N O T S

T O O N I P   H E C C I O

U G J E D   P U R M E I

149 | DIFFICULTY: ●●●●○○○○○○
COMPLETION: ☐ TIME: ______

DEFINITION FINDER

Using the clues below, find and circle the words concealed in the letter grid.

J	O	X	E	N	T	I	R	E
I	M	M	U	N	E	Z	Q	H
Q	N	J	I	N	G	L	E	U
V	I	L	L	A	G	E	G	N
Z	V	X	O	P	E	R	A	G
K	O	H	U	M	I	D	M	R
X	R	A	N	C	H	Q	A	Y
B	E	F	O	R	E	Z	D	X

- ○ Suffering because of a lack of food *(adjective)*
- ○ A drama set to music and made up of vocal pieces *(noun)*
- ○ To physically harm (something) *(verb)*
- ○ A short song that is easy to remember *(noun)*
- ○ Having no element or part left out *(adjective)*
- ○ An animal that eats both plants and other animals *(noun)*
- ○ Having a lot of moisture in the air *(adjective)*
- ○ A large farm for raising horses, cattle, or sheep *(noun)*
- ○ At an earlier time *(adverb)*
- ○ Not capable of being affected by a disease *(adjective)*
- ○ A small town in the country *(noun)*

150 | DIFFICULTY: ●●●●○○○○○○
COMPLETION: ☐ TIME: ________

WORD WINDER

Use the clue to help you find the answers word-winding their way through the grid. Each answer will connect the top of the grid to the bottom.

W	F	N	T	L	H
A	E	G	I	A	O
C	I	R	T	V	T
T	K	E	V	E	C
H	S	L	K	H	S
L	F	O	A	I	W
U	R	C	M	A	C
L	E	B	E	K	Y

Find five two-syllable words word-winding their way from top to bottom.

151 | DIFFICULTY: ●●●●○○○○○○ COMPLETION: ☐ TIME: ______

PRISM CROSS'D WORDS

Use the color-coded clues below to find words that fit in the like-colored portions of the puzzle grid below.

- ○ Somewhat or slightly wet (1-syllable adjective)
- ○ Pull apart by force (1-syllable verb)
- ○ The state of being frolicsome (3-syllable noun)

- ○ A large body of water (2-syllable noun)
- ○ To show what you have (2-syllable verb)

- ○ Any multisided figure (3-syllable noun)
- ○ In a time before the present (1-syllable adjective)

- ○ A long, thin, pointed flag (2-syllable noun)
- ○ To take a deep breath (1-syllable verb)

- ○ A tornado or dust devil (2-syllable noun)
- ○ Having excessive body fat (2-syllable adjective)

152 | DIFFICULTY: ●●●●○○○○○○
COMPLETION: ☐ TIME: ______

MAKE THE CONNECTION

Fill in the boxes with common two-word phrases with the help of the clues below. The last word in each pair will be the first word in the following pair.

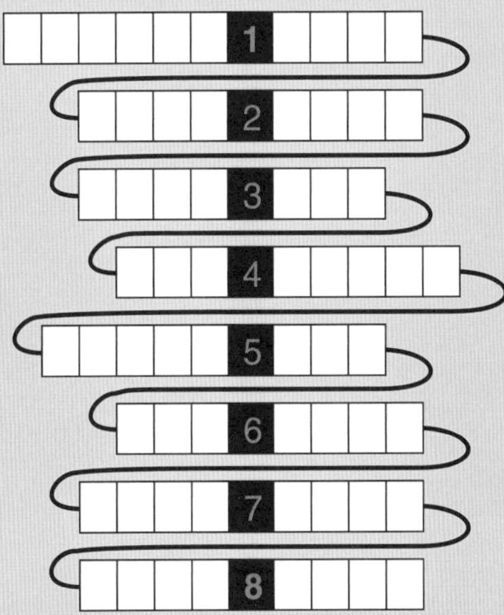

1 It's used to buy now and pay later
2 Uno or gin rummy
3 Handheld Nintendo
4 He's always prepared
5 Look for
6 Nevada, to Georgia
7 Disputed land near the River Jordan
8 Way to sink a ball in pool

153 | DIFFICULTY: ●●●●○○○○○○ COMPLETION: ☐ TIME: ______

SYLLABARY

Link word segments together in the grid below to create words, and enter them in the blanks.

I	A	TIVE	GO	RY
RON	NEG	CAT	E	OP
I	CAL	LY	DE	VEL
UN	ION	OP	ER	LUTE
RE	CO	AB	SO	ATE

Three-Syllable Adjective: _ _ _ O _ _ _

Four-Syllable Noun: _ _ _ _ _ O _ _

Five-Syllable Adverb: _ R _ _ _ _ _ _ _ _

Three-Syllable Noun: _ _ _ _ _ _ N

Four-Syllable Verb: _ _ _ _ _ _ _ T _

Three-Syllable Adjective: _ _ _ _ T _ _ _

Three-Syllable Verb: _ _ V _ _ _ _

154 | DIFFICULTY: ●●●●○○○○○○ COMPLETION: ☐ TIME: ______

SYNONYM FINDER

Find and circle the six pairs of SYNONYMS, one on each side, in the letter grids below.

C	F	T	D	E	E
B	C	U	S	D	K
X	D	A	U	H	I
K	H	L	T	G	L
C	E	D	Y	C	A
P	I	C	K	D	H

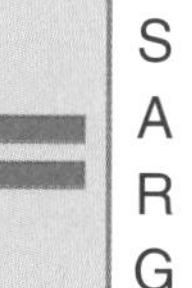

P	S	A	M	E	T
S	U	H	Y	C	P
A	D	R	E	T	O
R	P	L	S	C	L
G	E	R	R	U	F
S	E	V	A	D	E

○○○○○○

155 | DIFFICULTY: ●●●●○○○○○○ COMPLETION: ☐ TIME: ______

ANTONYM FINDER

Find and circle the six pairs of ANTONYMS, one on each side, in the letter grids below.

Y	D	I	R	T	Y
F	W	F	D	S	F
E	B	G	A	E	C
U	H	E	L	S	P
D	M	B	A	D	T
C	A	W	N	R	Y

H	V	N	D	W	F
A	M	C	O	E	K
R	W	L	G	C	A
D	S	E	C	A	E
E	V	A	D	E	W
B	G	N	F	P	W

○○○○○○

156 | DIFFICULTY: ●●●●○○○○○○
COMPLETION: ☐ TIME: ________

SYNONYM UNSCRAMBLE

Unscramble the letters below to form pairs of SYNONYMS. Watch out—some words can be unscrambled more than one way!

L S Y = F R Y T A C

L A A Y L = S T E O H O

C L I R R A C U = U D R N O

E N K E = R A S P H

K H N I T = D R O P E N

O M D H E T = Y T M E S S

N Y A M = I S A U R V O

157 | DIFFICULTY: ●●●●○○○○○○
COMPLETION: ☐ TIME: ______

MISSING DEFINITIONS FINDER

Using the clues below, find and circle the words concealed in the letter grid.

A	S	M	E	L	L	Z	E	B	N
L	C	J	P	A	A	G	Q	O	S
I	X	T	M	L	A	K	I	J	T
K	H	R	I	R	E	T	E	L	U
I	O	E	E	O	A	A	U	S	D
N	Z	V	A	C	N	S	S	V	Y
G	A	X	O	R	E	Q	Z	E	F
Q	J	L	B	R	I	V	E	R	S

ab·nor·mal *adjective* \(ˌ)ab-ˈnȯr-məl, əb-\
different from what is ________ or ________

con·se·quence *noun* \ˈkän(t)-sə-ˌkwen(t)s, -kwən(t)s\
something that happens as a ________ of a particular ________

dis·tinct *adjective* \di-ˈstiŋ(k)t\
different in a way that you can see, ________, ________, feel, etc.

fas·tid·i·ous *adjective* \fa-ˈsti-dē-əs, fə-\
________ few things : hard to ________

ge·og·ra·phy *noun* \jē-ˈä-grə-fē\
an area of ________ that deals with the ________ of countries, cities, ________, mountains, ________, etc.

158 | DIFFICULTY: ●●●●●○○○○○ COMPLETION: ☐ TIME: ______

CROSS'D WORDS UNSCRAMBLE

Unscramble the letters in each clue to fill in the puzzle grid below.

ACROSS

1 SMASI *(two-syllable word)*
3 UFOMR *(two-syllable word)*
5 BIEDLBR *(two-syllable word)*
7 HUSTO *(one-syllable word)*
8 RHEET *(one-syllable word)*
9 ICIMM *(two-syllable word)*
11 SCUFO *(two-syllable word)*
13 PLOTAIC *(three-syllable word)*
14 RHOON *(two-syllable word)*
15 TYLRU *(two-syllable word)*

DOWN

1 SASAM *(two-syllable word)*
2 TWFSI *(one-syllable word)*
3 LAFEB *(two-syllable word)*
4 YOMAR *(two-syllable word)*
5 TRAMODO *(two-syllable word)*
6 CLEAHIT *(three-syllable word)*
9 OHMTU *(one-syllable word)*
10 PRACE *(two-syllable word)*
11 TEAFC *(two-syllable word)*
12 ASCYU *(two-syllable word)*

159 | DIFFICULTY: ●●●●●○○○○○
COMPLETION: ☐ TIME: ______

ANTONYM UNSCRAMBLE

Unscramble the letters below to form pairs of ANTONYMS. Note: Some words can be unscrambled more than one way!

S P T O ≠ E N N C U T O I

N E E V ≠ D O D

T A I Y V N ≠ S M E T O Y D

P R E W O ≠ S K E E N S A W

L H E W O ≠ I V E D D I D

G E E H H I N T ≠ R O L E W

T R E E A S A P ≠ I O J N

160 | DIFFICULTY: ●●●●○○○○○○ COMPLETION: ☐ TIME: ______

MIXED-UP DEFINITION

Unscramble the letters below to reveal the definition of the given word.

em·blem *noun* \ˈem-bləm\
na jocteb dsue ot gussteg a ghitn ahtt tncona eb whnso

161 | DIFFICULTY: ●●●●●○○○○○ COMPLETION: ☐ TIME: ______

SYNONYM FINDER

Find and circle the six pairs of SYNONYMS, one on each side, in the letter grids below.

T	F	D	B	M	L
A	N	E	I	T	G
E	C	R	U	E	L
H	B	F	M	D	O
C	Y	K	C	H	O
H	G	L	E	E	M

=

T	E	D	G	E	L
L	C	P	C	A	W
W	J	H	T	M	E
A	O	U	E	P	H
R	R	E	U	E	W
B	W	D	N	P	R

○ ○ ○ ○ ○ ○

162 | DIFFICULTY: ●●●●○○○○○○
COMPLETION: ☐ TIME: ______

MAKE THE CONNECTION

Fill in the boxes with common two-word phrases with the help of the clues below. The last word in each pair will be the first word in the following pair.

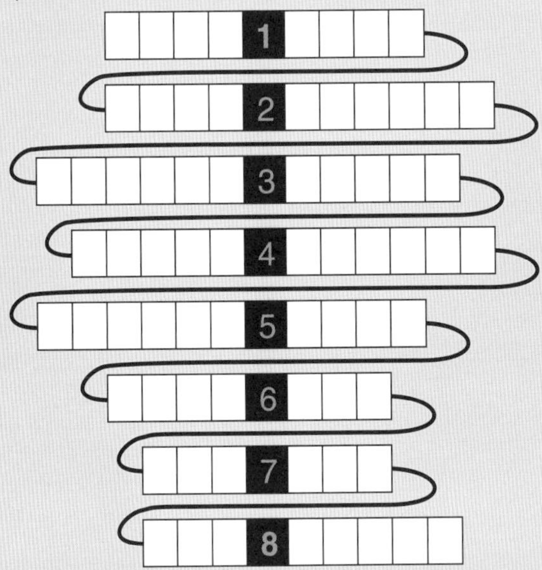

1 One-on-one meeting
2 Common sci-fi theme
3 Trip planner
4 Poison used in the Vietnam War
5 Sunkist, for one
6 Carbonated beverage
7 Easy catch for an outfielder
8 Do something without preparing

163 | DIFFICULTY: ●●●●●○○○○○
COMPLETION: ☐ TIME: ________

MISSING DEFINITIONS FINDER

Using the clues below, find and circle the words concealed in the letter grid.

R	Q	C	I	N	S	E	C	T	S
E	P	R	O	P	E	R	X	V	J
S	L	O	W	M	S	O	U	N	D
P	X	Z	K	J	F	V	H	X	A
E	N	O	U	G	H	O	S	Q	N
C	S	H	E	L	T	E	R	K	G
T	A	C	T	I	O	N	A	T	E
J	V	L	A	R	G	E	H	Z	R

ca·coph·o·ny *noun* \ka-ˈkä-fə-nē, -ˈkȯ- also -ˈka-\
_______ or discordant _______

flip·pant *adjective* \ˈfli-pənt\
lacking _______ _______ or seriousness

im·pede *transitive verb* \im-ˈpēd\
to _______ the movement, progress, or _______ of (someone or something)

mea·ger *adjective* \ˈmē-gər\
not having _______ of something (such as money or food) for _______ or happiness

ref·uge *noun* \ˈre-(ˌ)fyüj also -(ˌ)fyüzh\
_______ or protection from _______ or trouble

swarm *noun* \ˈswȯrm\
a very _______ number of _______ moving together

164 | DIFFICULTY: ●●●●○○○○○○
COMPLETION: ☐ TIME: ______

CROSS'D WORD CONNECTIONS

The crosswords below share common letters as indicated by the colored boxes. Use the clues to solve the puzzles.

ACROSS
1 A usually rectangular-shaped bag
4 Easily damaged or destroyed
5 To cause (something) to be seen
DOWN
1 A strong metal box with a lock that is used to store money or valuable things
2 To come into conflict
3 Not moving quickly

ACROSS
1 A strong feeling of anger that is difficult to control
4 A group of singers especially in a church
5 To cook slowly in hot liquid
DOWN
1 A contest of speed
2 To show in an improper way that you are happy with your own success
3 To increase in size, amount, etc.

ACROSS
1 Moving or able to move quickly
4 To decay or lose freshness especially because of being kept too long
5 A small area of a surface that is different from other areas
DOWN
1 To become joined by melting together
2 A small sailboat with one mast
3 A narrow opening or groove

165 | DIFFICULTY: ●●●●●●●○○○○
COMPLETION: ☐ TIME: ______

WORD WINDER

Use the clue to help you find the answers word-winding their way through the grid. Each answer will connect the top of the grid to the bottom.

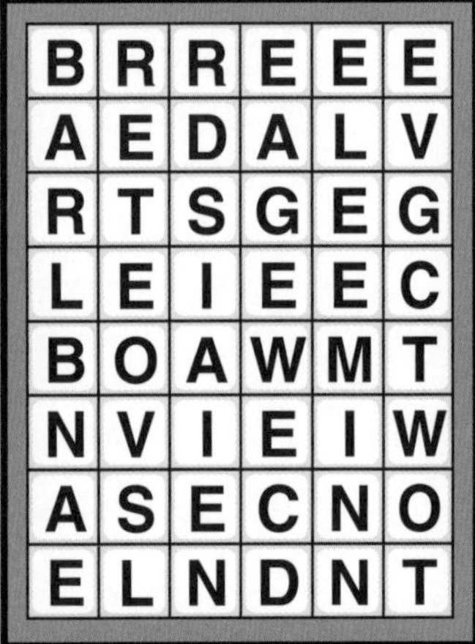

B	R	R	E	E	E
A	E	D	A	L	V
R	T	S	G	E	G
L	E	I	E	E	C
B	O	A	W	M	T
N	V	I	E	I	W
A	S	E	C	N	O
E	L	N	D	N	T

Find five words with the same number of consonants and vowels word-winding their way from top to bottom.

______

______

______

______

______

166 | DIFFICULTY: ●●●●○○○○○○
COMPLETION: ☐ TIME: ______

ANTONYM FINDER

Find and circle the seven pairs of ANTONYMS divided between the letter grids below.

R	A	C	O	A	R	S	E
A	E	V	J	X	Q	W	N
E	T	C	E	Z	K	Z	A
C	J	T	A	R	J	W	R
I	Q	Z	E	N	A	X	E
L	Z	M	Q	N	T	G	T
A	X	J	Z	X	D	P	E
M	D	A	P	P	E	R	V

Z	Q	J	M	D	T	E	Q
C	G	X	W	A	C	C	E
S	P	L	H	I	E	H	S
B	L	Z	V	N	L	A	R
J	Q	O	C	T	G	R	O
G	N	X	P	Y	E	I	D
X	Z	K	M	P	N	T	N
Q	U	I	R	K	Y	Y	E

○ ○ ○ ○ ○ ○ ○

167 | DIFFICULTY: ●●●●●●●○○○○
COMPLETION: ☐ TIME: ______

DICTIONARY CROSS'D WORDS

Fill in the puzzle using the Merriam-Webster definition clues below.

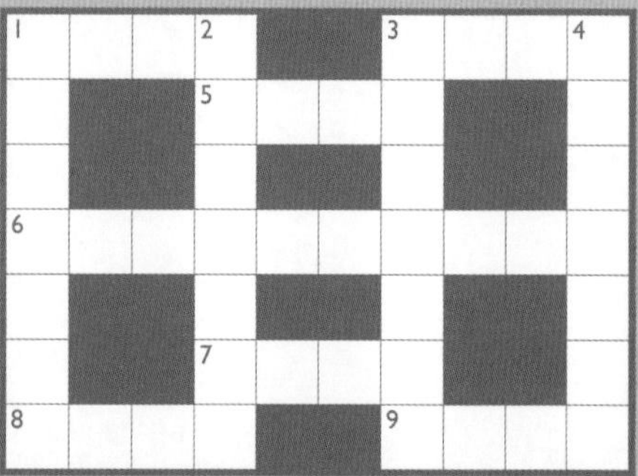

Across
1 Structure providing means of flight (1-syllable noun)
3 Trodden way (1-syllable noun)
5 In or at this place (1-syllable noun)
6 Unhelpful, unkind, or harmful act (3-syllable noun)
7 Diminished by (1-syllable preposition)
8 Lacking cheer or brightness (1-syllable adjective)
9 24th part of a day (1-syllable noun)

Down
1 Exhaustively talking person (2-syllable noun)
2 Horrible to the senses (2-syllable adjective)
3 Marked by ill temper (2-syllable adjective)
4 In whatever manner (3-syllable conjunction)

168 | DIFFICULTY: ●●●●○○○○○○
COMPLETION: ☐ TIME: ________

SYLLABARY

Link word segments together in the grid below to create words, and enter them in the blanks.

LI	GA	TOR	WIL	DER
AL	TE	RI	A	NESS
E	HIS	PAS	SION	MENT
CAF	TOR	ATE	ATE	I
OP	ER	IC	EX	PER

Three-Syllable Adjective: _ _ _ T _ _ _ _

Four-Syllable Noun: _ L _ _ _ _ _ _ _

Four-Syllable Verb: _ _ P _ _ _ _ _ _ _

Three-Syllable Verb: _ _ _ _ _ _ E

Three-Syllable Adjective: _ _ _ _ _ _ N _ _ _

Three-Syllable Noun: _ _ _ _ _ _ _ _ S _

Five-Syllable Noun: _ _ _ _ T _ _ _ _

169 | DIFFICULTY: ●●●●●●○○○○ COMPLETION: ☐ TIME: ______

DICTIONARY UNSCRAMBLE

Unscramble the letters below to form words that match the Merriam-Webster definitions.

noun Any one of the very large groups of stars that make up the universe

XAAGYL= ☐☐☐☐☐☐

adjective
Disposed to suspect rivalry or unfaithfulness

SLUJOAE= ☐☐☐☐☐☐☐

adjective Made in or representative of the work of an earlier period

QATENUI= ☐☐☐☐☐☐☐

adverb
Marked by little or no motion or activity

QIYELUT= ☐☐☐☐☐☐☐

adjective Often or easily becoming worried and afraid about what might happen

SRONUVE= ☐☐☐☐☐☐☐

transitive verb To talk or argue with someone especially in order to agree on a price

GEGHLA= ☐☐☐☐☐☐

170 | DIFFICULTY: ●●●●○○○○○○
COMPLETION: ☐ TIME: ______

DEFINITION FINDER

Using the clues below, find and circle the words concealed in the letter grid.

B	N	Z	N	E	V	E	R	X
E	L	U	X	U	R	Y	J	C
L	Q	A	M	O	U	N	T	O
A	V	X	W	E	A	V	E	M
H	Z	A	P	P	R	O	V	E
X	R	A	P	I	D	O	V	D
E	D	O	U	B	T	X	U	Y
J	U	S	T	I	F	Y	J	S

- ○ Happening in a short amount of time *(adjective)*
- ○ To interlace (as threads) into cloth *(verb)*
- ○ The total number or quantity *(noun)*
- ○ To provide or be a good reason for (something) *(verb)*
- ○ To be uncertain about (something) *(verb)*
- ○ Not ever : at no time *(adverb)*
- ○ A drama of light and amusing character *(noun)*
- ○ To breathe out *(verb)*
- ○ Something that is expensive and not necessary *(noun)*
- ○ To give formal or official sanction to *(verb)*
- ○ Existing in large numbers *(adjective)*

171 | DIFFICULTY: ●●●●●○○○○○
COMPLETION: ☐ TIME: ______

SYNONYM UNSCRAMBLE

Unscramble the letters below to form pairs of SYNONYMS. Watch out—some words can be unscrambled more than one way!

I F L A = U F L K N

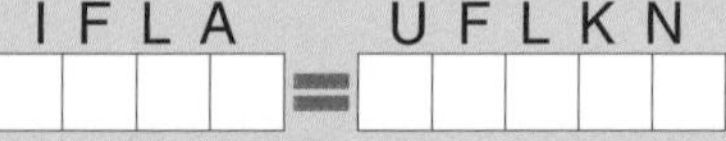

T H O S I = A L E E T E V

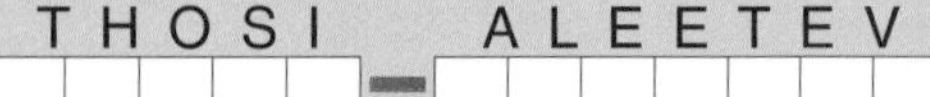

T R O S M A D = M F E A

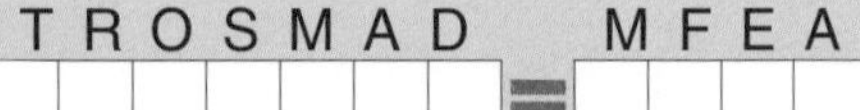

E O Y N M = R C C U Y N R E

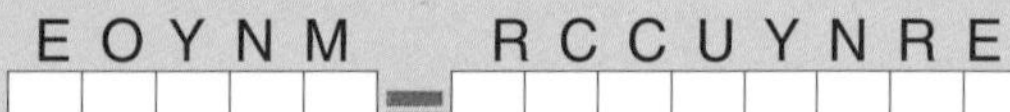

C E T H A = S C R I T T U N

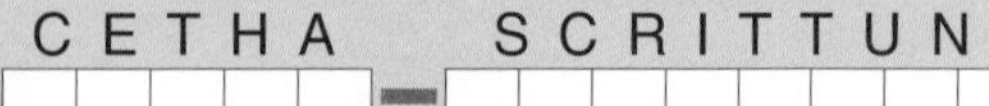

K R E B N O = A D M H E S S

C S E P H E = I N T O O A R

172 | DIFFICULTY: ●●●●●●○○○○
COMPLETION: ☐ TIME: ______

DICTIONARY WORD WINDER

Use the clues below to help you find the answers word-winding their way through the grid. Each answer will connect one side of the grid to the other—left to right, top to bottom, right to left, and bottom to top.

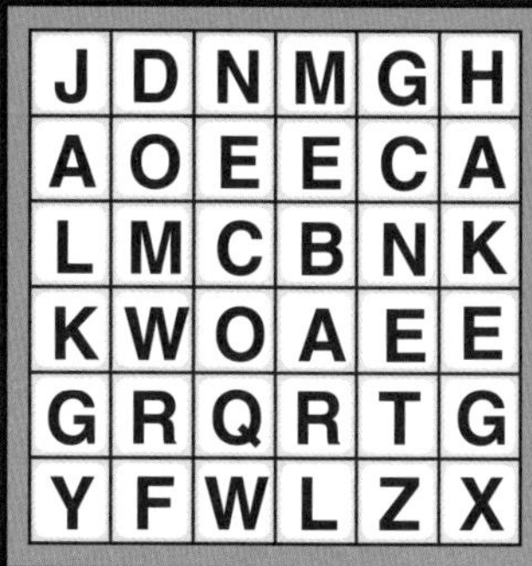

J	D	N	M	G	H
A	O	E	E	C	A
L	M	C	B	N	K
K	W	O	A	E	E
G	R	Q	R	T	G
Y	F	W	L	Z	X

→ To find the place or position of (something or someone) ______

↓ The things learned and kept in the mind ______

← A list or outline of things to be considered or done ______

↑ A tool consisting of a handle with one end designed to hold, twist, or turn an object (such as a bolt or nut) ______

173 | DIFFICULTY: ●●●●●○○○○○
COMPLETION: ☐ TIME: ______

PRISM WORD FINDER

Using the color-coded clues below, find and circle the words in the letter grid.

G	B	S	T	Q	D	M	O	V	I	E
N	S	S	P	E	U	W	K	L	C	Q
P	A	I	E	E	E	I	H	T	K	S
F	A	C	M	L	E	E	C	Z	R	U
O	X	R	D	P	Z	D	Y	K	Y	O
E	V	E	T	E	L	L	Y	L	J	I
K	E	E	E	L	E	Y	E	R	T	V
N	L	H	R	R	Y	R	W	M	F	I
B	W	G	A	L	U	H	J	G	I	L
Z	T	R	B	S	Y	F	M	C	W	B
A	C	T	I	V	A	T	E	D	S	O

Find five six-letter adverbs ending in "LY" starting with an orange letter ○○○○○

Find four antonyms for "slow" starting with a blue letter ○○○○

Find three words with "V" in the middle starting with a purple letter ○○○

Find three six-letter words with three "E's" starting with a red letter ○○○

174 | DIFFICULTY: ●●●●●●○○○○
COMPLETION: ☐ TIME: ______

PRISM CROSS'D WORDS

Use the color-coded clues below to find words that fit in the like-colored portions of the puzzle grid below.

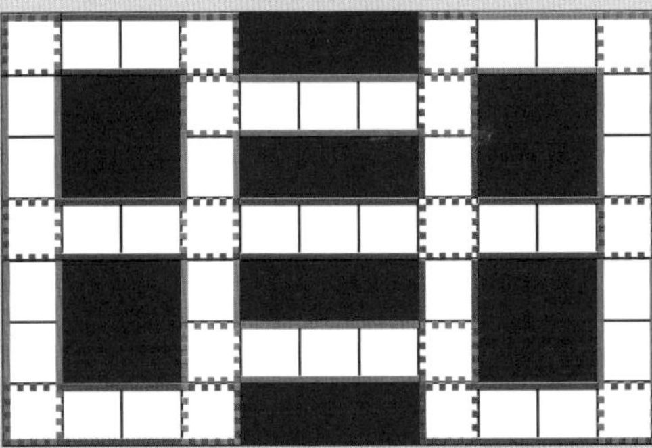

- ● Requirement as part of an agreement (4-syllable noun)
- ● A long, formal dress (1-syllable noun)
- ● Characterized by optimism (2-syllable adjective)

- ● Spectral, phantasmal (2-syllable adjective)
- ● To yearn for (1-syllable verb)

- ● Go continuously in one direction (1-syllable verb)
- ● To criticize for tiny faults (2-syllable verb)

- ● To flap the wings rapidly (2-syllable verb)
- ● The yellow part of an egg (1-syllable noun)

- ● Not according to truth or facts (2-syllable adverb)
- ● To urge or drive forward (2-syllable verb)

175 | DIFFICULTY: ●●●●●●●○○○
COMPLETION: ☐ TIME: ______

DICTIONARY UNSCRAMBLE

Unscramble the letters below to form words that match the Merriam-Webster definitions.

transitive verb To lose or give up (something) as a punishment or because of a rule or law

TREFFIO= ☐☐☐☐☐☐☐

noun
Something that you have to go around or over

BLOCSETA= ☐☐☐☐☐☐☐☐

adjective
Having a pleasant and usually sweet smell

ATGRRFAN= ☐☐☐☐☐☐☐☐

noun A written statement that promises the good condition of a product

RATRYAWN= ☐☐☐☐☐☐☐☐

adjective
Able to be touched or felt

ABGLINTE= ☐☐☐☐☐☐☐☐

transitive verb To make greater, more numerous, larger, or more intense

UTANGEM= ☐☐☐☐☐☐☐

176 | DIFFICULTY: ●●●●●●●●○○○ COMPLETION: ☐ TIME: ______

MIXED-UP DEFINITION

Unscramble the letters below to reveal the definition of the given word.

deb·o·nair *adjective* \ˌde-bə-ˈner\
sridgsen adn taigcn ni na plenagipa dan cottsiidsapeh awy

177 | DIFFICULTY: ●●●●●●●○○○○ COMPLETION: ☐ TIME: ______

COLOR WORD CHAINS

Use the clues and letters below to make word paths between like colors to fill the board.

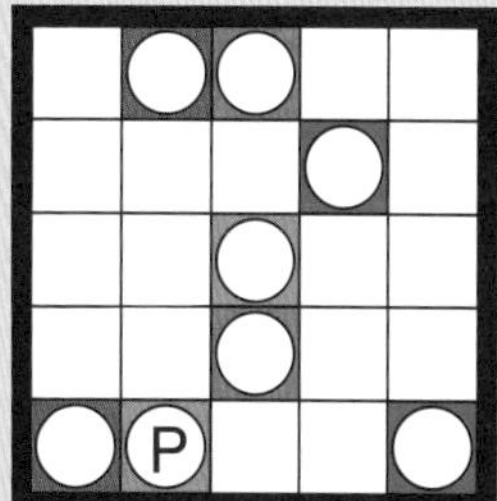

- A wrapped package
- A tough connective tissue
- To enter in order to take control by military force
- Of utmost importance

A	A	A	C	C	C
D	D	E	E	E	I
I	L	L	N	N	N
O	R	R	T	U	V

178 | DIFFICULTY: ●●●●●●●●○○○
COMPLETION: ☐ TIME: ______

ANTONYM FINDER

Find and circle the six pairs of ANTONYMS, one on each side, in the letter grids below.

E	H	A	Z	Y	H
D	L	W	N	C	A
I	B	Y	T	Y	P
B	D	A	I	C	P
A	C	P	H	N	Y
M	K	E	E	N	G

S	B	S	W	R	T
S	K	L	A	M	Y
I	M	E	U	D	N
M	L	O	H	N	S
C	M	T	V	L	T
J	T	R	U	E	B

○○○○○○

179 | DIFFICULTY: ●●●●●●●●○○○
COMPLETION: ☐ TIME: ______

SYNONYM FINDER

Find and circle the six pairs of SYNONYMS, one on each side, in the letter grids below.

C	Q	A	B	E	T
A	H	F	C	S	U
M	Z	O	I	J	O
E	Y	S	O	C	B
N	E	D	W	S	A
D	E	F	E	R	E

R	E	V	I	S	E
K	D	F	J	K	S
L	A	E	C	D	A
H	D	I	L	M	E
Y	P	G	D	A	C
N	E	A	R	L	Y

○○○○○○

180 | DIFFICULTY: ●●●●●●○○○○
COMPLETION: ☐ TIME: ______

SYNONYM FINDER

Find and circle the seven pairs of SYNONYMS divided between the letter grids below.

T	S	J	S	M	H	T	N
C	R	C	G	N	C	O	C
E	P	Q	A	E	I	D	E
T	F	Y	R	T	L	B	N
E	L	R	C	E	T	P	D
D	O	N	I	D	N	E	U
C	A	Y	W	T	K	T	R
S	U	P	P	O	S	E	E

A	Q	L	W	R	I	D	R
E	P	E	T	J	M	N	E
S	F	P	X	Y	P	T	F
I	W	S	R	P	R	G	F
M	P	I	H	O	O	M	U
R	F	D	K	B	V	S	S
U	J	C	G	L	E	A	E
S	U	B	M	I	T	Z	L

○○○○○○○

181 | DIFFICULTY: ●●●●●●●●○○○
COMPLETION: ☐ TIME: ______

CROSS'D WORDS UNSCRAMBLE

Unscramble the letters in each clue to fill in the puzzle grid below.

1				2		3				4
		5						6		
7						8				
9				10		11				12
		13								
14						15				

ACROSS

1 STRSU *(one-syllable word)*
3 SLAHF *(one-syllable word)*
5 UOQBETU *(two-syllable word)*
7 CIEPB *(two-syllable word)*
8 TRYID *(two-syllable word)*
9 TLBNU *(one-syllable word)*
11 FIMAA *(three-syllable word)*
13 TAXLYEC *(three-syllable word)*
14 NODER *(one-syllable word)*
15 VIEOL *(two-syllable word)*

DOWN

1 BRTOH *(one-syllable word)*
2 PLUSM *(one-syllable word)*
3 ULFID *(two-syllable word)*
4 NOYHE *(two-syllable word)*
5 SCEEBUA *(two-syllable word)*
6 FRYTTIH *(two-syllable word)*
9 NBALD *(one-syllable word)*
10 SEETA *(one-syllable word)*
11 TOOMT *(two-syllable word)*
12 RAAEW *(two-syllable word)*

182 | DIFFICULTY: ●●●●●○○○○○
COMPLETION: ☐ TIME: ______

MAKE THE CONNECTION

Fill in the boxes with common two-word phrases with the help of the clues below. The last word in each pair will be the first word in the following pair.

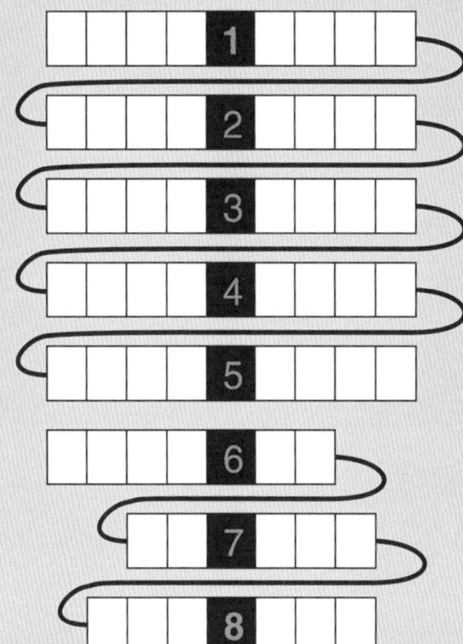

1 No longer using
2 Like "affectionately yours"
3 Sitcom about the Ricardos: "I ____ ____"
4 It featured Mr. Mooney: "The ____ ____"
5 Poster
6 "Charge it"
7 Statement of agreement
8 "Such a pity"

183 | DIFFICULTY: ●●●●●●○○○○
COMPLETION: ☐ TIME: ______

ANTONYM UNSCRAMBLE

Unscramble the letters below to form pairs of ANTONYMS. Note: Some words can be unscrambled more than one way!

ERRA ≠ MOONCM

DRAENW ≠ YSAT

TRNFO ≠ CAKB

FYSEAT ≠ GRAEND

NAITIGGC ≠ NYTI

EHED ≠ RINEOG

NSEEICL ≠ RACMLO

184 | DIFFICULTY: ●●●●●○○○○○
COMPLETION: ☐ TIME: ________

WORD WINDER

Use the clue to help you find the answers word-winding their way through the grid. Each answer will connect the top of the grid to the bottom.

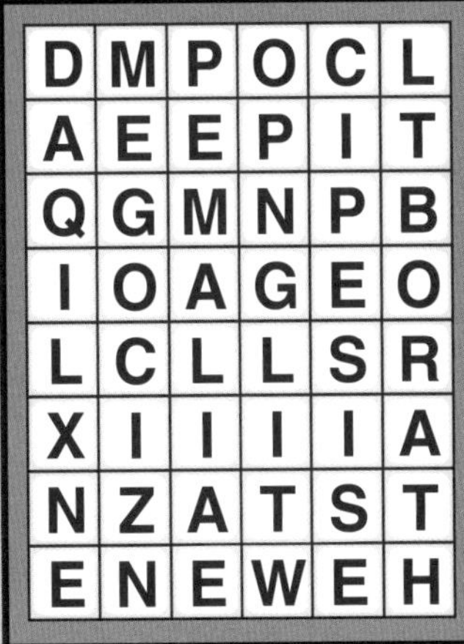

D	M	P	O	C	L
A	E	E	P	I	T
Q	G	M	N	P	B
I	O	A	G	E	O
L	C	L	L	S	R
X	I	I	I	I	A
N	Z	A	T	S	T
E	N	E	W	E	H

↓ Find five three-syllable words word-winding their way from top to bottom.

185 | DIFFICULTY: ●●●●●○○○○○
COMPLETION: ☐ TIME: ______

PRISM WORD FINDER

Using the color-coded clues below, find and circle the words in the letter grid.

I	N	E	P	T	W	B	S	T	C	G
P	S	J	L	G	R	M	L	I	H	K
S	R	N	V	D	P	E	V	O	L	V
J	C	O	O	Z	E	I	F	L	O	E
K	X	O	O	W	C	N	A	E	D	D
R	A	L	O	F	F	F	S	U	R	E
O	W	Y	Q	T	N	A	R	E	L	S
O	K	C	A	I	T	C	L	A	B	O
L	M	G	A	K	W	L	G	L	P	O
F	B	R	J	V	C	E	W	Q	X	M
R	O	T	O	R	R	L	E	V	E	L

Find five five-letter palindromes starting with an orange letter ○ ○ ○ ○ ○

Find five five-letter words with double "O's" starting with a blue letter ○ ○ ○ ○ ○

Find four five-letter adjectives starting with a purple letter ○ ○ ○ ○

Find two eight-letter weather terms starting with a red letter ○ ○

186 | DIFFICULTY: ●●●●●●●○○○ COMPLETION: ☐ TIME: ______

SYNONYM FINDER

Find and circle the six pairs of SYNONYMS, one on each side, in the letter grids below.

W	N	C	A	R	E
B	K	S	I	C	N
A	C	L	N	H	O
S	Y	A	E	P	L
I	H	C	P	K	A
C	B	K	T	B	C

=

○○○○○○

187 | DIFFICULTY: ●●●●●●○○○○ COMPLETION: ☐ TIME: ______

COLOR WORD CHAINS

Use the clues and letters below to make word paths between like colors to fill the board.

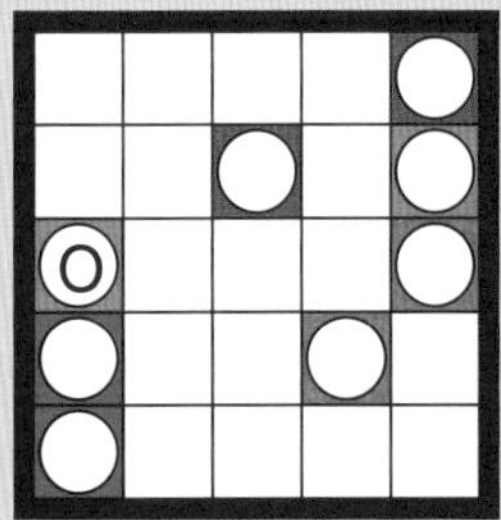

- To try to stop or defeat
- A lobby or entrance hall
- A written list of things and the times they will be done
- To pay no attention to

C	D	E	E	E	E
E	F	G	H	I	L
N	O	O	O	P	P
R	R	S	S	U	Y

188 | DIFFICULTY: ●●●●●●●○○○
COMPLETION: ☐ TIME: ______

SYLLABARY

Link word segments together in the grid below to create words, and enter them in the blanks.

ES	MOR	MATE	DEC	O
TO	TI	ROW	FOR	RA
CU	RI	OS	TIVE	TU
A	O	REL	I	NATE
POL	GIZE	A	TIVE	TY

Three-Syllable Noun: _ _ _ A _ _ _ _

Four-Syllable Adjective: _ _ C _ _ _ _ _ _ _

Five-Syllable Noun: _ U _ _ _ _ _ _ _

Three-Syllable Verb: _ _ _ _ _ _ _ E

Three-Syllable Noun: _ _ _ _ _ R _ _

Four-Syllable Verb: _ _ _ _ O _ _ _ _

Three-Syllable Adjective: _ _ _ T _ _ _ _ _

189 | DIFFICULTY: ●●●●●●●●○○○
COMPLETION: ☐ TIME: ______

SYNONYM UNSCRAMBLE

Unscramble the letters below to form pairs of SYNONYMS. Watch out—some words can be unscrambled more than one way!

R A N E = J E D T A A N C

L A D D E W = T R O L I E

T L Y Q I A U = S L S C A

S T U E P = V U R N E E N

R K H N I S = L I D D W E N

F R Y T I A = N I C M O R F

Y O L L A = L I F F H A U T

190 | DIFFICULTY: ●●●●●●○○○○
COMPLETION: ☐ TIME: ______

PRISM CROSS'D WORDS

Use the color-coded clues below to find words that fit in the like-colored portions of the puzzle grid below.

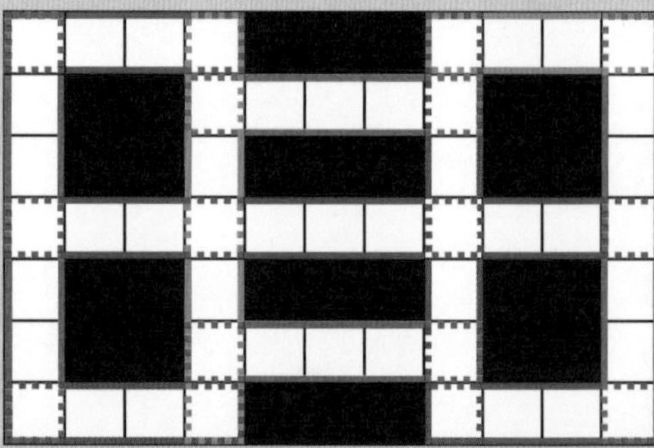

- ○ An instance of acting badly (4-syllable noun)
- ○ To suddenly pull something (1-syllable verb)
- ○ A plucked stringed instrument (1-syllable noun)

- ○ A hanging bed or couch (2-syllable noun)
- ○ Move on hands and knees (1-syllable verb)

- ○ A circle of light (2-syllable noun)
- ○ Punishment for a past deed (2-syllable noun)

- ○ To strike with the foot or feet (1-syllable verb)
- ○ To a great degree (3-syllable adverb)

- ○ To be more important than (2-syllable verb)
- ○ To show or cause astonishment (2-syllable verb)

191 | DIFFICULTY: ●●●●●●○○○○
COMPLETION: ☐ TIME: ______

DICTIONARY CROSS'D WORDS

Fill in the puzzle using the Merriam-Webster definition clues below.

Across
1 To touch with the lips (1-syllable verb)
3 Give way suddenly under strain (1-syllable verb)
5 To ascertain the heaviness (1-syllable verb)
6 Larva of a butterfly or moth (4-syllable noun)
7 A state of uncertainty (2-syllable noun)
8 Sympathetic sorrow (2-syllable noun)
9 To have a desire for (1-syllable verb)

Down
1 Thick sauce made with tomatoes (2-syllable noun)
2 In a gentle, kind, or friendly manner (2-syllable adverb)
3 Having little depth (2-syllable adjective)
4 A ruler of ancient Egypt (2-syllable noun)

192 | DIFFICULTY: ●●●●●○○○○○
COMPLETION: ☐ TIME: ______

DEFINITION FINDER

Using the clues below, find and circle the words concealed in the letter grid.

- ○ The essential or most vital part of something *(noun)*
- ○ Easy to see or understand *(adjective)*
- ○ The contractile aperture in the iris of the eye *(noun)*
- ○ Careful about spending money *(adjective)*
- ○ A slight irregularity, error, or malfunction *(noun)*
- ○ Lacking ease or grace *(adjective)*
- ○ A person who has just started a job or activity *(noun)*
- ○ A bright or shining quality *(noun)*
- ○ To be carried along by moving water or air *(verb)*
- ○ To view closely in critical appraisal *(verb)*
- ○ Few in number or little in amount *(adjective)*

193 | DIFFICULTY: ●●●●●●○○○○ COMPLETION: ☐ TIME: ______

CROSS'D WORD CONNECTIONS

The crosswords below share common letters as indicated by the colored boxes. Use the clues to solve the puzzles.

ACROSS
1 A rubber disk used in ice hockey
4 Used in Hawaii to say hello or good-bye
5 To stop doing work or an activity
DOWN
1 A method for achieving an end
2 A person or thing that appears to be an exact copy of another person or thing
3 A small wheeled vehicle

ACROSS
1 A male deer or antelope
4 Friend
5 A long pole rising from the keel or deck of a ship and supporting the yards, booms, and rigging
DOWN
1 A feeling of being bored, tired, etc.
2 Porcelain wares for domestic use
3 To separate and put in a particular order

ACROSS
1 A regular solid of six equal square sides
4 The large artery connected to the heart
5 A very untidy state or condition
DOWN
1 Applaud
2 Transported or transmitted by
3 Armed conflicts between countries or groups

194 | DIFFICULTY: ●●●●●○○○○○
COMPLETION: ☐ TIME: ______

PRISM WORD FINDER

Using the color-coded clues below, find and circle the words in the letter grid.

W	R	G	R	Z	M	C	H	E	E	P
B	D	E	H	A	Y	E	X	G	P	C
V	P	G	C	K	N	W	R	E	H	R
R	P	R	A	L	R	G	V	R	L	E
R	E	E	O	E	I	I	Y	W	Y	E
E	L	C	F	N	T	N	Y	B	R	L
N	V	E	E	C	O	V	E	E	C	D
D	R	Q	E	I	A	U	E	R	R	E
E	Z	J	K	E	V	H	N	L	E	E
R	D	L	H	K	C	E	L	T	E	R
A	R	A	T	H	E	R	R	B	K	C

Find five words that start and end with "R" starting with an orange letter ○○○○○

Find five five-letter words with double "E's" starting with a blue "C" ○○○○○

Find four five-letter adjectives ending in "Y" starting with a purple letter ○○○○

Find two parts of speech starting with a red letter ○○

195 | DIFFICULTY: ●●●●●●○○○○
COMPLETION: ☐ TIME: ______

WORD WINDER

Use the clue to help you find the answers word-winding their way through the grid. Each answer will connect the top of the grid to the bottom.

M	H	E	T	F	A
E	E	V	L	B	R
M	S	E	N	U	R
O	I	L	G	A	I
T	R	A	S	T	R
I	A	I	N	H	I
A	T	V	C	O	S
N	L	E	E	E	N

Find five words containing four vowels word-winding their way from top to bottom.

______

______

______

______

______

196 | DIFFICULTY: ●●●●●○○○○○
COMPLETION: ☐ TIME: ______

MAKE THE CONNECTION

Fill in the boxes with common two-word phrases with the help of the clues below. The last word in each pair will be the first word in the following pair.

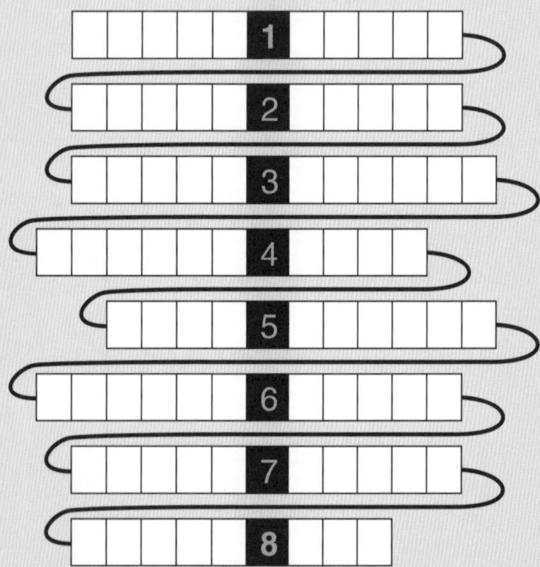

1 Eat
2 Serrated tool
3 Haft
4 Package warning: "_____ _____ care"
5 Burger-ordering option
6 It's often called "plain"
7 Piece of pie
8 Trim, cut

197 | DIFFICULTY: ●●●●●●○○○○ COMPLETION: ☐ TIME: ______

ANTONYM FINDER

Find and circle the six pairs of ANTONYMS, one on each side, in the letter grids below.

H	A	L	T	F	T
F	L	G	P	C	Y
R	T	O	A	C	D
A	B	X	N	I	L
F	E	A	J	G	N
N	F	C	M	H	K

≠

G	S	L	O	S	E
W	F	H	R	C	F
D	R	A	O	K	A
W	E	O	L	R	C
N	C	A	N	W	T
L	W	H	D	G	F

○○○○○○

198 | DIFFICULTY: ●●●●●○○○○○ COMPLETION: ☐ TIME: ______

MIXED-UP DEFINITION

Unscramble the letters below to reveal the definition of the given word.

no·mad·ic *adjective* \nō-ˈma-dik\
grianom uaotb mrof cleap ot lepca sillymase

☐☐☐☐☐☐☐
☐☐☐☐☐
☐☐☐☐ ☐☐☐☐☐
☐☐ ☐☐☐☐☐
☐☐☐☐☐☐☐☐☐

199 | DIFFICULTY: ●●●●●○○○○○ COMPLETION: ☐ TIME: ______

DICTIONARY UNSCRAMBLE

Unscramble the letters below to form words that match the Merriam-Webster definitions.

intransitive verb
To interfere without right or propriety

DEEMLD= ☐☐☐☐☐☐

adverb
Almost never

MOSLED= ☐☐☐☐☐☐

transitive verb
To refuse to buy, use, or participate in (something)

COOTBYT= ☐☐☐☐☐☐☐

adjective
Having a bad temper or complaining often

PRYMUG= ☐☐☐☐☐☐

noun A person who works for another person or for a company

LEYPEOME= ☐☐☐☐☐☐☐☐

adjective Having an old-fashioned or unusual quality or appearance

TAQNUI= ☐☐☐☐☐☐

200 | DIFFICULTY: ●●●●●○○○○○
COMPLETION: ☐ TIME: ________

MISSING DEFINITIONS FINDER

Using the clues below, find and circle the words concealed in the letter grid.

O	J	D	A	N	G	E	R	J	K
X	C	P	O	W	E	R	Z	F	W
P	O	C	A	P	T	U	R	E	O
E	V	E	A	R	I	S	K	E	L
O	E	A	E	S	V	Z	N	L	L
P	R	R	V	V	I	O	Q	I	O
L	E	T	I	X	O	O	Z	N	F
E	D	H	G	M	J	Q	N	G	X

cal·lous *adjective* \ˈka-ləs\
not ________ or showing any concern about the problems or suffering of other ________

eclipse *noun* \i-ˈklips\
an ________ when the sun looks like it is completely or partially ________ with a dark circle because the ________ is between the sun and the ________

jeop·ar·dize *transitive verb* \ˈje-pər-ˌdīz\
to expose to ________ or ________

man·date *transitive verb* \ˈman-ˌdāt\
to officially ________ (someone) the ________ to do something

pur·sue *verb* \pər-ˈsü, -ˈsyü\
to ________ and try to catch or ________ (someone or something)

201 | DIFFICULTY: ●●●●●○○○○○
COMPLETION: ☐ TIME: ______

ANTONYM UNSCRAMBLE

Unscramble the letters below to form pairs of ANTONYMS. Note: Some words can be unscrambled more than one way!

T R I H B ≠ T E H A D

L U L F ≠ P Y E T M

S R Y O M T ≠ M C L A

D R O E A ≠ D I S S E E P

N S Y N U ≠ D L U C Y O

W L O ≠ G I H H

S M N I E E M ≠ T I N U E M

202 | DIFFICULTY: ●●●●●○○○○○
COMPLETION: ☐ TIME: ______

DICTIONARY WORD WINDER

Use the clues below to help you find the answers word-winding their way through the grid. Each answer will connect one side of the grid to the other– left to right, top to bottom, right to left, and bottom to top.

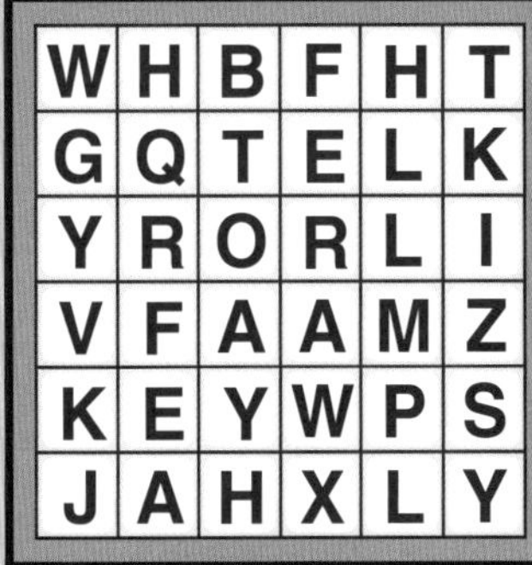

W	H	B	F	H	T
G	Q	T	E	L	K
Y	R	O	R	L	I
V	F	A	A	M	Z
K	E	Y	W	P	S
J	A	H	X	L	Y

→ To cross a street carelessly or at an illegal or dangerous place ______

↓ Easily broken, torn, etc. ______

← An idea or set of ideas that is intended to explain facts or events ______

↑ A brick, stone, or concrete area in front of a fireplace ______

203 | DIFFICULTY: ●●●●●○○○○○
COMPLETION: ☐ TIME: ______

ANTONYM FINDER

Find and circle the seven pairs of ANTONYMS divided between the letter grids below.

N	P	F	O	R	G	E	T
R	Q	R	Z	C	X	D	C
O	E	X	E	Y	Z	I	H
C	Y	V	P	C	T	K	A
S	X	M	I	P	I	Q	S
Z	U	J	E	V	P	S	T
B	Z	K	N	B	E	M	E
G	S	W	X	Z	Q	J	N

R	W	R	Q	H	R	B	R
E	I	Z	E	X	W	E	P
S	N	N	X	C	V	J	Y
P	E	K	E	E	A	A	T
E	K	X	I	X	L	L	A
C	A	L	F	E	A	N	L
T	E	B	D	M	Z	C	F
B	W	N	X	G	B	L	T

○○○○○○○

204 | DIFFICULTY: ●●●●●●○○○○ COMPLETION: ☐ TIME: ______

SYNONYM FINDER

Find and circle the six pairs of SYNONYMS, one on each side, in the letter grids below.

K	Y	A	M	L	G
C	E	N	T	E	R
L	X	N	P	A	A
L	Q	O	Z	S	N
U	R	Y	K	E	T
D	S	L	E	E	K

=

K	P	S	I	R	K
S	T	U	P	I	D
N	Y	C	M	T	W
W	K	O	I	L	Y
G	I	F	T	G	F
K	A	L	L	A	Y

○○○○○○

205 | DIFFICULTY: ●●●●●●○○○○ COMPLETION: ☐ TIME: ______

MIXED-UP DEFINITION

Unscramble the letters below to reveal the definition of the given word.

quix·ot·ic *adjective* \kwik-ˈsä-tik\
slohyolfi tricciaplam sleepyacil ni het stuuipr fo adseil

206 | DIFFICULTY: ●●●●●●○○○○
COMPLETION: ☐ TIME: ______

MAKE THE CONNECTION

Fill in the boxes with common two-word phrases with the help of the clues below. The last word in each pair will be the first word in the following pair.

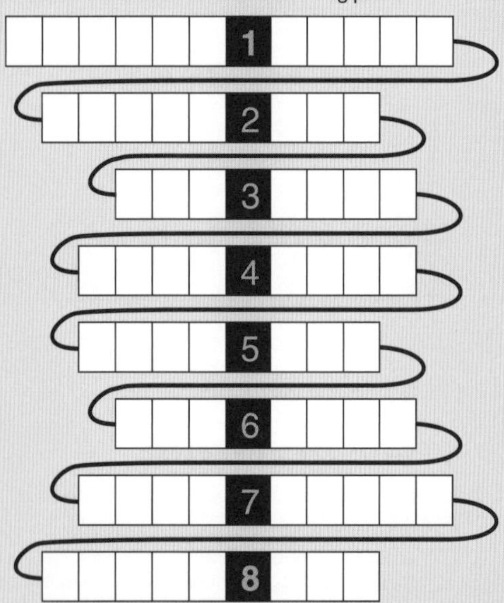

1 Certain North American waterfowl
2 The numeral zero
3 Appetizer option at a Chinese restaurant
4 Time to say "here!"
5 Summon
6 Available for purchase
7 Discounted amount
8 Competition that leads to lower costs

207 | DIFFICULTY: ●●●●●●●○○○○
COMPLETION: ☐ TIME: ______

PRISM WORD FINDER

Using the color-coded clues below, find and circle the words in the letter grid.

B	R	E	P	O	R	T	I	N	G	A
F	G	W	G	L	O	O	M	Y	K	R
S	A	Z	I	P	V	Q	O	V	C	I
H	K	U	H	N	K	E	D	B	L	A
X	E	J	L	P	T	E	N	Y	O	R
D	N	A	F	T	L	R	H	E	Q	E
E	E	V	R	E	Y	S	Y	A	E	A
R	E	J	E	T	A	R	M	D	Q	R
E	D	H	G	L	Y	I	D	E	A	J
E	E	V	F	S	E	C	E	D	E	W
V	D	Q	U	E	N	C	H	I	N	G

Find five six-letter adjectives ending in "Y" starting with an orange letter ○○○○○

Find five six-letter words with three "E's" starting with a blue letter ○○○○○

Find four four-letter words with three vowels starting with a purple letter ○○○○

Find two nine-letter verbs ending in "ING" starting with a red letter ○○

208 | DIFFICULTY: ●●●●●●●○○○○
COMPLETION: ☐ TIME: ______

WORD WINDER

Use the clue to help you find the answers word-winding their way through the grid. Each answer will connect the top of the grid to the bottom.

A	A	A	A	A	A
Q	D	G	V	U	L
E	U	I	L	I	D
G	Q	A	A	I	E
N	R	U	T	N	T
I	A	I	A	I	R
T	U	D	O	T	O
N	E	M	E	N	N

↓ Find five words containing five vowels word-winding their way from top to bottom.

______

______

______

______

______

209 | DIFFICULTY: ●●●●●●○○○○
COMPLETION: ☐ TIME: ______

SYNONYM UNSCRAMBLE

Unscramble the letters below to form pairs of SYNONYMS. Watch out—some words can be unscrambled more than one way!

Y P T I = M A P H Y Y S T

S R T E = P R O E S E

T U F A N L = P S I Y L D A

T O W U A L = T A D N I B

C O E T N I = B E E S R O V

L I G A N E = C L I O D A R

L A C C E N = S R I D E N C

210 | DIFFICULTY: ●●●●●●○○○○ COMPLETION: ☐ TIME: ________

ANTONYM FINDER

Find and circle the six pairs of ANTONYMS, one on each side, in the letter grids below.

M	S	O	B	E	R
R	C	F	J	B	O
I	E	P	L	M	A
F	D	H	F	O	M
Q	U	I	C	K	W
G	R	B	K	D	N

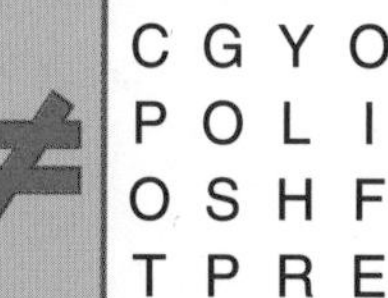

W	E	A	K	W	P
C	G	Y	O	K	L
P	O	L	I	T	E
O	S	H	F	D	W
T	P	R	E	S	T
S	D	R	U	N	K

○○○○○○

211 | DIFFICULTY: ●●●●●○○○○○ COMPLETION: ☐ TIME: ________

SYNONYM FINDER

Find and circle the six pairs of SYNONYMS, one on each side, in the letter grids below.

T	C	F	H	G	G
S	V	A	N	N	Y
E	K	I	I	F	E
H	L	R	F	V	M
C	A	A	I	P	F
D	D	G	L	P	G

A	K	L	H	M	Y
C	D	Y	O	K	K
E	L	H	N	N	C
D	O	K	E	U	A
E	B	Y	S	R	W
J	U	S	T	T	E

○○○○○○

212 | DIFFICULTY: ●●●●●○○○○○ COMPLETION: ☐ TIME: ______

CROSS'D WORDS UNSCRAMBLE

Unscramble the letters in each clue to fill in the puzzle grid below.

ACROSS

1 SRSBA *(one-syllable word)*
3 RELNA *(one-syllable word)*
5 RAQLURE *(two-syllable word)*
7 PRGHA *(one-syllable word)*
8 LEBCA *(two-syllable word)*
9 MOTTE *(two-syllable word)*
11 TREME *(two-syllable word)*
13 TARROLE *(three-syllable word)*
14 LOLYF *(two-syllable word)*
15 BLOBY *(two-syllable word)*

DOWN

1 GRBNI *(one-syllable word)*
2 THSAS *(one-syllable word)*
3 CRILY *(two-syllable word)*
4 UNGED *(one-syllable word)*
5 TURRQAE *(two-syllable word)*
6 SLERTBO *(two-syllable word)*
9 EHFIT *(one-syllable word)*
10 EMTYA *(two-syllable word)*
11 TOELM *(two-syllable word)*
12 NUNYR *(two-syllable word)*

213 | DIFFICULTY: ●●●●●○○○○○ COMPLETION: ☐ TIME: ______

DICTIONARY CROSS'D WORDS

Fill in the puzzle using the Merriam-Webster definition clues below.

Across

1 To stop being frozen (1-syllable verb)
3 To blow in short gusts (1-syllable verb)
5 To wash with clean water (1-syllable verb)
6 Made to look like an exact copy, as money (3-syllable adjective)
7 Physical or mental effort (2-syllable noun)
8 A contest of speed (1-syllable noun)
9 A large but indefinite number (2-syllable adjective)

Down

1 One whose occupation is to instruct (2-syllable noun)
2 A small line or fold (2-syllable noun)
3 To entertain an audience (2-syllable verb)
4 Far removed from normal reality (3-syllable noun)

214 | DIFFICULTY: ●●●●●○○○○○
COMPLETION: ☐ TIME: ______

DEFINITION FINDER

Using the clues below, find and circle the words concealed in the letter grid.

Q	T	X	E	E	K	B	G	N
V	S	T	V	Z	L	R	O	H
Z	E	A	I	J	U	I	R	C
X	R	B	A	Q	T	T	G	T
C	R	O	N	C	Z	T	E	O
J	A	O	N	X	J	L	V	N
B	M	U	M	B	L	E	X	J
K	J	K	I	C	K	O	F	F

- ○ The start of something *(noun)*
- ○ Showing a lack of experience or knowledge *(adjective)*
- ○ To take or keep in custody by authority of law *(verb)*
- ○ A place where two things join *(noun)*
- ○ Easily broken, cracked, or snapped *(adjective)*
- ○ A V-shaped indentation *(noun)*
- ○ A clumsy person *(noun)*
- ○ Not acceptable to talk about or do *(adjective)*
- ○ To utter with a low, inarticulate voice *(verb)*
- ○ A narrow steep-walled canyon *(noun)*
- ○ To have a very strong desire for (something) *(verb)*

215 | DIFFICULTY: ●●●●●●○○○○
COMPLETION: ☐ TIME: ______

SYLLABARY

Link word segments together in the grid below to create words, and enter them in the blanks.

EX	MO	CON	VATE	U
PERT	LY	TI	SID	NI
IM	BET	IZE	VER	ER
PUL	PHA	SI	FOR	MA
SIVE	AL	IN	TY	TION

Four-Syllable Noun: _ _ _ _ R _ _ _ _ _ _

Three-Syllable Adjective: _ _ _ _ _ _ I _ _

Three-Syllable Adverb: _ _ P _ _ _ _ _

Five-Syllable Noun: _ _ _ _ _ _ _ _ T _

Four-Syllable Verb: _ _ _ _ _ B _ _ _ _ _

Three-Syllable Verb: _ _ T _ _ _ _ _

Three-Syllable Verb: _ _ _ S _ _ _ _

216 | DIFFICULTY: ●●●●●●●○○○○
COMPLETION: ☐ TIME: ________

WORD WINDER

Use the clue to help you find the answers word-winding their way through the grid. Each answer will connect the top of the grid to the bottom.

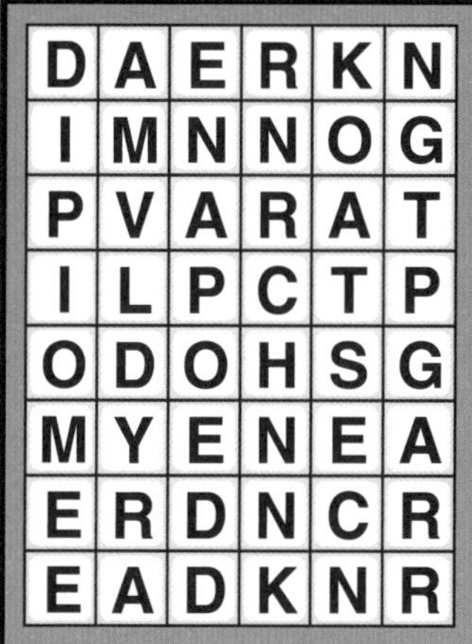

Find five words starting and ending with the same letter word-winding their way from top to bottom.

____

____

____

____

____

217 | DIFFICULTY: ●●●●●○○○○○
COMPLETION: ☐ TIME: ______

SYNONYM FINDER

Find and circle the six pairs of SYNONYMS, one on each side, in the letter grids below.

V	L	V	R	C	L
E	Y	B	A	E	A
S	D	N	C	S	S
U	T	N	V	L	T
A	A	B	Y	S	S
C	B	O	U	N	D

=

O	H	U	G	E	D
R	L	B	H	L	E
I	U	E	E	D	P
G	N	H	A	G	T
I	N	L	C	S	H
N	A	V	F	P	T

○○○○○○

218 | DIFFICULTY: ●●●●●○○○○○
COMPLETION: ☐ TIME: ______

MIXED-UP DEFINITION

Unscramble the letters below to reveal the definition of the given word.

stri·dent *adjective* \ˈstrī-dənt\
speergixns spoonnii ro stimcciir ni a yevr cloffure awy

219 | DIFFICULTY: ●●●●●○○○○○
COMPLETION: ☐ TIME: ______

PRISM CROSS'D WORDS

Use the color-coded clues below to find words that fit in the like-colored portions of the puzzle grid below.

- The side of a door or window (1-syllable noun)
- The ability to think of new things (5-syllable noun)
- To stop doing work or an activity (1-syllable verb)

- A very thin cloth (1-syllable noun)
- A special anniversary (3-syllable noun)

- Personal belongings of travelers (2-syllable noun)
- Not true or real (1-syllable adjective)

- Overhanging portion of a roof (1-syllable noun)
- Component of a bird's plumage (2-syllable noun)

- Not asleep (2-syllable adjective)
- Serious and sincere (2-syllable adjective)

220 | DIFFICULTY: ●●●●●●○○○○
COMPLETION: ☐ TIME: ______

SYNONYM FINDER

Find and circle the seven pairs of SYNONYMS divided between the letter grids below.

F L I N G E R A
F L B Z J T M S
E M O Y A M G J
E C D U E N P K
L Y W L R A Y N
I X I F L I R L
N D H M C Z S N
G A L L E G E H

=

○○○○○○○

221 | DIFFICULTY: ●●●●●●○○○○
COMPLETION: ☐ TIME: ______

CROSS'D WORD CONNECTIONS

The crosswords below share common letters as indicated by the colored boxes. Use the clues to solve the puzzles.

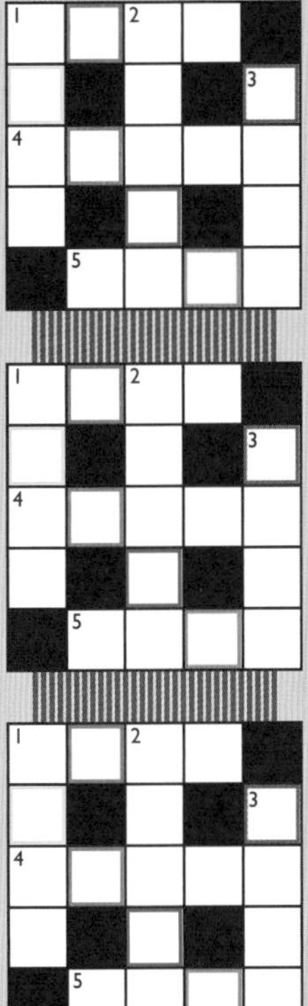

ACROSS
1 A hollow elongated cylinder
4 To move (something) back to an original place or position
5 A fraudulent act or operation

DOWN
1 To become weary
2 Not including anything extra
3 The main trunk of a plant

ACROSS
1 Wet dirt or mud
4 Horizontal condition
5 To beat wings

DOWN
1 A unit equal to 1.609344 kilometers
2 Only as polite as a person needs to be in order to not be rude
3 Food waste (as garbage) fed to animals

ACROSS
1 Covered with healthy green plants
4 Lustrous object formed by some mollusks
5 Marine bivalve living in sand or mud

DOWN
1 The soft parts surrounding the mouth
2 A small animal that lives in a shell that it carries on its back
3 A noisy violent closing

222 | DIFFICULTY: ●●●●●●○○○○
COMPLETION: ☐ TIME: ______

DICTIONARY WORD WINDER

Use the clues below to help you find the answers word-winding their way through the grid. Each answer will connect one side of the grid to the other—left to right, top to bottom, right to left, and bottom to top.

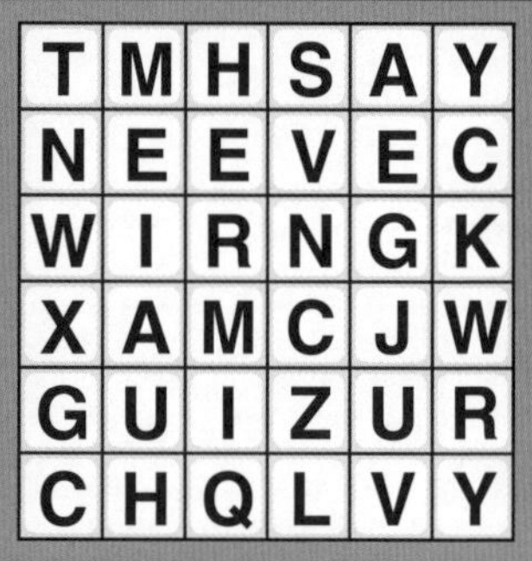

T	M	H	S	A	Y
N	E	E	V	E	C
W	I	R	N	G	K
X	A	M	C	J	W
G	U	I	Z	U	R
C	H	Q	L	V	Y

→ A vertical structure incorporated into a building and enclosing a flue or flues that carry off smoke ______

↓ A silver metal that is liquid at normal temperatures ______

← A type of roasted nut that has a curved shape ______

↑ Having an old-fashioned or unusual quality or appearance that is usually attractive or appealing ______

223 | DIFFICULTY: ●●●●●●○○○○
COMPLETION: ☐ TIME: ______

SYNONYM UNSCRAMBLE

Unscramble the letters below to form pairs of SYNONYMS. Watch out—some words can be unscrambled more than one way!

P J M U = P A E L

M E T R I P = W A O L L

C O T T R E P = F E E D D N

U F A Q I D E I L = B A E L

D R W H S E = N I C G U N N

T E E R D = S A D D S E U I

N A M H Y R O = C R A D O C

224 | DIFFICULTY: ●●●●●●○○○○
COMPLETION: ☐ TIME: ______

DEFINITION FINDER

Using the clues below, find and circle the words concealed in the letter grid.

H	E	C	K	L	E	Q	Y	J
E	A	Q	A	T	X	R	L	X
S	Z	R	A	B	E	J	A	L
I	I	R	M	V	O	T	V	A
O	I	Z	I	O	N	O	I	T
P	Z	L	Z	I	N	X	S	N
V	E	Q	O	L	Z	Y	H	E
D	X	J	A	D	E	D	X	D

- ○ A hissing sound (as of something frying over a fire) *(noun)*
- ○ Of or relating to teeth *(adjective)*
- ○ A point where two bones meet in the body *(noun)*
- ○ To interrupt someone by shouting comments *(verb)*
- ○ Someone who attacks and steals from a ship at sea *(noun)*
- ○ Easy self-possessed assurance of manner *(noun)*
- ○ A part of a train that is attached at the back end *(noun)*
- ○ Made dull, apathetic, or cynical by experience *(adjective)*
- ○ A pleasing arrangement of different things *(noun)*
- ○ The act of taking something to a person or place *(noun)*
- ○ Having a very rich and expensive quality *(adjective)*

225 | DIFFICULTY: ●●●●●●○○○○
COMPLETION: ☐ TIME: ______

ANTONYM UNSCRAMBLE

Unscramble the letters below to form pairs of ANTONYMS. Note: Some words can be unscrambled more than one way!

C F A T ≠ I N I T F O C

O T P ≠ M O O B T T

M H E S A ≠ S T E E P R C

A L R C E ≠ Q O E P U A

P R I A D ≠ L W O S

S N I T E L ≠ R I N E G O

J A R O D U N ≠ I B G N E

226 | DIFFICULTY: ●●●●●●○○○○ COMPLETION: ☐ TIME: ______

SYNONYM FINDER

Find and circle the six pairs of SYNONYMS, one on each side, in the letter grids below.

N	B	F	Y	E	W
R	R	W	D	E	V
O	X	I	N	M	T
D	B	I	V	O	H
A	H	D	R	A	X
S	H	O	W	Y	L

O	D	E	C	A	Y
B	P	K	W	Y	K
E	H	P	D	R	C
A	Y	U	O	T	E
R	A	M	P	S	D
G	G	L	A	R	E

○○○○○○

227 | DIFFICULTY: ●●●●●○○○○○ COMPLETION: ☐ TIME: ______

ANTONYM FINDER

Find and circle the six pairs of ANTONYMS, one on each side, in the letter grids below.

H	F	E	E	D	G
M	C	H	I	C	T
W	R	P	F	M	N
R	E	A	D	Y	I
G	C	L	N	K	H
M	E	A	N	K	G

S	T	A	R	V	E
Y	N	M	J	L	F
D	C	I	I	V	R
R	L	E	C	H	E
A	V	T	D	E	S
T	A	C	K	Y	H

○○○○○○

228 | DIFFICULTY: ●●●●●○○○○○
COMPLETION: ☐ TIME: ______

PRISM WORD FINDER

Using the color-coded clues below, find and circle the words in the letter grid.

R	B	T	S	S	P	A	N	I	E	L
T	W	E	N	L	L	O	U	D	L	Y
C	E	Z	A	X	O	D	F	A	B	Y
H	M	R	K	G	N	W	N	V	L	J
C	I	N	R	U	L	A	L	D	K	Y
A	U	G	O	I	U	E	A	Y	L	A
L	T	H	H	G	E	L	A	D	P	Z
C	O	W	I	L	G	R	L	G	N	A
I	P	M	X	K	Y	O	H	M	U	L
U	I	Q	V	H	B	N	G	W	J	E
M	A	K	C	O	B	A	L	T	K	A

Find five six-letter adverbs ending in "LY" starting with an orange letter ○○○○○

Find four six-letter words with four vowels starting with a blue letter ○○○○

Find four breeds of dogs starting with a purple letter ○○○○

Find two elements starting with a red "C" ○○

229 | DIFFICULTY: ●●●●●●○○○○ COMPLETION: ☐ TIME: ______

WORD WINDER

Use the clue to help you find the answers word-winding their way through the grid. Each answer will connect the top of the grid to the bottom.

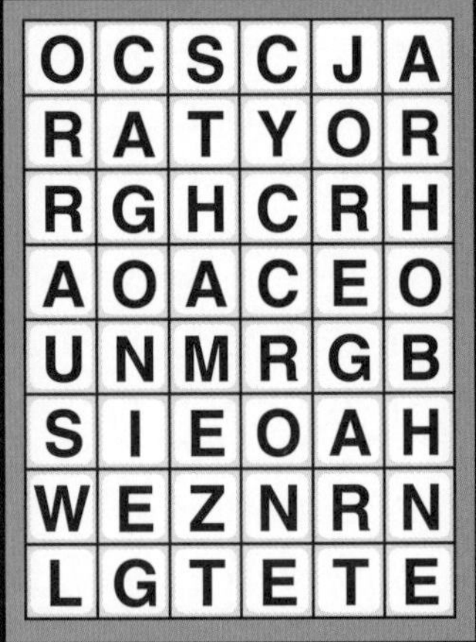

O	C	S	C	J	A
R	A	T	Y	O	R
R	G	H	C	R	H
A	O	A	C	E	O
U	N	M	R	G	B
S	I	E	O	A	H
W	E	Z	N	R	N
L	G	T	E	T	E

↓ Find five three-syllable words word-winding their way from top to bottom.

230 | DIFFICULTY: ●●●●●●○○○○
COMPLETION: ☐ TIME: ______

DICTIONARY UNSCRAMBLE

Unscramble the letters below to form words that match the Merriam-Webster definitions.

adjective
Completely correct or accurate

CREEPTF= ☐☐☐☐☐☐☐

noun A document, chart, etc., that shows the days, weeks, and months

DANCLEAR= ☐☐☐☐☐☐☐☐

transitive verb To have or include (someone or something) as a part of something

LOVEIVN= ☐☐☐☐☐☐☐

adverb
With speed

TWYSLFI= ☐☐☐☐☐☐☐

adjective
Lacking ease or grace

DARKAWW= ☐☐☐☐☐☐☐

intransitive verb To pass usually periodically from one region or climate to another

TRIMAGE= ☐☐☐☐☐☐☐

231 | DIFFICULTY: ●●●●●○○○○○
COMPLETION: ☐ TIME: ______

SYLLABARY

Link word segments together in the grid below to create words, and enter them in the blanks.

NA	SI	Y	EN	ON
GYM	LAR	UM	BAND	ER
SION	U	A	IC	GET
FU	CAB	EST	SUIT	A
CON	MOD	VO	LY	BLE

Five-Syllable Noun: _ _ C _ _ _ _ _ _ _

Three-Syllable Adjective: _ _ _ _ _ B _ _

Four-Syllable Noun: _ _ _ N _ _ _ _ _

Four-Syllable Adjective: _ _ _ _ _ _ _ _ C

Three-Syllable Adverb: _ _ _ _ _ T _ _

Three-Syllable Verb: _ _ _ _ D _ _

Three-Syllable Noun: _ O _ _ _ _ _ _ _

232 | DIFFICULTY: ●●●●●●●○○○○ COMPLETION: ☐ TIME: ______

ANTONYM FINDER

Find and circle the six pairs of ANTONYMS, one on each side, in the letter grids below.

F	B	R	E	A	K
S	I	M	P	L	E
I	L	E	T	Z	P
N	Y	N	R	E	W
X	A	M	E	C	P
W	Q	K	T	N	E

V	I	R	T	U	E
M	C	G	Y	E	X
I	N	E	S	F	I
L	V	I	D	C	F
D	W	H	P	E	M
P	L	E	N	T	Y

○○○○○○

233 | DIFFICULTY: ●●●●●●○○○○○ COMPLETION: ☐ TIME: ______

SYNONYM FINDER

Find and circle the six pairs of SYNONYMS, one on each side, in the letter grids below.

C	Y	A	C	M	E
L	O	V	I	D	V
B	N	M	I	R	L
E	P	C	P	C	Y
N	E	Y	D	L	E
D	M	D	E	F	Y

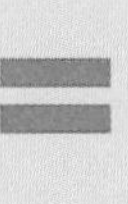

A	G	R	E	E	E
M	L	F	M	L	D
D	N	I	T	P	L
G	R	T	G	N	O
C	E	C	L	H	M
S	D	A	R	E	T

○○○○○○

234 | DIFFICULTY: ●●●●●○○○○○
COMPLETION: ☐ TIME: ______

CROSS'D WORDS UNSCRAMBLE

Unscramble the letters in each clue to fill in the puzzle grid below.

ACROSS

1 ESNWI *(two-syllable word)*
3 RWHLI *(one-syllable word)*
5 GEENHIY *(two-syllable word)*
7 SRANO *(two-syllable word)*
8 CRETU *(one-syllable word)*
9 KESLE *(one-syllable word)*
11 TACTI *(two-syllable word)*
13 KEENRSA *(two-syllable word)*
14 NODUP *(one-syllable word)*
15 MEYEN *(three-syllable word)*

DOWN

1 SNUAA *(two-syllable word)*
2 OWANG *(two-syllable word)*
3 ETHWA *(one-syllable word)*
4 EALES *(one-syllable word)*
5 STOSHSE *(two-syllable word)*
6 TRQEOAU *(three-syllable word)*
9 OTPSO *(one-syllable word)*
10 ANDKE *(one-syllable word)*
11 NEALK *(two-syllable word)*
12 DAYCN *(two-syllable word)*

235 | DIFFICULTY: ●●●●●●●●○○○
COMPLETION: ☐ TIME: ______

DICTIONARY CROSS'D WORDS

Fill in the puzzle using the Merriam-Webster definition clues below.

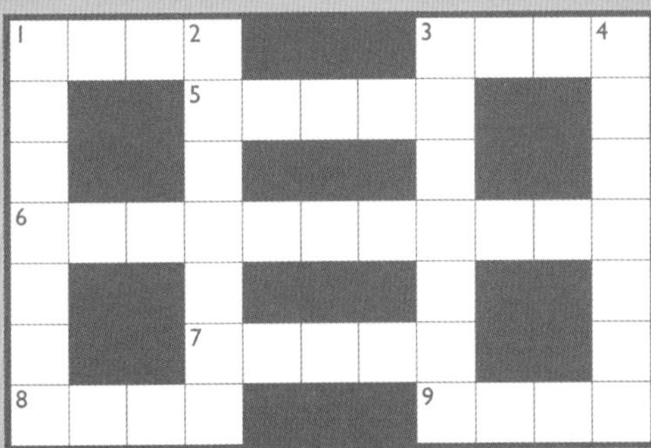

Across
1 Space that is used for something (1-syllable noun)
3 Having the shape of an egg (2-syllable adjective)
5 Being away from a center (2-syllable adjective)
6 Disadvantageous (5-syllable adjective)
7 A small pepper with a very hot flavor (2-syllable noun)
8 Every one of two or more (1-syllable adjective)
9 A small restaurant (2-syllable noun)

Down
1 Have a compelling need for (2-syllable verb)
2 A person who reigns over a kingdom (2-syllable noun)
3 Not using artificial chemicals (3-syllable adjective)
4 To give official permission for (2-syllable verb)

236 | DIFFICULTY: ●●●●●●○○○○
COMPLETION: ☐ TIME: _______

MAKE THE CONNECTION

Fill in the boxes with common two-word phrases with the help of the clues below. The last word in each pair will be the first word in the following pair.

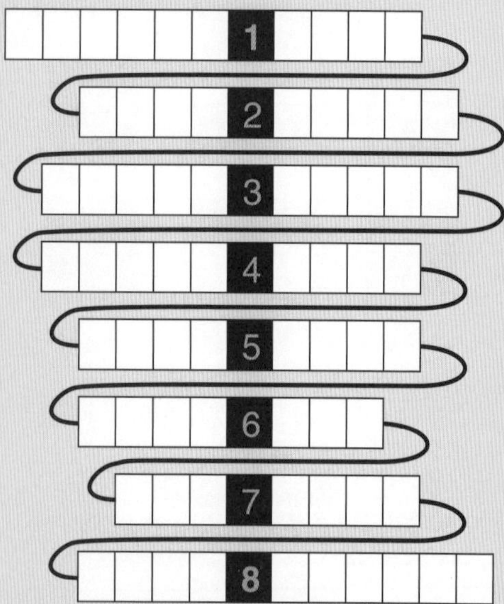

1 A North American country capital
2 Urban unit
3 Neighborhood gathering
4 Twister or Pictionary
5 Where to see Pat Sajak or Alex Trebek
6 Attention seeker
7 Michael Jackson album: "____ the ____"
8 New York City financial district

237 | DIFFICULTY: ●●●●●●●○○○○
COMPLETION: ☐ TIME: ________

MISSING DEFINITIONS FINDER

Using the clues below, find and circle the words concealed in the letter grid.

S	K	J	E	Q	C	H	A	V	E
L	Z	S	A	H	F	A	O	J	F
E	E	I	G	S	B	I	U	L	X
V	D	L	E	I	J	L	G	S	D
A	I	L	R	L	Q	Z	O	H	E
R	V	Y	Z	O	V	X	J	W	T
T	I	M	P	O	R	T	A	N	T
Q	D	V	B	F	K	H	O	M	E

ab·surd *adjective* \əb-ˈsərd, -ˈzərd\
extremely ________, ________, or unreasonable : completely ridiculous

cleave *intransitive verb* \ˈklēv\
to ________ by or as if by a cutting ________

grapple *verb* \ˈgra-pəl\
to ________ and ________ with another person

in·still *transitive verb* \in-ˈstil\
to gradually ________ someone to ________ (an attitude, feeling, etc.)

ob·se·qui·ous *adjective* \əb-ˈsē-kwē-əs, äb-\
too ________ to help or obey someone ________

vag·a·bond *noun* \ˈva-gə-ˌbänd\
a person who ________ from place to place and does not have a ________

238 | DIFFICULTY: ●●●●●●○○○○ COMPLETION: ☐ TIME: ______

SYNONYM FINDER

Find and circle the six pairs of SYNONYMS, one on each side, in the letter grids below.

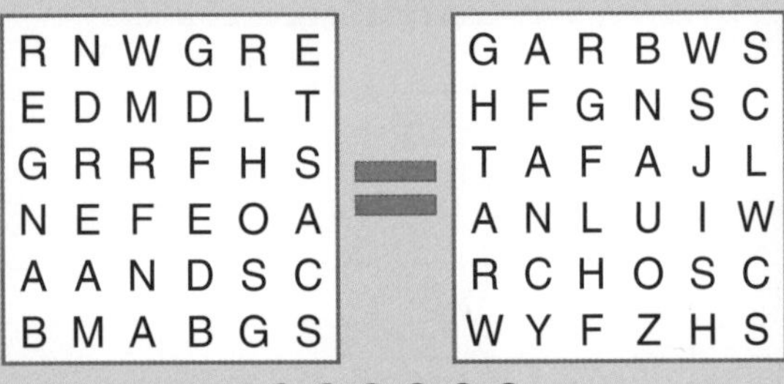

239 | DIFFICULTY: ●●●●●○○○○○ COMPLETION: ☐ TIME: ______

COLOR WORD CHAINS

Use the clues and letters below to make word paths between like colors to fill the board.

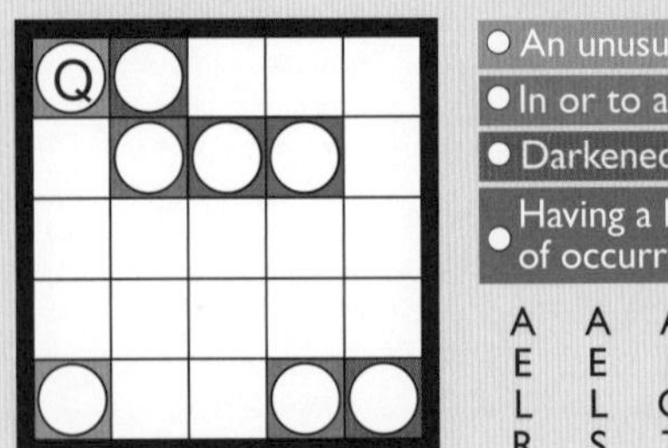

- An unusual way of behaving
- In or to a foreign country
- Darkened by clouds
- Having a high probability of occurring or being true

A A A B C D
E E I I K K
L L O O R R
R S T U V Y

240 | DIFFICULTY: ●●●●●●●○○○
COMPLETION: ☐ TIME: ______

DICTIONARY WORD WINDER

Use the clues below to help you find the answers word-winding their way through the grid. Each answer will connect one side of the grid to the other—left to right, top to bottom, right to left, and bottom to top.

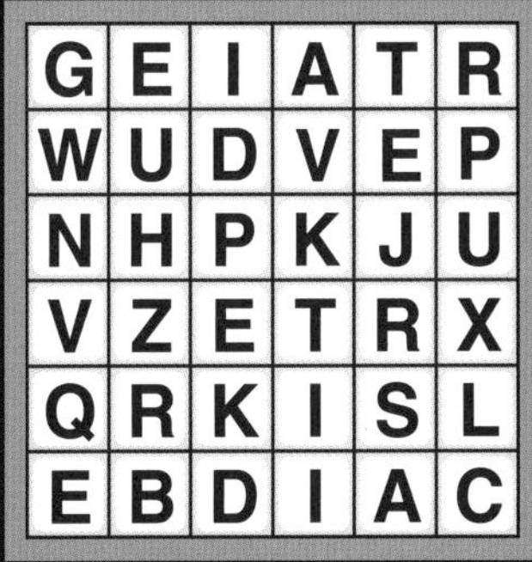

G	E	I	A	T	R
W	U	D	V	E	P
N	H	P	K	J	U
V	Z	E	T	R	X
Q	R	K	I	S	L
E	B	D	I	A	C

→ Of or relating to marriage or a wedding ceremony ______

↓ To hold fast or stick by, or as if by, gluing, suction, grasping, or fusing ______

← To look at or examine (something) carefully; especially before making a decision or judgment ______

↑ To interrupt the normal progress or activity of (something) ______

241 | DIFFICULTY: ●●●●●●○○○○
COMPLETION: ☐ TIME: ______

MISSING DEFINITIONS FINDER

Using the clues below, find and circle the words concealed in the letter grid.

B	C	F	Z	J	R	Y	E	A	G
D	I	I	Y	K	E	L	Z	C	N
N	T	S	V	N	B	B	F	C	I
O	I	H	O	I	M	U	I	O	H
C	E	M	S	K	U	R	R	U	C
E	S	S	V	X	N	N	E	N	T
S	O	P	E	O	P	L	E	T	A
P	E	L	E	C	T	I	O	N	C

de·pos·it *verb* \di-ˈpä-zət\
to put (______) in a bank ______

ig·nite *verb* \ig-ˈnīt\
to set (something) on ______ : to cause (something) to ______

lure *noun* \ˈlu̇r\
a device used for attracting and ______ animals, birds, or especially ______

max·i·mum *noun* \ˈmak-s(ə-)məm\
the highest ______ or amount that is ______ or allowed

re·count *noun* \ˈrē-ˌkau̇nt, (ˌ)rē-ˈ\
a ______ count of the votes in a close ______

ur·ban *adjective* \ˈər-bən\
relating to ______ and the ______ who live in them

242 | DIFFICULTY: ●●●●●●●○○○○
COMPLETION: ☐ TIME: ________

PRISM CROSS'D WORDS

Use the color-coded clues below to find words that fit in the like-colored portions of the puzzle grid below.

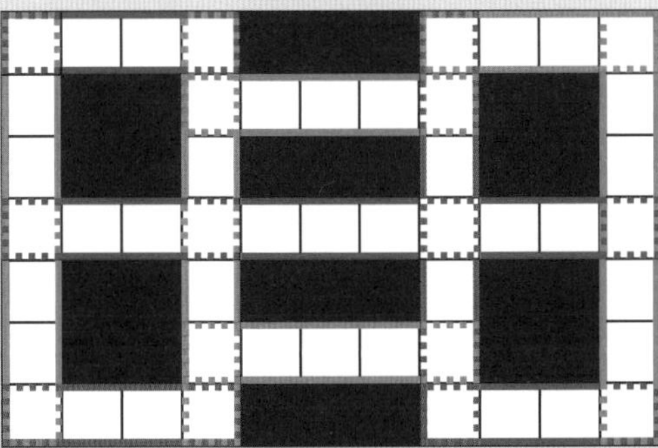

- A single-wheeled cart (3-syllable noun)
- Needless bustle or excitement (1-syllable noun)
- Very small (2-syllable adjective)

- Animal with black & white stripes (2-syllable noun)
- Toward what is ahead (2-syllable adverb)

- Exert pressure on opposite sides (1-syllable verb)
- The cover of a building (1-syllable noun)

- To stupefy especially by a blow (1-syllable verb)
- Movement away from a place (2-syllable verb)

- Marked by rhetorical elegance (3-syllable adjective)
- To write or say the exact words (1-syllable verb)

243 | DIFFICULTY: ●●●●●●●○○○○
COMPLETION: ☐ TIME: ______

WORD WINDER

Use the clue to help you find the answers word-winding their way through the grid. Each answer will connect the top of the grid to the bottom.

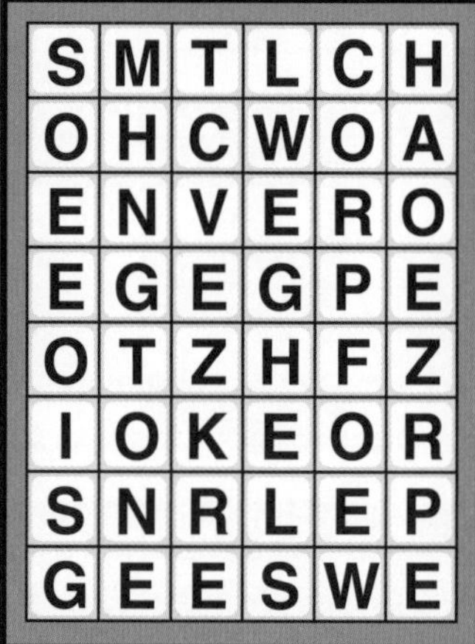

Find five words containing double vowels word-winding their way from top to bottom.

244 | DIFFICULTY: ●●●●●●○○○○
COMPLETION: ☐ TIME: ______

MAKE THE CONNECTION

Fill in the boxes with common two-word phrases with the help of the clues below. The last word in each pair will be the first word in the following pair.

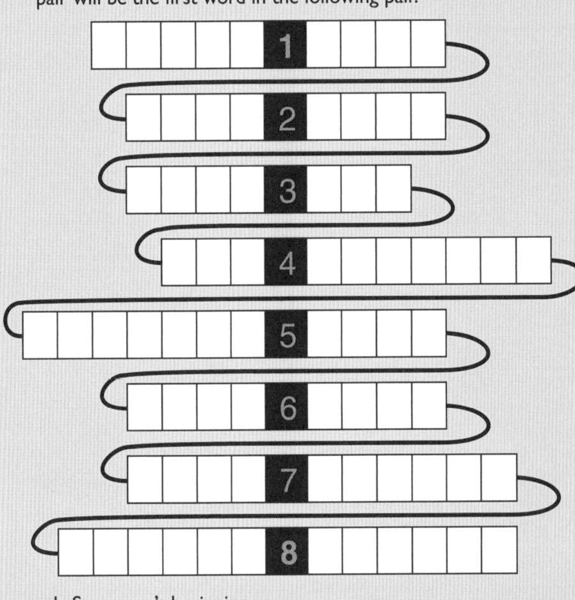

1 Superman's beginning
2 Group of readers
3 Lounge, on a train
4 It can be jump-started
5 Corrosive material
6 Polluted precipitation
7 Area of lush vegetation
8 Park official

245 | DIFFICULTY: ●●●●●●●○○○○
COMPLETION: ☐ TIME: ______

PRISM WORD FINDER

Using the color-coded clues below, find and circle the words in the letter grid.

E	Q	E	B	D	O	D	G	I	N	G
J	M	W	C	L	O	V	E	L	Y	P
E	L	B	X	L	E	H	W	C	E	U
Z	W	G	R	L	I	Y	N	P	T	M
I	T	A	G	A	L	P	V	Q	A	P
M	W	A	R	R	C	Y	S	E	G	I
O	E	G	O	M	L	E	V	E	N	N
N	V	O	J	N	L	I	Z	K	O	G
O	P	C	I	N	T	Y	B	P	L	H
C	W	A	H	C	F	A	S	T	E	T
E	V	M	A	M	I	L	D	L	Y	F

Find five six-letter adverbs ending in "LY" starting with an orange letter ○○○○○

Find five words that start and end with "E" starting with a blue letter ○○○○○

Find two antonyms for slow starting with a purple letter ○○

Find two seven-letter verbs ending in "ING" starting with a red letter ○○

246 | DIFFICULTY: ●●●●●●○○○○
COMPLETION: ☐ TIME: ______

DEFINITION FINDER

Using the clues below, find and circle the words concealed in the letter grid.

N	O	B	L	E	X	E	Z	E
O	V	N	N	Z	D	Q	G	T
G	E	I	U	O	J	A	T	W
A	R	G	R	N	K	I	O	I
X	D	E	S	C	F	L	X	C
E	O	B	E	O	L	O	Q	E
H	X	R	R	E	J	Z	L	V
Z	W	P	Y	Z	Q	V	X	D

- ○ Having the color of the sun or of ripe lemons *(adjective)*
- ○ The excess of returns over expenditure *(noun)*
- ○ Of high birth or exalted rank *(adjective)*
- ○ To spread or straighten out *(verb)*
- ○ To do (something) in an excessive or extreme way *(verb)*
- ○ A polygon of six angles and six sides *(noun)*
- ○ Doubled in amount or degree *(adverb)*
- ○ Place where plants are grown for transplanting *(noun)*
- ○ The broken parts of a vehicle, building, etc. *(noun)*
- ○ To do the first part of an action *(verb)*
- ○ To wear away by the action of water or wind *(verb)*

247 | DIFFICULTY: ●●●●●●●●○○○
COMPLETION: ☐ TIME: ________

DICTIONARY UNSCRAMBLE

Unscramble the letters below to form words that match the Merriam-Webster definitions.

transitive verb To move things or people into a different order or into different positions

FLUSFHE= ☐☐☐☐☐☐☐

---

noun
A place where sick or injured people are given care

SLAPTHIO= ☐☐☐☐☐☐☐☐

---

adjective
Having pleasant or appealing qualities

BALLIEEK= ☐☐☐☐☐☐☐☐

---

adverb
So soon

DRAALYE= ☐☐☐☐☐☐☐

---

intransitive verb
To tread heavily so as to bruise, crush, or injure

PRETMAL= ☐☐☐☐☐☐☐

---

adjective
Very small or too small in amount

GRAMEE= ☐☐☐☐☐☐

248 | DIFFICULTY: ●●●●●●○○○○
COMPLETION: ☐ TIME: ______

SYNONYM FINDER

Find and circle the seven pairs of SYNONYMS divided between the letter grids below.

V	O	C	A	L	H	Y	X
I	E	Y	L	Q	M	E	F
C	Y	R	B	G	L	X	W
T	D	A	D	P	R	O	W
O	Y	W	M	I	L	C	J
R	P	O	K	L	C	N	M
Y	C	Z	A	E	F	T	P
D	I	S	C	L	O	S	E

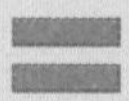

C	O	N	Q	U	E	S	T
A	R	M	I	X	E	D	N
U	V	E	H	Y	C	T	E
T	Y	E	V	T	N	R	M
I	Z	K	R	E	M	P	G
O	G	P	S	B	A	J	D
U	B	S	L	D	A	L	U
S	A	G	N	F	M	L	J

○○○○○○○

249 | DIFFICULTY: ●●●●●●●○○○
COMPLETION: ☐ TIME: ______

SYNONYM UNSCRAMBLE

Unscramble the letters below to form pairs of SYNONYMS. Watch out—some words can be unscrambled more than one way!

L A O E N = T R O Y S L A I

I V L D A = N O D S U

T R E A O T = E L E O R V V

D A N P O R = L E E S R A E

H A R T T E = C M N E E A

R O N G E V = T O O C L R N

O R R R E = O P L E O R B

250 | DIFFICULTY: ●●●●●●●○○○ COMPLETION: ☐ TIME: ______

ANTONYM FINDER

Find and circle the six pairs of ANTONYMS, one on each side, in the letter grids below.

H	C	W	L	Z	H
D	V	L	O	S	G
M	E	A	E	R	N
Y	E	R	G	I	K
P	F	E	H	U	N
F	M	T	T	Z	E

A	V	O	I	D	E
T	T	C	G	L	T
E	H	I	F	Z	S
R	X	I	R	D	E
U	T	R	C	E	R
S	J	Z	Q	K	D

○○○○○○

251 | DIFFICULTY: ●●●●●●○○○○ COMPLETION: ☐ TIME: ______

SYNONYM FINDER

Find and circle the six pairs of SYNONYMS, one on each side, in the letter grids below.

E	T	Y	G	C	E
M	F	C	W	R	Y
P	M	F	A	D	B
T	R	C	O	L	N
Y	S	B	F	R	M
B	R	A	W	L	T

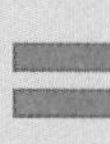

F	R	A	C	A	S
T	F	L	D	H	S
E	B	A	U	S	K
I	A	R	Q	M	T
U	R	M	K	B	P
Q	E	W	O	R	K

○○○○○○

252 | DIFFICULTY: ●●●●●●○○○○
COMPLETION: ☐ TIME: ______

CROSS'D WORD CONNECTIONS

The crosswords below share common letters as indicated by the colored boxes. Use the clues to solve the puzzles.

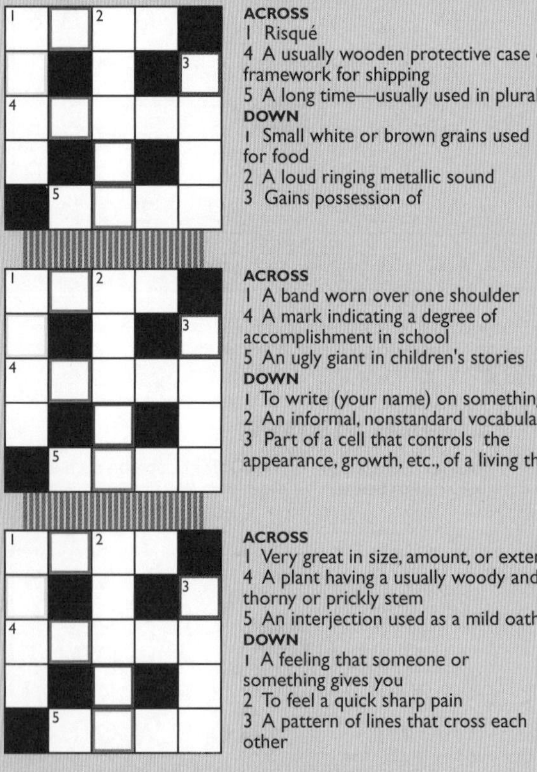

ACROSS
1 Risqué
4 A usually wooden protective case or framework for shipping
5 A long time—usually used in plural

DOWN
1 Small white or brown grains used for food
2 A loud ringing metallic sound
3 Gains possession of

ACROSS
1 A band worn over one shoulder
4 A mark indicating a degree of accomplishment in school
5 An ugly giant in children's stories

DOWN
1 To write (your name) on something
2 An informal, nonstandard vocabulary
3 Part of a cell that controls the appearance, growth, etc., of a living thing

ACROSS
1 Very great in size, amount, or extent
4 A plant having a usually woody and thorny or prickly stem
5 An interjection used as a mild oath

DOWN
1 A feeling that someone or something gives you
2 To feel a quick sharp pain
3 A pattern of lines that cross each other

253 | DIFFICULTY: ●●●●●●●○○○
COMPLETION: ☐ TIME: ______

ANTONYM UNSCRAMBLE

Unscramble the letters below to form pairs of ANTONYMS. Note: Some words can be unscrambled more than one way!

S U T T R ≠ B O T D U

D R A B O ≠ R N O A W R

A Z L E ≠ P H A Y A T

P R O T E Y V ≠ T W A H E L

G L E N P U ≠ O R S A

S M E Y I R ≠ S L B S I

M U L T O R I ≠ M L C A

254 | DIFFICULTY: ●●●●●●○○○○ COMPLETION: ☐ TIME: ______

PRISM CROSS'D WORDS

Use the color-coded clues below to find words that fit in the like-colored portions of the puzzle grid below.

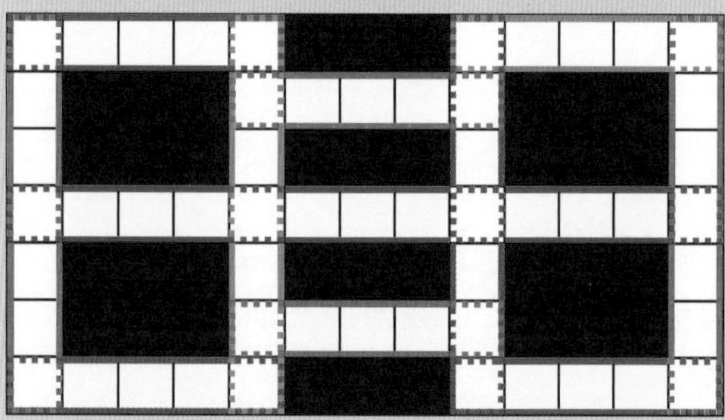

- To put clothes on (1-syllable verb)
- Act of searching for facts (5-syllable noun)
- To cook by exposing to dry heat (1-syllable verb)

- Excess of spending over revenue (3-syllable noun)
- Very silly or stupid (2-syllable adjective)

- To cut with care or precision (1-syllable verb)
- Relating to an earthquake (2-syllable adjective)

- A heavy knife with a wide blade (2-syllable noun)
- The subject of a discourse (2-syllable noun)

- To be better than others (2-syllable verb)
- Well-known and respected (3-syllable adjective)

255 | DIFFICULTY: ●●●●●●●○○○
COMPLETION: ☐ TIME: ______

DICTIONARY CROSS'D WORDS

Fill in the puzzle using the Merriam-Webster definition clues below.

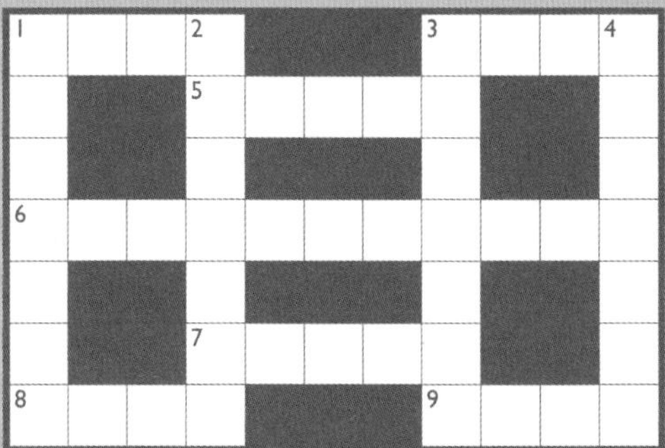

Across
1 A list of the foods that may be ordered (2-syllable noun)
3 A strong need or desire (1-syllable noun)
5 An eating or cooking tool (1-syllable noun)
6 A terrible disaster (4-syllable noun)
7 The utmost extent (2-syllable noun)
8 Word used in hailing (2-syllable interjection)
9 Of great size or area (1-syllable adjective)

Down
1 A type of makeup (3-syllable noun)
2 Normally or regularly (4-syllable adverb)
3 Behaving in a rude way (2-syllable adjective)
4 Financial burden or outlay (2-syllable noun)

256 | DIFFICULTY: ●●●●●○○○○○
COMPLETION: ☐ TIME: ______

SYNONYM FINDER

Find and circle the six pairs of SYNONYMS, one on each side, in the letter grids below.

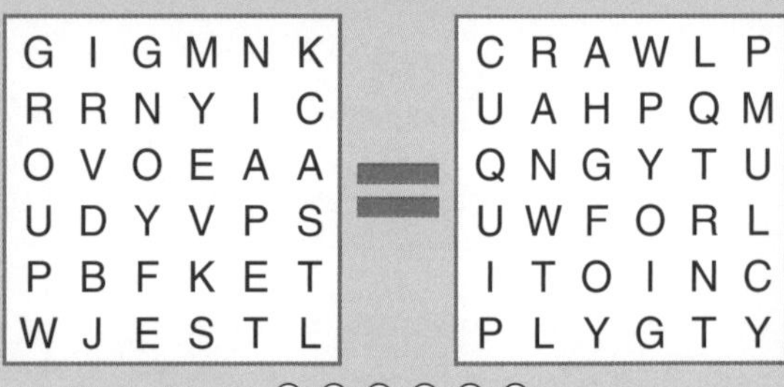

G	I	G	M	N	K
R	R	N	Y	I	C
O	V	O	E	A	A
U	D	Y	V	P	S
P	B	F	K	E	T
W	J	E	S	T	L

=

C	R	A	W	L	P
U	A	H	P	Q	M
Q	N	G	Y	T	U
U	W	F	O	R	L
I	T	O	I	N	C
P	L	Y	G	T	Y

○○○○○○

257 | DIFFICULTY: ●●●●●○○○○○
COMPLETION: ☐ TIME: ______

MIXED-UP DEFINITION

Unscramble the letters below to reveal the definition of the given word.

mus·ter *verb* \ˈməs-tər\
ot grateh troteegh slcyaeeilp rfo tebtla ro rwa

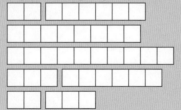

258 | DIFFICULTY: ●●●●●○○○○○
COMPLETION: ☐ TIME: ______

SYLLABARY

Link word segments together in the grid below to create words, and enter them in the blanks.

LY	AM	PLI	TER	PU
A	FUL	FY	PAR	COM
PLAY	POL	O	GET	TIC
IL	STAM	ATE	IC	I
LIT	ER	I	NA	PATE

Three-Syllable Adverb: _ _ _ Y _ _ _ _ _

Five-Syllable Adjective: _ _ _ _ _ G _ _ _ _

Three-Syllable Noun: _ O _ _ _ _ _ _

Three-Syllable Noun: _ _ _ _ I _ _

Four-Syllable Verb: _ _ _ _ _ _ _ _ A _ _

Three-Syllable Verb: _ _ P _ _ _ _

Four-Syllable Adjective: _ _ _ _ _ _ _ A _ _

259 | DIFFICULTY: ●●●●●●●○○○
COMPLETION: ☐ TIME: ______

WORD WINDER

Use the clue to help you find the answers word-winding their way through the grid. Each answer will connect the top of the grid to the bottom.

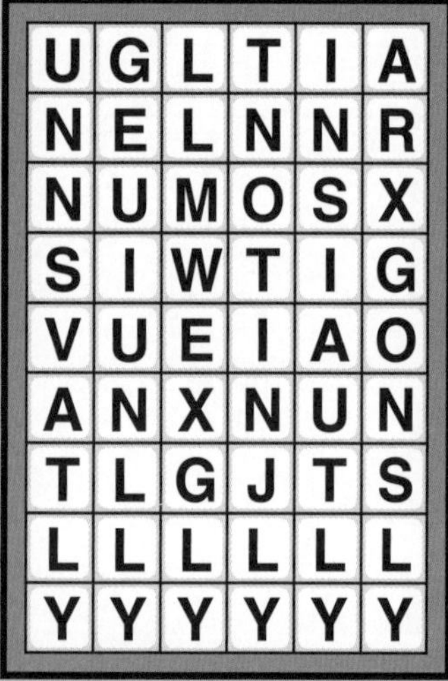

Find five adverbs word-winding their way from top to bottom.

______

______

______

______

______

260 | DIFFICULTY: ●●●●●●○○○○ COMPLETION: ☐ TIME: ______

SYNONYM FINDER

Find and circle the seven pairs of SYNONYMS divided between the letter grids below.

C	P	R	O	P	E	R	P
R	L	P	F	L	W	S	E
E	U	T	R	M	U	C	R
T	S	W	Y	O	X	K	F
L	H	D	I	D	M	Z	E
A	N	V	P	N	K	P	C
C	B	J	T	A	G	Y	T
O	M	H	N	R	M	R	N

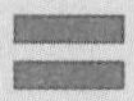

S	U	I	T	A	B	L	E
E	P	D	Y	T	W	Y	C
K	V	O	F	B	F	L	H
M	Y	I	T	I	Z	K	A
H	W	C	D	L	G	P	N
S	L	O	M	E	E	T	C
R	M	J	F	B	N	S	E
E	L	E	G	A	N	T	S

○○○○○○○

261 | DIFFICULTY: ●●●●●●○○○○
COMPLETION: ☐ TIME: ______

DEFINITION FINDER

Using the clues below, find and circle the words concealed in the letter grid.

J	K	A	R	U	G	G	E	D
E	N	U	D	X	Q	L	N	M
T	A	Q	N	V	B	N	E	A
A	C	Z	X	I	A	N	X	L
C	K	V	L	I	O	N	Q	I
O	J	L	V	R	Z	N	C	C
L	U	A	D	E	L	U	X	E
G	E	N	E	R	I	C	Z	Q

- ○ Quick to believe something that is not true *(adjective)*
- ○ An organization of workers *(noun)*
- ○ To find the place or position of something *(verb)*
- ○ Having a rough, uneven surface *(adjective)*
- ○ To bring or move forward *(verb)*
- ○ Being or having a nonproprietary name *(adjective)*
- ○ Of or relating to birds *(adjective)*
- ○ To make a continuous low humming sound *(verb)*
- ○ A talent or special skill needed to do something *(noun)*
- ○ Notably luxurious, elegant, or expensive *(adjective)*
- ○ A desire to cause harm to another person *(noun)*

262 | DIFFICULTY: ●●●●●●●●○○○
COMPLETION: ☐ TIME: ________

DICTIONARY WORD WINDER

Use the clues below to help you find the answers word-winding their way through the grid. Each answer will connect one side of the grid to the other—left to right, top to bottom, right to left, and bottom to top.

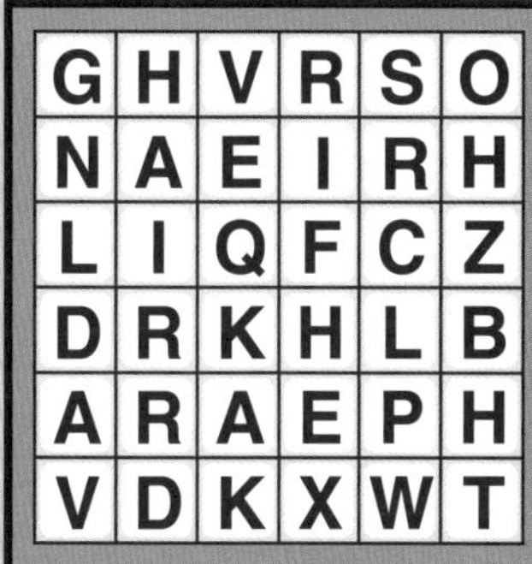

G	H	V	R	S	O
N	A	E	I	R	H
L	I	Q	F	C	Z
D	R	K	H	L	B
A	R	A	E	P	H
V	D	K	X	W	T

→ Marked by profusion or excess ________

↓ An action or movement of the body that happens automatically as a reaction to something ________

← A planting of fruit trees, nut trees, or sugar maples ________

↑ Willing to do dangerous or difficult things ________

263 | DIFFICULTY: ●●●●●●●●○○○
COMPLETION: ☐ TIME: ______

MISSING DEFINITIONS FINDER

Using the clues below, find and circle the words concealed in the letter grid.

Y	J	C	H	A	N	G	E	V	Y
R	Q	N	Z	E	L	X	D	R	Q
T	X	O	E	N	I	V	E	S	Z
N	I	I	V	E	V	V	N	O	S
U	D	S	O	C	E	Z	N	O	K
O	E	Y	M	S	V	Q	A	N	R
C	A	R	E	F	U	L	L	Y	O
V	S	C	A	U	S	E	P	Z	W

ad·vo·cate *noun* \ˈad-və-kət, -ˌkāt\
a person who ______ for a ______ or group

bed·lam *noun* \ˈbed-ləm\
a very ______ and confused state or ______

elab·o·rate *adjective* \i-ˈla-b(ə-)rət\
having many parts that are ______ arranged or ______

im·mi·nent *adjective* \ˈi-mə-nənt\
happening ______ ______

mi·grate *intransitive verb* \ˈmī-ˌgrāt, mī-ˈ\
to ______ from one ______ or place to ______ or work in another

ob·sti·nate *adjective* \ˈäb-stə-nət\
refusing to ______ your behavior or your ______

264 | DIFFICULTY: ●●●●●●●○○○ COMPLETION: ☐ TIME: ______

SYNONYM FINDER

Find and circle the six pairs of SYNONYMS, one on each side, in the letter grids below.

C	D	P	P	Y	T
H	A	Y	D	R	A
M	N	R	A	Q	G
W	A	P	R	P	E
T	M	G	L	Y	D
I	D	R	E	A	D

=

A	T	E	L	L	G
E	L	M	Y	N	T
T	H	A	I	D	O
A	F	R	R	G	L
L	B	P	C	M	P
S	E	N	I	L	E

○○○○○○

265 | DIFFICULTY: ●●●●●○○○○○ COMPLETION: ☐ TIME: ______

COLOR WORD CHAINS

Use the clues and letters below to make word paths between like colors to fill the board.

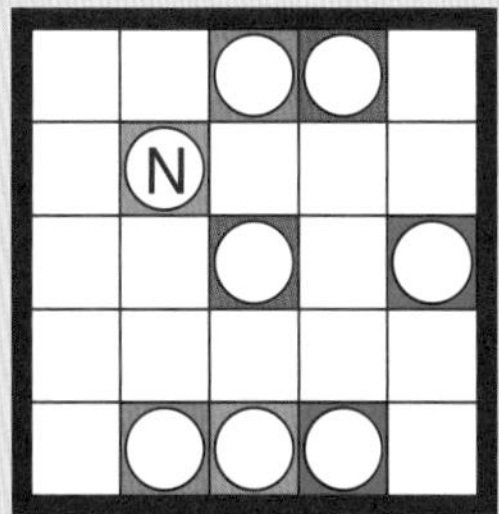

- Connection, link
- A buyer and seller
- An appearance that belies the truth
- Exaggerated self-confidence

A	A	A	B	C	C
D	E	E	E	F	H
H	I	M	N	R	R
S	S	T	U	U	X

266 | DIFFICULTY: ●●●●●●●●●○○
COMPLETION: ☐ TIME: ______

MAKE THE CONNECTION

Fill in the boxes with common two-word phrases with the help of the clues below. The last word in each pair will be the first word in the following pair.

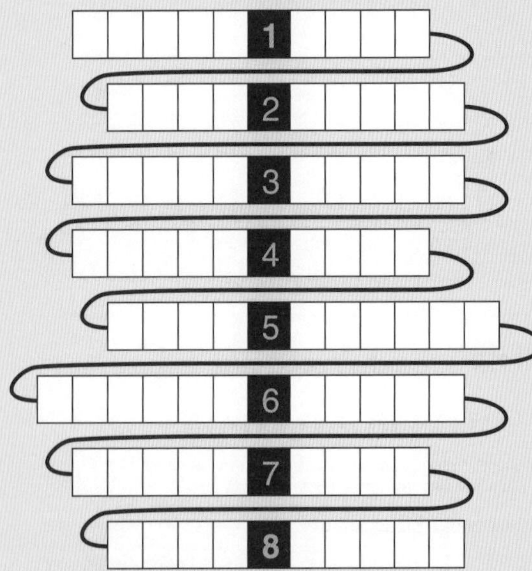

1 Showing neither a profit or a loss
2 Proportionate swap
3 Labor guild
4 U.K. flag
5 Monterey ____ ____
6 Appetizer option with a gooey topping
7 Queue for the hungry
8 Straight shot, in baseball

267 | DIFFICULTY: ●●●●●●●○○○ COMPLETION: ☐ TIME: ______

ANTONYM FINDER

Find and circle the six pairs of ANTONYMS, one on each side, in the letter grids below.

R	S	H	T	B	K
J	A	F	E	E	A
R	I	C	S	M	E
G	A	A	K	R	L
F	E	N	K	E	B
D	W	E	L	L	T

G	R	I	E	F	Y
L	A	K	F	N	L
L	L	V	N	M	E
I	O	U	O	V	J
T	S	G	O	I	L
S	S	M	H	N	D

○○○○○○

268 | DIFFICULTY: ●●●●●○○○○○ COMPLETION: ☐ TIME: ______

SYNONYM FINDER

Find and circle the six pairs of SYNONYMS, one on each side, in the letter grids below.

D	A	D	E	P	T
I	P	K	C	P	N
P	F	L	A	H	I
A	W	R	O	N	A
R	C	M	D	T	F
S	G	H	A	R	D

N	B	F	T	L	F
A	Y	F	M	P	A
L	G	I	Q	K	S
P	M	T	N	A	T
M	A	S	T	E	R
W	B	R	A	W	L

○○○○○○

269 | DIFFICULTY: ●●●●●○○○○○
COMPLETION: ☐ TIME: ______

ANTONYM FINDER

Find and circle the seven pairs of ANTONYMS divided between the letter grids below.

G	T	Z	M	Q	N	Y	T
X	E	B	X	O	D	N	S
W	Z	N	R	R	M	C	I
J	I	T	U	E	J	G	S
Z	A	T	D	I	B	Q	S
P	S	N	T	Z	N	D	A
X	O	M	F	Y	P	E	M
C	H	E	E	R	F	U	L

R	B	G	L	O	O	M	Y
A	I	X	P	H	L	D	V
S	P	C	R	Q	T	P	E
O	K	P	K	R	J	H	N
L	Z	Z	R	E	Z	O	D
E	X	C	Q	O	T	N	O
M	W	F	N	J	V	Y	R
N	I	M	P	E	D	E	T

○○○○○○○

270 | DIFFICULTY: ●●●●●●●●○○○
COMPLETION: ☐ TIME: ______

PRISM WORD FINDER

Using the color-coded clues below, find and circle the words in the letter grid.

J	E	R	N	P	S	G	P	E	B	P
W	K	L	L	E	D	E	L	E	E	W
C	E	U	E	E	R	B	T	V	E	L
S	P	A	D	V	I	V	I	T	A	P
L	E	E	V	G	A	T	O	P	E	D
P	E	R	E	I	A	T	I	U	E	E
W	U	L	V	L	N	C	E	D	S	F
H	L	M	U	A	I	G	E	L	V	Q
I	K	M	P	N	N	E	G	W	K	C
N	U	W	U	J	S	T	P	R	O	P
C	V	M	A	L	U	M	I	N	U	M

Find four seven-letter words with "V" in the middle starting with an orange letter ○○○○

Find four four-syllable words starting with a blue letter ○○○○

Find four four-letter words starting and ending with "P" starting with a purple letter ○○○○

Find three six-letter words with three "E's" starting with a red letter ○○○

271 | DIFFICULTY: ●●●●●●●●○○○
COMPLETION: ☐ TIME: ______

PRISM CROSS'D WORDS

Use the color-coded clues below to find words that fit in the like-colored portions of the puzzle grid below.

- Keeping clean and organized (2-syllable adjective)
- Devotion to one's country (5-syllable noun)
- To turn over quickly (1-syllable verb)

- In an honest and direct way (2-syllable adverb)
- The nut of the oak tree (2-syllable noun)

- A formal and serious promise (1-syllable noun)
- Adherent to strict moral rules (3-syllable noun)

- Twisted strand used for knitting (1-syllable noun)
- Very wealthy (3-syllable adjective)

- Pleasing arrangement of parts (3-syllable noun)
- To take power in a violent way (2-syllable verb)

272 | DIFFICULTY: ●●●●●●●○○○
COMPLETION: ☐ TIME: ______

DICTIONARY UNSCRAMBLE

Unscramble the letters below to form words that match the Merriam-Webster definitions.

preposition
Throughout the entire time of

RUGDIN= ☐☐☐☐☐☐

adjective
Positive and cheerful

ETUBAP= ☐☐☐☐☐☐

noun A barbed spear or javelin used especially in hunting large fish

PHORNAO= ☐☐☐☐☐☐☐

intransitive verb To lie or creep with the body prostrate in token of subservience

LOVGER= ☐☐☐☐☐☐

adjective
Morally bad

KWEDCI= ☐☐☐☐☐☐

transitive verb
To sit back or lie down in a relaxed manner

CREELNI= ☐☐☐☐☐☐☐

273 | DIFFICULTY: ●●●●●●●○○○○
COMPLETION: ☐ TIME: ________

WORD WINDER

Use the clue to help you find the answers word-winding their way through the grid. Each answer will connect the top of the grid to the bottom.

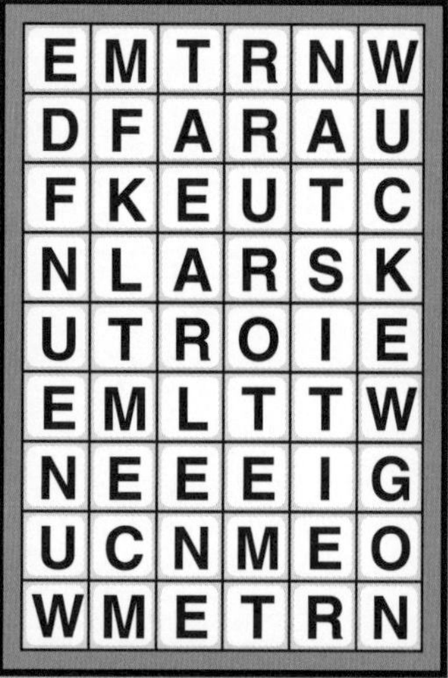

E	M	T	R	N	W
D	F	A	R	A	U
F	K	E	U	T	C
N	L	A	R	S	K
U	T	R	O	I	E
E	M	L	T	T	W
N	E	E	E	I	G
U	C	N	M	E	O
W	M	E	T	R	N

Find five words starting and ending with the same letter word-winding their way from top to bottom.

274 | DIFFICULTY: ●●●●●●●●○○○
COMPLETION: ☐ TIME: ______

SYNONYM UNSCRAMBLE

Unscramble the letters below to form pairs of SYNONYMS.
Watch out—some words can be unscrambled more than one way!

M I C E N O = N E E U V R E

M H E S A = C R I E D S A G

G K E C A A P = C A L R P E

N A L E = C W R Y S N A

S N I T E L = R E L O L N

S P E R I A = T R A E F T L

C P A T E C = E E R V I E C

275 | DIFFICULTY: ●●●●●●●○○○○
COMPLETION: ☐ TIME: ______

DICTIONARY CROSS'D WORDS

Fill in the puzzle using the Merriam-Webster definition clues below.

Across
1 To unite (metallic parts) by heating (1-syllable verb)
3 One who directs or supervises workers (1-syllable noun)
5 Very excited and interested (2-syllable adjective)
6 State of being old and in bad condition (4-syllable noun)
7 A disagreeable sensation of coldness (1-syllable noun)
8 A special ability (1-syllable noun)
9 A circular movement of air or water (2-syllable noun)

Down
1 A marriage ceremony (2-syllable noun)
2 To diminish the importance (2-syllable verb)
3 Easily broken or cracked (2-syllable adjective)
4 Making a sharp, shrill cry (2-syllable adjective)

276 | DIFFICULTY: ●●●●●●○○○○
COMPLETION: ☐ TIME: ________

ANTONYM UNSCRAMBLE

Unscramble the letters below to form pairs of ANTONYMS. Note: Some words can be unscrambled more than one way!

ENDY ≠ GLIDEUN

TLNUB ≠ STELBU

ATTSR ≠ LECCUODN

NEETRD ≠ GOHTU

SHOCA ≠ MANRYHO

MUGL ≠ ELCFEUHR

SAECU ≠ FEETCF

277 | DIFFICULTY: ●●●●●●○○○○ COMPLETION: ☐ TIME: ______

SYNONYM FINDER

Find and circle the six pairs of SYNONYMS, one on each side, in the letter grids below.

F	A	B	L	E	T
K	S	P	D	P	I
R	L	O	U	M	D
O	C	R	L	Y	Y
W	B	N	D	I	W
A	B	E	A	R	D

=

L	A	B	O	R	M
D	T	K	F	I	Y
L	H	A	R	D	H
B	M	T	L	C	P
S	U	D	D	E	N
G	C	A	R	R	Y

○○○○○○

278 | DIFFICULTY: ●●●●○○○○○○ COMPLETION: ☐ TIME: ______

MIXED-UP DEFINITION

Unscramble the letters below to reveal the definition of the given word.

con·sci·en·tious *adjective* \ˌkän(t)-shē-ˈen(t)-shəs\
rvye flaurce toaub igdno athw uyo rae pessdpuo ot od

☐☐☐☐ ☐☐☐☐☐☐☐
☐☐☐☐☐
☐☐☐☐☐ ☐☐☐☐
☐☐☐ ☐☐☐
☐☐☐☐☐☐☐☐ ☐☐ ☐☐

279 | DIFFICULTY: ●●●●●●●○○○○
COMPLETION: ☐ TIME: ______

CROSS'D WORDS UNSCRAMBLE

Unscramble the letters in each clue to fill in the puzzle grid below.

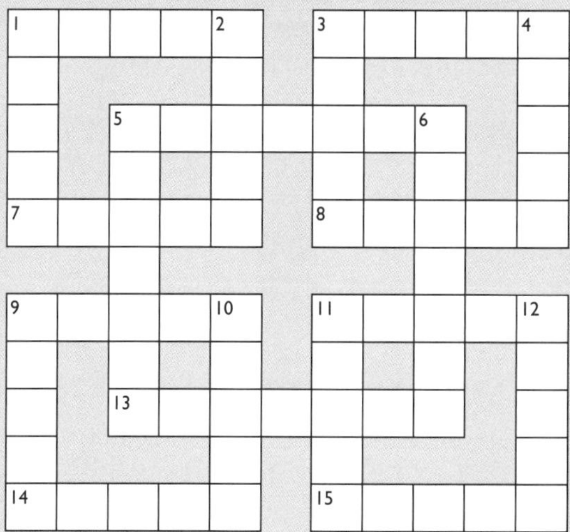

ACROSS

1 ALDSA *(two-syllable word)*
3 REFIB *(one-syllable word)*
5 PHIMACE *(two-syllable word)*
7 TIHFF *(one-syllable word)*
8 SIKKO *(two-syllable word)*
9 FIFSK *(one-syllable word)*
11 LYPPU *(two-syllable word)*
13 STORMUI *(three-syllable word)*
14 FDTAR *(one-syllable word)*
15 QLAUE *(two-syllable word)*

DOWN

1 FNSFI *(one-syllable word)*
2 PHEDT *(one-syllable word)*
3 CLAKB *(one-syllable word)*
4 SLAKF *(one-syllable word)*
5 FILTINC *(two-syllable word)*
6 OLOMHUD *(two-syllable word)*
9 CLOSD *(one-syllable word)*
10 ATFLU *(one-syllable word)*
11 DRIEP *(one-syllable word)*
12 LEOYD *(two-syllable word)*

280 | DIFFICULTY: ●●●●●●○○○○ COMPLETION: ☐ TIME: ______

SYNONYM FINDER

Find and circle the seven pairs of SYNONYMS divided between the letter grids below.

F	E	R	V	E	N	T	E
N	T	M	J	Y	H	T	R
P	O	W	D	G	I	E	T
Z	H	V	U	N	U	L	E
C	P	O	I	Q	U	M	S
G	N	F	N	C	X	F	U
E	N	O	C	K	E	L	A
I	C	O	R	N	T	C	P

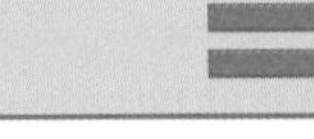

A	R	D	E	N	T	N	L
L	Y	E	B	J	T	P	A
C	E	U	S	E	C	L	N
H	T	A	R	P	M	E	R
W	K	C	R	W	I	N	E
R	E	Q	D	N	F	T	T
S	U	B	D	U	E	Y	E
G	V	L	L	C	N	R	Z

281 | DIFFICULTY: ●●●○○○○○○○ COMPLETION: ☐ TIME: ______

COLOR WORD CHAINS

Use the clues and letters below to make word paths between like colors to fill the board.

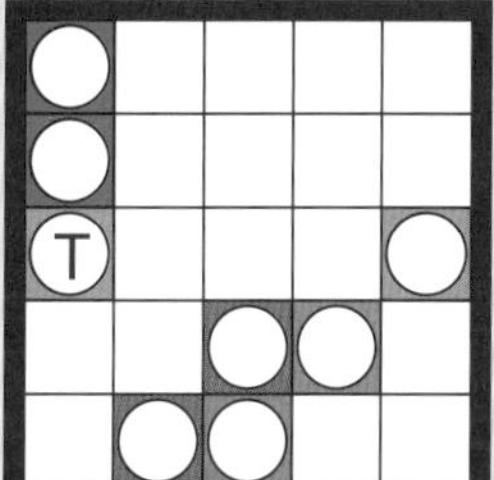

- Something that tastes good and is not eaten often
- To fall or rest on the knees
- To measure heaviness
- Strange or unknown

A	E	E	E	E	E
G	H	I	I	K	L
M	N	O	R	R	S
S	T	T	U	W	Y

282 | DIFFICULTY: ●●●●●●●●○○ COMPLETION: ☐ TIME: ______

ANTONYM FINDER

Find and circle the six pairs of ANTONYMS, one on each side, in the letter grids below.

L	I	T	T	L	E
H	W	I	Q	T	G
S	U	L	B	D	M
Q	R	A	S	H	E
C	O	M	M	O	N
R	T	L	Y	T	D

R	E	M	A	I	N
D	H	L	K	W	B
L	A	R	G	E	Y
O	R	B	M	R	C
C	M	J	A	A	D
Q	P	W	L	R	N

○ ○ ○ ○ ○ ○

283 | DIFFICULTY: ●●●●●●●○○○○
COMPLETION: ☐ TIME: ______

WORD WINDER

Use the clue to help you find the answers word-winding their way through the grid. Each answer will connect the top of the grid to the bottom.

D	I	I	M	D	H
D	E	A	M	E	T
E	F	P	N	R	A
N	O	E	V	D	R
R	T	N	C	T	A
I	T	T	F	T	P
C	I	A	O	E	J
V	A	R	N	W	L
L	E	T	Y	T	G

↓ Find five adjectives word-winding their way from top to bottom.

______

______

______

______

______

284 | DIFFICULTY: ●●●●●●●○○○ COMPLETION: ☐ TIME: ______

PRISM CROSS'D WORDS

Use the color-coded clues below to find words that fit in the like-colored portions of the puzzle grid below.

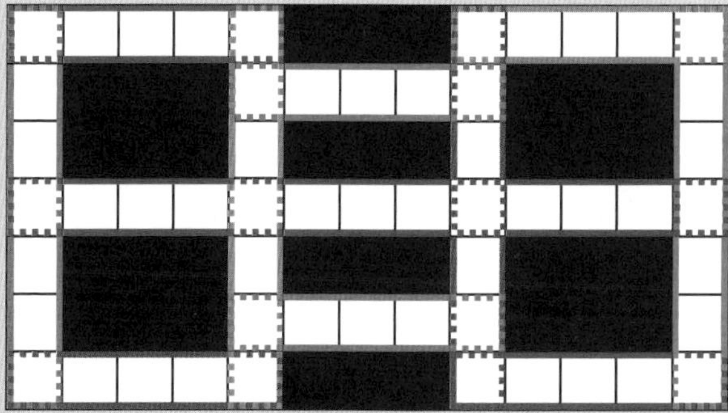

- Complete happiness (1-syllable noun)
- A hard, heavy, blackish wood (3-syllable noun)
- To form an idea in your mind (5-syllable verb)

- Polite but not friendly (2-syllable adjective)
- Seating area above the main floor (3-syllable noun)

- The thick part of milk (1-syllable noun)
- To completely suppress (1-syllable verb)

- Period prior to maturity (1-syllable noun)
- Skilled at doing something (3-syllable adjective)

- A fixed number or percentage (2-syllable noun)
- Royal bearing or aspect (3-syllable noun)

285 | DIFFICULTY: ●●●●●●●●●○○
COMPLETION: ☐ TIME: ______

CROSS'D WORD CONNECTIONS

The crosswords below share common letters as indicated by the colored boxes. Use the clues to solve the puzzles.

ACROSS
1 Piece of material that is sticky on one side
4 Fold of fabric that is on the front of a coat or jacket
5 Having had a previous owner

DOWN
1 To cause to have an inclination
2 Long, hollow tubes for carrying water
3 A lump of dirt or clay

ACROSS
1 To become less bright : to lose color
4 Keen-edged instrument for shaving
5 Particular amount of length, time, money, etc., used for counting

DOWN
1 Placed in a way that is not easily moved
2 Group of 12 people or things
3 Moderately fast gait of a horse

ACROSS
1 One of two equal or nearly equal parts
4 To provide food and drinks at a party
5 Containers to hold cremated remains

DOWN
1 Uneducated person from a small town
2 At a time in the future
3 People paid to participate in a sport or activity

286 | DIFFICULTY: ●●●●●●●●●○○
COMPLETION: ☐ TIME: ______

MAKE THE CONNECTION

Fill in the boxes with common two-word phrases with the help of the clues below. The last word in each pair will be the first word in the following pair.

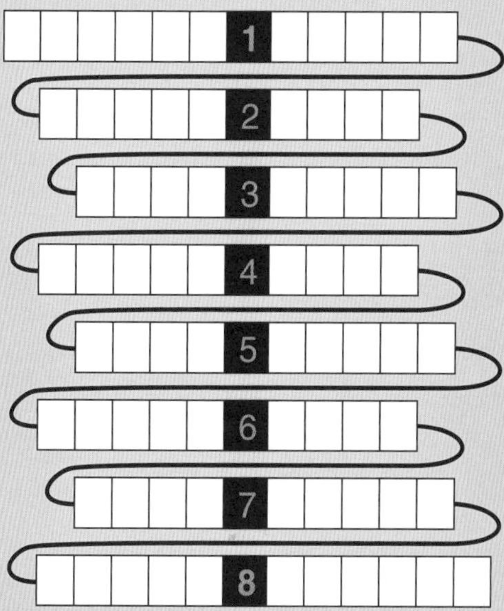

1 Where tip-off occurs
2 Event with a judge and jury
3 Example
4 Cram
5 Jolly Rancher, for one
6 Christmas treat
7 Major export of Hawaii
8 It's like a snickerdoodle

287 | DIFFICULTY: ●●●●●●●●●○○ COMPLETION: ☐ TIME: ______

ANTONYM FINDER

Find and circle the six pairs of ANTONYMS, one on each side, in the letter grids below.

T	P	T	A	K	E
S	B	L	E	N	L
A	H	G	U	A	D
V	A	A	U	M	H
R	C	S	R	T	P
F	U	A	G	P	H

B	D	U	L	L	E
F	C	K	X	W	V
L	Y	A	N	G	I
S	M	A	L	L	G
W	E	H	Y	M	C
L	N	R	A	R	E

○○○○○○

288 | DIFFICULTY: ●●●●●●●○○○○ COMPLETION: ☐ TIME: ______

COLOR WORD CHAINS

Use the clues and letters below to make word paths between like colors to fill the board.

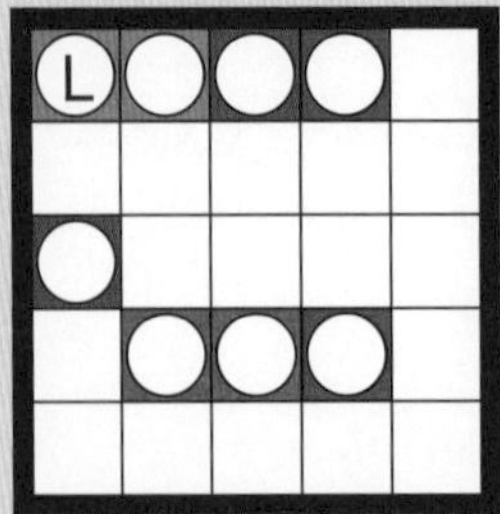

- A symbol used to identify a company
- To sell from place to place
- Regional way of speaking
- To earn a degree or diploma

A	A	A	C	D	D
D	D	E	E	E	E
G	G	I	L	L	O
O	P	R	T	T	U

289 | DIFFICULTY: ●●●●●●●●●○○
COMPLETION: ☐ TIME: ______

DEFINITION FINDER

Using the clues below, find and circle the words concealed in the letter grid.

M	X	O	F	F	B	E	A	T
Z	E	Q	N	X	O	Z	I	Q
E	S	D	O	A	G	E	N	T
D	A	U	I	X	E	J	F	X
I	R	P	L	U	Y	Q	A	J
C	H	P	L	A	M	O	N	G
E	P	E	I	X	A	Z	T	V
D	X	R	B	A	N	N	E	X

- ○ Located at or near the top *(adjective)*
- ○ To make a choice about (something) *(verb)*
- ○ Something that is the middle size *(noun)*
- ○ One thousand million *(noun)*
- ○ Different from the ordinary, usual, or expected *(adjective)*
- ○ A terrifying or dreaded person or thing *(noun)*
- ○ To add (an area or region) to a country, state, etc. *(verb)*
- ○ A brief expression that is commonly used *(noun)*
- ○ In or through (a group of people or things) *(preposition)*
- ○ A person who does business for another person *(noun)*
- ○ A child in the first period of life *(noun)*

290 | DIFFICULTY: ●●●●●●●○○○
COMPLETION: ☐ TIME: ______

DICTIONARY CROSS'D WORDS

Fill in the puzzle using the Merriam-Webster definition clues below.

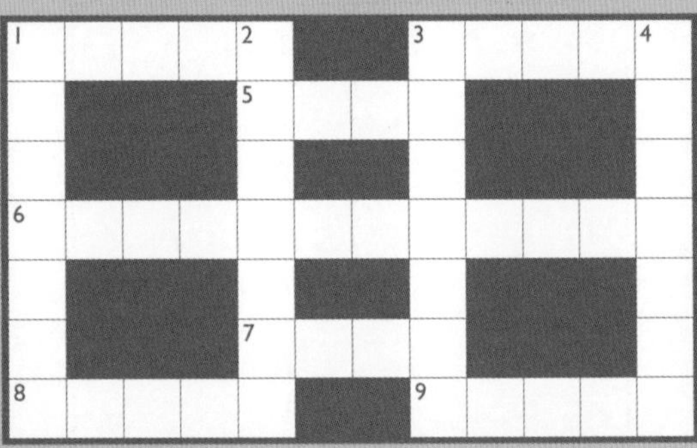

Across
1 Hair that grows on a man's face (1-syllable noun)
3 Firmly restraining response to pain (2-syllable adjective)
5 A group of red spots on the skin (1-syllable noun)
6 With a desire that is too strong to resist (4-syllable adverb)
7 A nest for bees (1-syllable noun)
8 A place where birds rest or sleep (1-syllable noun)
9 Smallest in amount or degree (1-syllable adjective)

Down
1 A dealer in meat (2-syllable noun)
2 Lack or insufficiency of rain (1-syllable noun)
3 To become dry and wrinkled (2-syllable verb)
4 An imitative act or product (3-syllable noun)

291 | DIFFICULTY: ●●●●●●○○○○
COMPLETION: ☐ TIME: ______

DICTIONARY WORD WINDER

Use the clues below to help you find the answers word-winding their way through the grid. Each answer will connect one side of the grid to the other—left to right, top to bottom, right to left, and bottom to top.

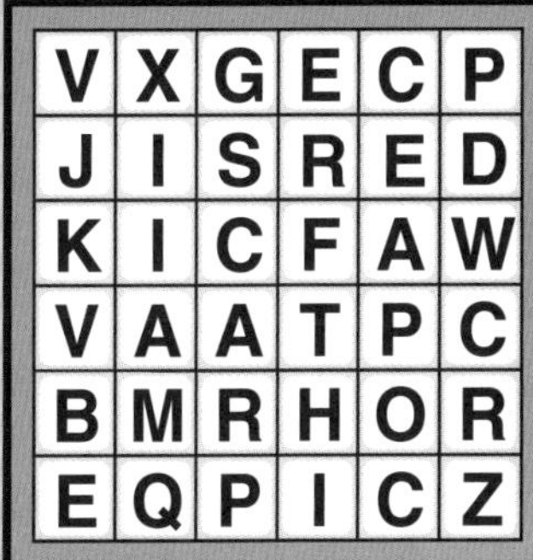

V	X	G	E	C	P
J	I	S	R	E	D
K	I	C	F	A	W
V	A	A	T	P	C
B	M	R	H	O	R
E	Q	P	I	C	Z

→ One that defeats an enemy or opponent ______

↓ Relating to the artistic use of pictures, shapes, and words, especially in books and magazines ______

← To hurt the reputation of (someone or something), especially by saying things that are false or unfair ______

↑ To express approval of (someone or something) ______

292 | DIFFICULTY: ●●●●●●●●○○○
COMPLETION: ☐ TIME: ______

PRISM WORD FINDER

Using the color-coded clues below, find and circle the words in the letter grid.

S	T	N	R	D	A	R	R	I	V	E
R	W	A	B	A	R	Q	V	J	F	S
H	A	K	T	E	D	A	O	R	T	A
B	L	T	N	T	R	I	C	Z	P	W
G	A	N	T	E	L	R	U	E	V	M
S	A	T	T	L	E	E	L	M	U	C
B	U	T	T	T	E	P	K	I	A	A
N	U	L	T	L	P	Q	L	V	M	T
M	Z	O	F	I	E	E	N	B	O	T
K	H	C	R	U	H	G	L	X	R	L
A	L	P	H	A	R	J	H	D	A	E

Find five six-letter words with double consonants starting with an orange letter ○○○○○

Find four six-letter words that rhyme with "prattle" starting with a blue letter ○○○○

Find three six-letter elements starting with a purple letter ○○○

Find three five-letter nouns that start and end with "A" starting with a red letter ○○○

293 | DIFFICULTY: ●●●●●●●●○○○ COMPLETION: ☐ TIME: ______

ANTONYM FINDER

Find and circle the six pairs of ANTONYMS, one on each side, in the letter grids below.

K	D	U	L	L	F
B	P	R	E	J	L
N	R	V	I	A	D
D	E	E	U	V	A
L	G	Q	A	M	E
H	E	C	L	K	H

≠

E	H	M	F	T	N
K	C	B	L	K	H
I	E	A	A	G	L
L	H	E	U	S	G
N	X	O	N	D	E
U	R	M	E	N	D

○○○○○○

294 | DIFFICULTY: ●●●●●●●○○○○ COMPLETION: ☐ TIME: ______

MIXED-UP DEFINITION

Unscramble the letters below to reveal the definition of the given word.

guile *noun* \ˈgī(-ə)l\

eth seu fo leervc dan sluuyal ntossdhei stomhed

☐☐☐ ☐☐☐ ☐☐

☐☐☐☐☐☐ ☐☐☐

☐☐☐☐☐☐☐

☐☐☐☐☐☐☐☐☐

☐☐☐☐☐☐☐

295 | DIFFICULTY: ●●●●●●○○○○
COMPLETION: ☐ TIME: ______

MISSING DEFINITIONS FINDER

Using the clues below, find and circle the words concealed in the letter grid.

S	K	E	L	S	E	E	Y	J	L
L	A	J	W	P	K	R	Q	U	A
I	E	Q	A	I	T	X	F	Z	R
A	P	C	L	N	T	E	J	K	G
T	S	N	U	V	R	H	V	C	E
E	U	O	Z	A	Q	Z	O	I	S
D	C	X	C	H	E	L	D	U	T
J	L	O	Y	A	L	T	Y	Q	T

al·le·giance *noun* \ə-ˈlē-jən(t)s\
______ to a person, ______, group, etc.

ca·pac·i·ty *noun* \kə-ˈpa-sə-tē, -ˈpas-tē\
the ______ amount or number that can be ______ or contained

elude *transitive verb* \ē-ˈlüd\
to avoid or ______ by being ______, skillful, or clever

im·pro·vise *verb* \ˈim-prə-ˌvīz also ˌim-prə-ˈ\
to ______ or perform ______ preparation

pre·cise *adjective* \pri-ˈsīs\
very ______ and exact about the ______

unique *adjective* \yu̇-ˈnēk\
used to say that something or someone is ______ anything or anyone ______

296 | DIFFICULTY: ●●●●●●●●○○○
COMPLETION: ☐ TIME: ______

SYLLABARY

Link word segments together in the grid below to create words, and enter them in the blanks.

TAGE	UT	AD	LY	TER
PROB	VAN	TER	COP	RY
A	BLY	MEN	TA	I
SEC	E	Y	EX	HEL
EL	OND	AR	CITE	MENT

Four-Syllable Noun: ☐☐☐ I ☐☐☐☐☐☐

Three-Syllable Adverb: ☐☐☐☐ A ☐☐☐

Four-Syllable Adjective: ☐ E ☐☐☐☐☐☐☐

Three-Syllable Noun: ☐☐ V ☐☐☐☐☐☐

Three-Syllable Noun: ☐☐☐☐☐☐☐ E ☐☐

Three-Syllable Adverb: ☐☐☐☐☐ L ☐

Five-Syllable Adjective: ☐☐☐ M ☐☐☐☐☐☐

297 | DIFFICULTY: ●●●●●●●●●○○
COMPLETION: ☐ TIME: ______

ANTONYM UNSCRAMBLE

Unscramble the letters below to form pairs of ANTONYMS. Note: Some words can be unscrambled more than one way!

P H L E ≠ D R I E H N

T H E G L D I ≠ R O O S W R

R E G A S N T ≠ M O O C M N

V Y I C T A ≠ D O N U M

P Y P S L U ≠ E R R S E E V

T E S S R I ≠ P O L Y M C

C R Y M E ≠ T U L C Y R E

298 | DIFFICULTY: ●●●●●●●●○○○ COMPLETION: ☐ TIME: ______

WORD WINDER

Use the clue to help you find the answers word-winding their way through the grid. Each answer will connect the top of the grid to the bottom.

C	M	T	D	T	A
A	E	I	S	D	E
L	R	F	V	M	K
E	S	N	F	A	P
N	P	E	A	E	N
H	R	T	X	T	R
O	E	I	A	A	D
N	W	N	O	G	T
G	E	N	T	E	E

Find five three-syllable words word-winding their way from top to bottom.

299 | DIFFICULTY: ●●●●●●●○○○
COMPLETION: ☐ TIME: ______

DICTIONARY UNSCRAMBLE

Unscramble the letters below to form words that match the Merriam-Webster definitions.

adjective
Not false or fake

INNEEGU= ☐☐☐☐☐☐☐

noun A writing acknowledging the receiving of goods or money

PRICTEE= ☐☐☐☐☐☐☐

adjective
Free from error especially as the result of care

CARECUTA= ☐☐☐☐☐☐☐☐

adjective
Not paid at an expected or required time

VUEEROD= ☐☐☐☐☐☐☐

noun
To shake or move with a slight trembling motion

VQRIEU= ☐☐☐☐☐☐

adjective
Low or lower in quality

NORREIFI= ☐☐☐☐☐☐☐☐

300 | DIFFICULTY: ●●●●●●●○○○
COMPLETION: ☐ TIME: ______

SYNONYM UNSCRAMBLE

Unscramble the letters below to form pairs of SYNONYMS. Watch out—some words can be unscrambled more than one way!

V Y I C T A = L O O W H L

E S E D P = T E C V O Y I L

B I O N T A = C R E P R O U

T F I G = W E E D T O N N M

S E E D N = T O P M C C A

S N A T F E = D B N I

L S E L K D I = I R A T O D

301 | DIFFICULTY: ●●●●●●●●○○○
COMPLETION: ☐ TIME: ______

PRISM CROSS'D WORDS

Use the color-coded clues below to find words that fit in the like-colored portions of the puzzle grid below.

- Coming from ancient tales (5-syllable adjective)
- An occurrence of bad weather (1-syllable noun)
- A line for leading an animal (1-syllable noun)

- To cause to sleep or rest (1-syllable verb)
- Liquid for cleaning hair (2-syllable noun)

- A single round lens for one eye (3-syllable noun)
- Cloth worn around the neck (1-syllable noun)

- Bird that lives near the ocean (2-syllable noun)
- Upper atmospheric oxygen (2-syllable noun)

- A double-reed woodwind (2-syllable noun)
- Showing a lack of good sense (2-syllable adjective)

302 | DIFFICULTY: ●●●●●●●●●○○ COMPLETION: ☐ TIME: ______

SYNONYM FINDER

Find and circle the seven pairs of SYNONYMS divided between the letter grids below.

C	O	N	D	O	N	E	N
R	G	Y	P	D	L	I	L
E	I	W	H	I	A	A	K
D	Y	M	T	L	G	L	S
N	C	S	P	E	N	U	H
I	O	M	L	A	O	F	K
H	O	L	C	I	R	J	M
C	I	T	P	M	H	T	R

C	I	L	L	I	C	I	T
R	O	Q	M	B	J	C	N
E	C	N	Z	G	U	P	E
V	P	Y	T	R	A	S	M
E	R	L	T	R	U	T	A
A	F	S	W	C	A	K	L
L	B	N	X	H	B	R	M
O	D	E	V	O	U	T	Y

○ ○ ○ ○ ○ ○ ○

303 | DIFFICULTY: ●●●●●●●●●○○
COMPLETION: ☐ TIME: ______

CROSS'D WORDS UNSCRAMBLE

Unscramble the letters in each clue to fill in the puzzle grid below.

ACROSS

1 ICAML *(one-syllable word)*
3 WREEF *(two-syllable word)*
5 NOFTFIP *(two-syllable word)*
7 WHYCE *(two-syllable word)*
8 PIGER *(one-syllable word)*
9 NEWIH *(one-syllable word)*
11 COAOH *(two-syllable word)*
13 DOLLYWR *(two-syllable word)*
14 LADYE *(two-syllable word)*
15 BOTRI *(two-syllable word)*

DOWN

1 VICCI *(two-syllable word)*
2 OYEMN *(two-syllable word)*
3 NLFGI *(one-syllable word)*
4 SRIEA *(one-syllable word)*
5 VEERWIP *(two-syllable word)*
6 GLYFITH *(two-syllable word)*
9 REDWI *(one-syllable word)*
10 LAYRE *(two-syllable word)*
11 OUADI *(three-syllable word)*
12 HOTUG *(one-syllable word)*

304 | DIFFICULTY: ●●●●●●●○○○
COMPLETION: ☐ TIME: ______

MAKE THE CONNECTION

Fill in the boxes with common two-word phrases with the help of the clues below. The last word in each pair will be the first word in the following pair.

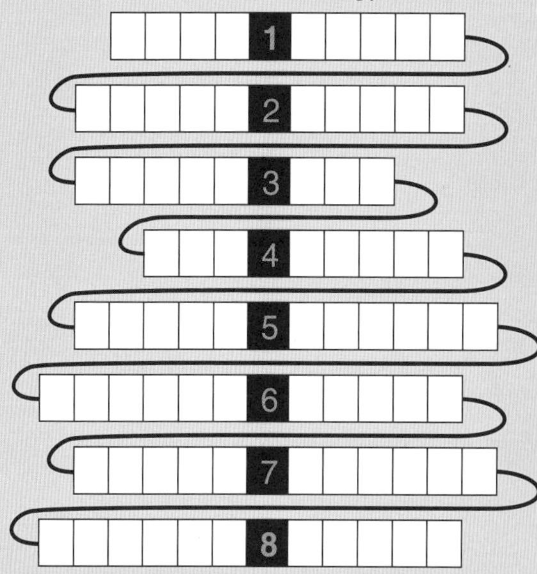

1 Drinking container for merlot
2 Certain lizard
3 Cure-all potion
4 Place to find black gold
5 Summer Olympic sport
6 Tool for Gretzky
7 Simplistic drawing
8 Skater's maneuver

305 | DIFFICULTY: ●●●●●●●●○○
COMPLETION: ☐ TIME: ______

ANTONYM FINDER

Find and circle the six pairs of ANTONYMS, one on each side, in the letter grids below.

T	H	A	S	T	Y
O	A	B	F	F	T
L	M	N	N	A	S
L	D	E	G	M	A
A	V	W	H	E	N
E	G	T	Y	C	R

S	S	T	Y	N	E
P	L	H	C	C	S
D	U	O	A	P	W
E	M	E	W	M	E
N	P	Y	H	D	E
Y	Y	R	T	N	T

○○○○○○

306 | DIFFICULTY: ●●●●●●○○○○
COMPLETION: ☐ TIME: ______

COLOR WORD CHAINS

Use the clues and letters below to make word paths between like colors to fill the board.

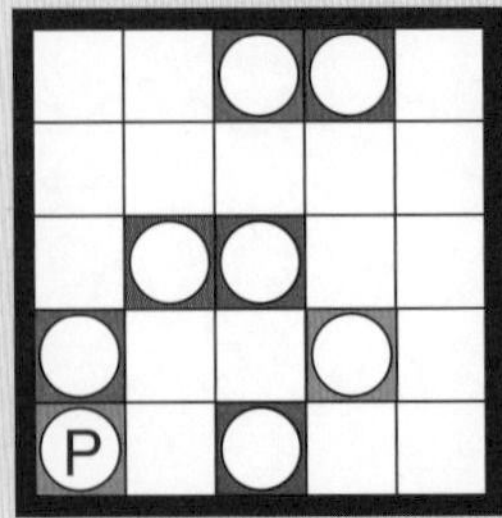

- A part of a whole
- To explain the meaning of
- To set someone or something free
- An article of clothing

A	A	C	D	E	E
E	E	E	E	E	E
F	G	I	I	L	M
N	N	R	R	S	T

307 | DIFFICULTY: ●●●●●●●●●○○
COMPLETION: ☐ TIME: ________

MISSING DEFINITIONS FINDER

Using the clues below, find and circle the words concealed in the letter grid.

S	T	J	E	L	H	E	A	V	Y
X	T	I	M	F	A	V	Z	S	R
S	A	R	M	I	F	R	S	J	E
T	T	G	E	E	S	E	G	Z	K
S	Q	U	R	N	L	T	C	E	A
A	A	Z	P	E	G	V	A	T	E
L	J	M	S	I	E	T	Z	K	W
Z	V	U	E	X	D	D	H	Q	E

abate *verb* \ə-ˈbāt\
to become ________ : to decrease in ________

blun·der *verb* \ˈblən-dər\
to make a ________ or careless ________

du·ra·tion *noun* \dü-ˈrā-shən also dyü-\
the length of ________ that something exists or ________

fu·tile *adjective* \ˈfyü-təl, ˈfyü-ˌtī(-ə)l\
having no result or ________ : pointless or ________

mas·sive *adjective* \ˈma-siv\
very ________ and ________

unan·i·mous *adjective* \yü-ˈna-nə-məs\
________ to by everyone : having the ________ opinion

308 | DIFFICULTY: ●●●●●●●○○○
COMPLETION: ☐ TIME: ______

DICTIONARY WORD WINDER

Use the clues below to help you find the answers word-winding their way through the grid. Each answer will connect one side of the grid to the other—left to right, top to bottom, right to left, and bottom to top.

T	D	A	W	E	K
B	G	E	J	M	T
I	N	T	Z	C	P
T	S	F	E	A	Q
N	E	H	T	V	D
I	Y	K	C	A	P

→ To cause (someone or something) to become sick or affected by disease ______

↓ The feeling that you understand and share another person's experiences and emotions ______

← A small bundle or parcel ______

↑ As an alternative to something expressed or implied ______

309 | DIFFICULTY: ●●●●●●●●○○○
COMPLETION: ☐ TIME: ______

DEFINITION FINDER

Using the clues below, find and circle the words concealed in the letter grid.

J	L	E	I	S	U	R	E	C
B	X	Z	S	X	A	R	N	A
Z	I	E	Q	L	O	O	O	N
J	U	Z	O	D	I	N	G	Y
G	X	H	A	Z	Q	A	R	O
K	C	F	O	R	E	M	A	N
S	Q	J	Z	X	R	Z	J	Q
J	X	M	O	L	T	E	N	Z

- ○ A learned person *(noun)*
- ○ A large country house on a large piece of land *(noun)*
- ○ A person who is in charge of a group of workers *(noun)*
- ○ Time when you can do whatever you want to do *(noun)*
- ○ Dark and dirty *(adjective)*
- ○ Strikingly out of the ordinary *(adjective)*
- ○ The language used for a particular activity *(noun)*
- ○ To love or admire (someone) very much *(verb)*
- ○ Fused or liquefied by heat *(adjective)*
- ○ To suppose or think (something) *(verb)*
- ○ A deep narrow valley with steep sides *(noun)*

310 | DIFFICULTY: ●●●●●●●●●○○
COMPLETION: ☐ TIME: ________

DICTIONARY CROSS'D WORDS

Fill in the puzzle using the Merriam-Webster definition clues below.

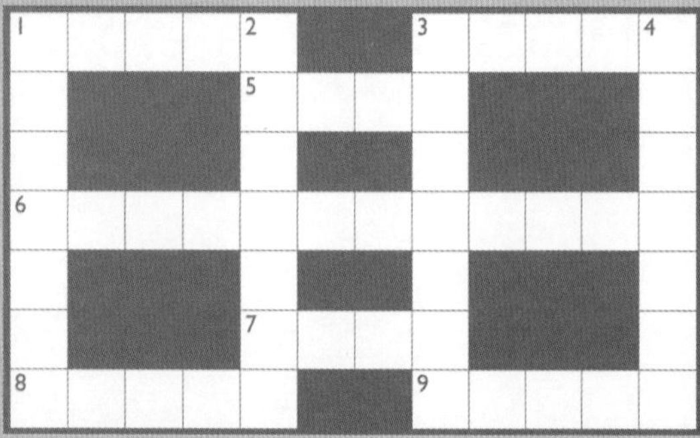

Across

1 Desirably firm and crunchy (1-syllable adjective)
3 A definite authoritative tenet (2-syllable noun)
5 A bar on which a wheel turns (2-syllable noun)
6 Completely and sincerely devoted (3-syllable adjective)
7 Of, being, or relating to zero (1-syllable noun)
8 A machine that looks like a human being (2-syllable noun)
9 Each individual or part of a group (2-syllable adjective)

Down

1 A thick soup or stew (2-syllable noun)
2 An elaborate, colorful exhibition (2-syllable noun)
3 A great disaster or complete failure (3-syllable noun)
4 A society of learned persons (4-syllable noun)

311 | DIFFICULTY: ●●●●●●●●○○○ COMPLETION: ☐ TIME: ________

PRISM WORD FINDER

Using the color-coded clues below, find and circle the words in the letter grid.

H	A	A	M	P	U	T	E	E	J	T
A	J	G	A	M	O	E	B	A	S	K
E	S	W	E	Y	B	A	Z	O	L	G
E	N	T	X	N	C	Q	O	W	P	R
T	J	A	H	A	D	R	F	Y	L	A
O	W	B	P	M	A	A	X	Y	E	N
V	G	L	X	D	A	O	X	X	D	T
E	A	Q	A	Y	R	O	F	B	G	E
D	W	M	X	P	P	Z	X	V	E	E
N	R	O	J	E	G	A	L	A	X	Y
A	F	F	O	R	E	S	E	E	W	S

Find five six-letter nouns that start and end with A starting with an orange letter ○○○○○

Find five words ending in "XY" starting with a blue letter ○○○○○

Find four seven-letter words ending with double "E's" starting with a purple letter ○○○○

Find two five-letter one-syllable words starting with a red letter ○○

312 | DIFFICULTY: ●●●●●●●●●○○
COMPLETION: ☐ TIME: ______

ANTONYM FINDER

Find and circle the six pairs of ANTONYMS, one on each side, in the letter grids below.

E	L	A	C	K	C
K	V	D	K	I	E
E	L	A	N	H	T
E	Q	A	D	F	I
M	P	G	J	E	R
H	E	A	V	Y	T

≠

Y	F	R	E	S	H
T	M	C	P	E	S
N	G	E	C	W	R
E	M	A	E	N	A
L	E	R	D	T	H
P	L	I	G	H	T

○○○○○○

313 | DIFFICULTY: ●●●●●●●●○○○
COMPLETION: ☐ TIME: ______

MIXED-UP DEFINITION

Unscramble the letters below to reveal the definition of the given word.

ad·van·tage *noun* \əd-ˈvan-tij\
a traocf ro sniccmeatru fo bteenif ot sti spoosress

☐ ☐☐☐☐☐☐

☐☐

☐☐☐☐☐☐☐☐☐☐☐☐

☐☐ ☐☐☐☐☐☐☐

☐☐ ☐☐☐ ☐☐☐☐☐☐☐☐☐

314 | DIFFICULTY: ●●●●●●●○○○○ COMPLETION: ☐ TIME: ______

WORD WINDER

Use the clue to help you find the answers word-winding their way through the grid. Each answer will connect the top of the grid to the bottom.

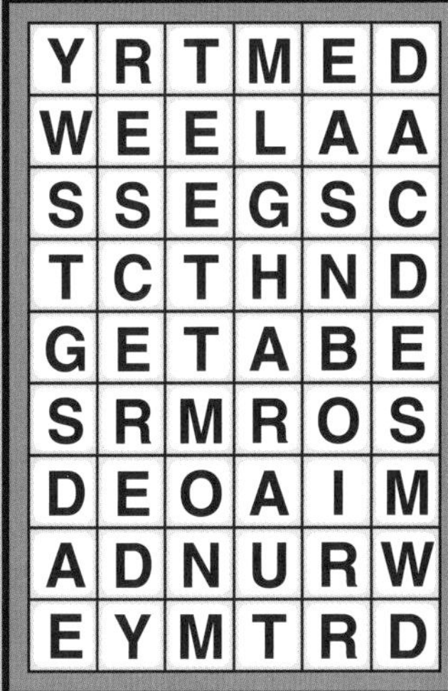

Y	R	T	M	E	D
W	E	E	L	A	A
S	S	E	G	S	C
T	C	T	H	N	D
G	E	T	A	B	E
S	R	M	R	O	S
D	E	O	A	I	M
A	D	N	U	R	W
E	Y	M	T	R	D

Find five words starting and ending with the same letter word-winding their way from top to bottom.

315 | DIFFICULTY: ●●●●●●●●●○○ COMPLETION: ☐ TIME: ______

SYNONYM FINDER

Find and circle the six pairs of SYNONYMS, one on each side, in the letter grids below.

C	Y	B	L	O	T
F	A	M	U	S	E
F	T	N	L	M	T
U	C	F	D	C	N
L	D	W	A	I	B
B	G	R	A	N	D

S	F	G	Y	K	G
Y	T	A	N	R	R
K	L	A	E	T	U
P	R	E	I	L	F
F	H	Y	C	N	F
C	L	O	F	T	Y

○○○○○○

316 | DIFFICULTY: ●●●●●●●○○○○ COMPLETION: ☐ TIME: ______

ANTONYM FINDER

Find and circle the six pairs of ANTONYMS, one on each side, in the letter grids below.

D	F	O	R	M	T
I	I	E	Z	H	R
G	H	S	C	M	A
I	P	I	M	X	T
R	T	A	D	A	S
N	Y	R	N	E	L

C	G	J	D	R	K
M	H	A	E	C	C
D	L	W	E	D	A
G	O	R	N	F	L
L	W	E	K	L	S
E	X	P	O	S	E

○○○○○○

317 | DIFFICULTY: ●●●●●●●●○○○
COMPLETION: ☐ TIME: ________

MISSING DEFINITIONS FINDER

Using the clues below, find and circle the words concealed in the letter grid.

G	H	A	P	P	E	N	G	G	Y
N	E	J	M	V	X	Q	O	N	R
O	V	Z	O	K	C	V	O	I	O
L	E	Q	N	X	H	Q	D	Y	G
L	I	T	E	R	A	T	U	R	E
I	H	V	Y	Z	N	Z	K	T	T
K	C	K	Q	A	G	A	I	N	A
S	A	T	A	L	E	N	T	X	C

bar·ter *verb* \ˈbär-tər\
to ________ things (such as products or services) for other things instead of for ________

du·ra·ble *adjective* \ˈdu̇r-ə-bəl also ˈdyu̇r-\
staying strong and in ________ condition over a ________ period of time

genre *noun* \ˈzhän-rə, ˈzhä^{n}-; ˈzhä^{n}r; ˈjän-rə\
a particular type or ________ of ________ or art

knack *noun* \ˈnak\
an ability, ________, or special ________ needed to do something

ob·jec·tive *noun* \əb-ˈjek-tiv, äb-\
something you are ________ to do or ________

re·cur *intransitive verb* \ri-ˈkər\
to ________ or appear ________

318 | DIFFICULTY: ●●●●●●●○○○
COMPLETION: ☐ TIME: ______

DICTIONARY CROSS'D WORDS

Fill in the puzzle using the Merriam-Webster definition clues below.

Across
1 Not the same (2-syllable adjective)
3 Easily damaged or destroyed (1-syllable adjective)
5 Morally bad (2-syllable adjective)
6 In a reluctant or unwilling way (4-syllable adverb)
7 To travel on water in a ship or boat (1-syllable verb)
8 To make a chirping sound (1-syllable verb)
9 In an early stage of life (1-syllable adjective)

Down
1 Different from the ordinary (2-syllable adjective)
2 Something that a person asks for (2-syllable noun)
3 With a smooth and easy style (3-syllable adverb)
4 A type of small flying insect (3-syllable noun)

319 | DIFFICULTY: ●●●●●●●○○○
COMPLETION: ☐ TIME: ________

SYNONYM FINDER

Find and circle the six pairs of SYNONYMS, one on each side, in the letter grids below.

T	K	B	M	G	N
A	C	L	F	N	O
E	B	E	L	C	M
N	R	A	Q	E	E
T	H	K	T	D	N
D	P	A	C	E	G

=

B	A	R	E	D	N
M	N	D	L	E	H
F	W	E	S	S	T
H	I	S	G	I	I
Y	E	M	A	G	D
L	W	G	C	N	Y

○○○○○○

320 | DIFFICULTY: ●●●●●●●○○○
COMPLETION: ☐ TIME: ________

COLOR WORD CHAINS

Use the clues and letters below to make word paths between like colors to fill the board.

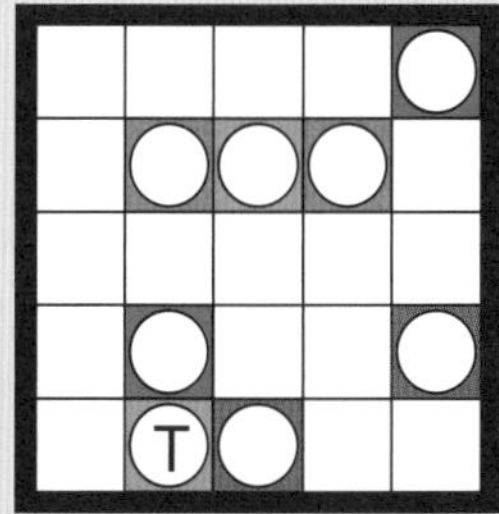

- A destructive storm
- A branch of mathematics using letters and numbers
- A moral fault or failing
- To meet the requirements

A	A	A	B	C	E
E	F	G	H	I	I
L	L	N	O	O	P
Q	R	U	V	Y	Y

321 | DIFFICULTY: ●●●●●●●●●○○
COMPLETION: ☐ TIME: ______

ANTONYM UNSCRAMBLE

Unscramble the letters below to form pairs of ANTONYMS. Note: Some words can be unscrambled more than one way!

T I O M ≠ S T I E N R

N Y E E M ≠ D R E F I N

D I A S U Q L ≠ E L A C N

S U Y C M L ≠ D A Y H N

V E E R I G ≠ J I E O R E C

A L E E E S R ≠ P R T A N E

D R A S N E L ≠ S P E I R A

322 | DIFFICULTY: ●●●●●●●○○○○
COMPLETION: ☐ TIME: ______

SYLLABARY

Link word segments together in the grid below to create words, and enter them in the blanks.

VAN	A	LATE	TRIC	I
CU	MU	CAR	LEC	TY
AC	WEA	HOW	E	ER
AF	RI	LY	EV	DEL
TER	WARD	CY	CA	I

Four-Syllable Noun: _ _ L _ _ _ _ _

Three-Syllable Noun: _ _ _ _ V _ _

Three-Syllable Adverb: _ O _ _ _ _ _

Four-Syllable Verb: _ _ _ _ _ _ _ _ T _

Three-Syllable Adverb: _ _ _ _ I _ _

Five-Syllable Noun: _ _ _ C _ _ _ _ _ _ _

Three-Syllable Adverb: _ _ T _ _ _ _ _ _

323 | DIFFICULTY: ●●●●●●●○○○
COMPLETION: ☐ TIME: ______

WORD WINDER

Use the clue to help you find the answers word-winding their way through the grid. Each answer will connect the top of the grid to the bottom.

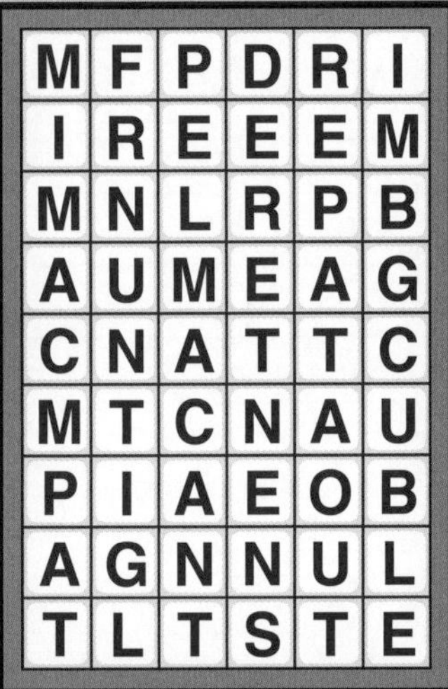

↓ Find five adjectives word-winding their way from top to bottom.

______

______

______

______

______

324 | DIFFICULTY: ●●●●●●●●○○○
COMPLETION: ☐ TIME: ________

DICTIONARY UNSCRAMBLE

Unscramble the letters below to form words that match the Merriam-Webster definitions.

adjective
Having always the same form, manner, or degree

FRUMION= ☐☐☐☐☐☐☐

---

noun
A specific military or naval task

SMOINIS= ☐☐☐☐☐☐☐

---

adjective
Pleasing to look at; especially of a person

SMAHEDON= ☐☐☐☐☐☐☐☐

---

transitive verb To prevent (someone) from doing something or being a part of a group

LEECUXD= ☐☐☐☐☐☐☐

---

adjective
Able to float

NYOUBAT= ☐☐☐☐☐☐☐

---

transitive verb To allow (yourself) to have or do something as a special pleasure

GNUILED= ☐☐☐☐☐☐☐

325 | DIFFICULTY: ●●●●●●●○○○○
COMPLETION: ☐ TIME: ______

PRISM CROSS'D WORDS

Use the color-coded clues below to find words that fit in the like-colored portions of the puzzle grid below.

- Strong cotton cloth (2-syllable noun)
- Fully and completely correct (2-syllable adjective)
- A drug that causes calm (4-syllable noun)

- At any time (2-syllable adverb)
- Far away in space or time (2-syllable adjective)

- Sign over a theater's entrance (2-syllable noun)
- Creamy coating for baked goods (2-syllable noun)

- An agreement to stop fighting (1-syllable noun)
- To make a very serious request (2-syllable verb)

- A connoisseur of food and drink (2-syllable noun)
- A tiny particle (2-syllable noun)

326 | DIFFICULTY: ●●●●●●●●○○○ COMPLETION: ☐ TIME: ______

CROSS'D WORDS UNSCRAMBLE

Unscramble the letters in each clue to fill in the puzzle grid below.

ACROSS

1 PSRAH *(one-syllable word)*
3 TRACO *(two-syllable word)*
5 SILVEBI *(three-syllable word)*
7 TPYAR *(two-syllable word)*
8 CRAHE *(one-syllable word)*
9 LSIKL *(one-syllable word)*
11 PALEM *(two-syllable word)*
13 TOOMEUC *(two-syllable word)*
14 RUTTO *(two-syllable word)*
15 EXYOP *(three-syllable word)*

DOWN

1 ESPHE *(one-syllable word)*
2 SPYHU *(two-syllable word)*
3 BEARM *(two-syllable word)*
4 GOHRU *(one-syllable word)*
5 TOREVGI *(three-syllable word)*
6 LEEMPAX *(three-syllable word)*
9 HITSG *(one-syllable word)*
10 EATRL *(two-syllable word)*
11 OABEV *(two-syllable word)*
12 NYETR *(two-syllable word)*

327 | DIFFICULTY: ●●●●●●●○○○
COMPLETION: ☐ TIME: ________

SYNONYM UNSCRAMBLE

Unscramble the letters below to form pairs of SYNONYMS. Watch out—some words can be unscrambled more than one way!

S W I E = B E S S L I N E

U S O T T = D R U O N T

C E E C A D = S T O N N C E

T A H L H Y E = S R U O T B

C E H F T = C E R R P U O

D N D H E I = S T R E E C

S R E G S O N = S R A O B B

328 | DIFFICULTY: ●●●●●●●○○○
COMPLETION: ☐ TIME: ________

DICTIONARY WORD WINDER

Use the clues below to help you find the answers word-winding their way through the grid. Each answer will connect one side of the grid to the other—left to right, top to bottom, right to left, and bottom to top.

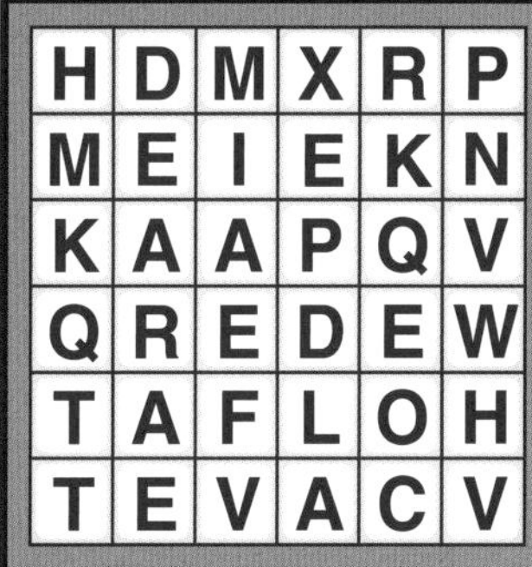

H	D	M	X	R	P
M	E	I	E	K	N
K	A	A	P	Q	V
Q	R	E	D	E	W
T	A	F	L	O	H
T	E	V	A	C	V

→ A usually flat area of land that is covered with tall grass ________

↓ To say (something) after someone else has said it ________

← A soft type of cloth that has short raised fibers on one side ________

↑ Filled with fear or apprehension ________

329 | DIFFICULTY: ●●●●●●●○○○
COMPLETION: ☐ TIME: ______

COLOR WORD CHAINS

Use the clues and letters below to make word paths between like colors to fill the board.

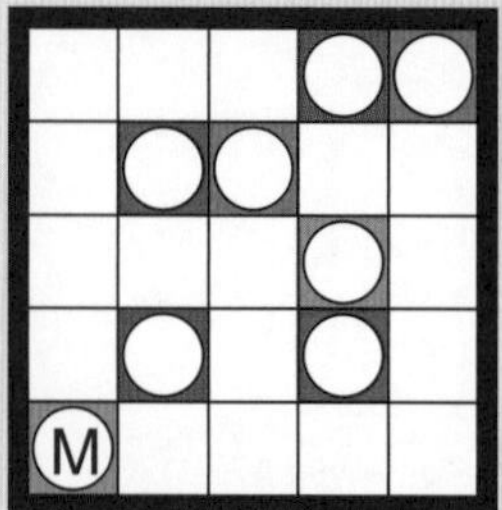

- To keep in good condition
- The feeling of wanting what someone else has
- Academic instruction period
- Complete disorder

A	A	A	C	E	E
E	E	H	I	I	M
N	N	N	O	R	S
S	S	T	T	V	Y

330 | DIFFICULTY: ●●●●●●●●○○
COMPLETION: ☐ TIME: ______

ANTONYM FINDER

Find and circle the six pairs of ANTONYMS, one on each side, in the letter grids below.

D	R	E	A	D	T
T	M	B	P	N	E
L	O	Q	U	M	E
U	O	A	A	C	D
A	L	L	I	X	Z
F	G	V	J	N	F

V	I	R	T	U	E
G	A	I	N	K	H
D	H	L	C	Q	T
G	V	I	O	M	R
R	U	P	D	R	I
Q	C	N	F	E	M

○ ○ ○ ○ ○ ○

331 | DIFFICULTY: ●●●●●●●○○○○
COMPLETION: ☐ TIME: ______

MISSING DEFINITIONS FINDER

Using the clues below, find and circle the words concealed in the letter grid.

P	A	I	D	J	M	H	B	C	J
Y	D	Z	E	X	P	L	A	I	N
H	A	R	M	B	J	L	T	R	X
Y	M	D	D	Z	K	S	K	V	D
E	A	N	S	T	R	A	N	G	E
N	G	I	J	O	P	O	I	N	T
O	E	K	W	S	I	L	L	Y	Z
M	G	E	N	E	R	O	U	S	V

be·nign *adjective* \bi-ˈnīn\
not causing ______ or ______

enig·ma *noun* \i-ˈnig-mə, e-\
something ______ to understand or ______

gra·tis *adverb or adjective* \ˈgra-təs, ˈgrā-\
used to indicate that no ______ is ______ for something

mag·nan·i·mous *adjective* \mag-ˈna-nə-məs\
having or showing a ______ and ______ nature

na·dir *noun* \ˈnā-ˌdir, ˈnā-dər\
the ______ or lowest ______ of something

zany *adjective* \ˈzā-nē\
very ______ and ______

332 | DIFFICULTY: ●●●●●●●○○○
COMPLETION: ☐ TIME: ________

ANTONYM FINDER

Find and circle the seven pairs of ANTONYMS divided between the letter grids below.

I	N	V	O	L	V	E	L
Z	M	J	A	V	C	A	H
J	M	P	K	C	U	G	T
X	H	P	A	Q	A	X	U
L	F	Z	E	I	J	N	R
Q	Z	N	D	C	R	W	T
X	U	C	E	A	S	E	M
L	I	F	E	L	E	S	S

X	B	E	N	E	F	I	T
M	A	T	C	H	E	D	S
L	Q	L	F	X	E	C	I
Z	Y	J	I	L	M	G	S
K	H	I	L	V	W	Q	R
R	D	I	N	K	E	N	E
C	F	T	P	G	H	L	P
Q	E	X	C	L	U	D	E

○ ○ ○ ○ ○ ○ ○

333 | DIFFICULTY: ●●●●●●●●●○○
COMPLETION: ☐ TIME: ________

PRISM WORD FINDER

Using the color-coded clues below, find and circle the words in the letter grid.

L C O U G A R G J R L
E S G V R T N N X B A
R V J O O A I E W G V
R N A V R A N Z E R I
I D I L T G N G K D R
U D I N L O E E Y B Y
Q V U R Y E N W C A E
S O B O T I Y L P B N
M W R N V Y G X N O V
V R X A M U S H Y O O
A J R M E A T Y B N Y

Find five land formations starting with an orange letter ○ ○ ○ ○ ○

Find five five-letter adjectives ending in "Y" starting with a blue letter ○ ○ ○ ○ ○

Find three two-syllable animals starting with a purple letter ○ ○ ○

Find three five-letter words with "V" in the middle starting with a red letter ○ ○ ○

334 | DIFFICULTY: ●●●●●●●●●○○
COMPLETION: ☐ TIME: ________

DEFINITION FINDER

Using the clues below, find and circle the words concealed in the letter grid.

M	T	X	S	C	H	A	F	E
U	Z	W	Q	P	C	Z	E	X
E	T	J	I	I	L	D	A	H
S	X	O	N	L	A	I	S	E
U	G	O	P	G	I	I	T	R
M	C	L	I	I	N	G	Z	M
I	Z	R	W	A	A	X	H	I
Q	B	J	V	T	E	M	P	T

- ○ To disappear entirely without a clear explanation *(verb)*
- ○ Period when day is ending and night is beginning *(noun)*
- ○ Widely recognized and well-established *(adjective)*
- ○ A large group of soldiers that is part of an army *(noun)*
- ○ A place of ideal perfection *(noun)*
- ○ To divide lengthwise usually along the grain *(verb)*
- ○ A building where things are collected and shown *(noun)*
- ○ A special meal with large amounts of food *(noun)*
- ○ To entice to do wrong by promise or gain *(verb)*
- ○ One that retires from society and lives in solitude *(noun)*
- ○ To become sore or damaged from rubbing *(verb)*

335 | DIFFICULTY: ●●●●●●●●●○○ COMPLETION: ☐ TIME: ______

DICTIONARY CROSS'D WORDS

Fill in the puzzle using the Merriam-Webster definition clues below.

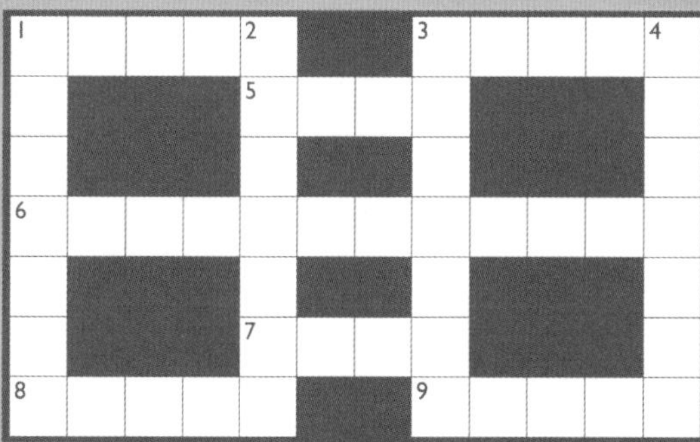

Across
1 A public square in a city or town (2-syllable noun)
3 Devoted to a particular religion (2-syllable adjective)
5 To become unclear or difficult to see (1-syllable verb)
6 The power or right to govern an area (4-syllable noun)
7 A chemical with a sour taste (2-syllable noun)
8 A gullible inhabitant of a rural area (2-syllable noun)
9 To remove something written (2-syllable verb)

Down
1 Telling a lie in a court of law (3-syllable noun)
2 Extremely poor or bad (3-syllable adjective)
3 To be, go, or come ahead or in front of (2-syllable verb)
4 To obtain money or property by deceit (2-syllable verb)

336 | DIFFICULTY: ●●●●●●●●●○○
COMPLETION: ☐ TIME: ______

MAKE THE CONNECTION

Fill in the boxes with common two-word phrases with the help of the clues below. The last word in each pair will be the first word in the following pair.

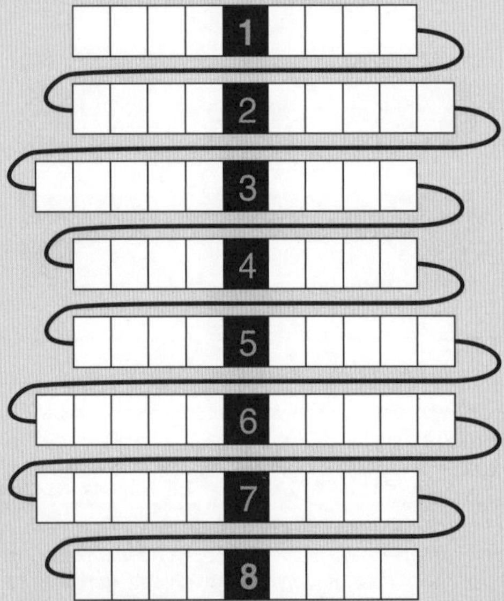

1 Item in a Rolodex
2 Furniture with folding legs
3 Common seasoning
4 Soothing soak
5 It might have lots of bubbles
6 Pool perk
7 Scoot to one side
8 Done

337 | DIFFICULTY: ●●●●●●●○○○
COMPLETION: ☐ TIME: ______

ANTONYM FINDER

Find and circle the six pairs of ANTONYMS, one on each side, in the letter grids below.

C	X	D	Q	G	Y
L	R	I	C	J	T
E	A	R	N	N	M
V	C	A	A	Q	R
E	Y	I	F	Z	A
R	G	L	E	E	W

S	O	R	R	O	W
L	P	C	O	L	D
L	C	Y	I	C	E
U	U	L	G	M	L
D	X	S	A	M	W
S	P	T	H	D	Y

○○○○○○

338 | DIFFICULTY: ●●●●●●●○○○
COMPLETION: ☐ TIME: ______

SYNONYM FINDER

Find and circle the six pairs of SYNONYMS, one on each side, in the letter grids below.

C	A	L	I	V	E
P	R	O	F	I	T
W	F	A	L	L	D
A	C	P	N	Y	G
R	Y	F	W	K	R
D	E	N	E	M	Y

S	K	E	T	C	H
A	T	B	Y	R	N
L	D	R	E	O	I
E	N	O	F	S	A
R	F	W	C	S	G
T	U	M	B	L	E

○○○○○○

339 | DIFFICULTY: ●●●●●●●●○○○
COMPLETION: ☐ TIME: ______

WORD WINDER

Use the clue to help you find the answers word-winding their way through the grid. Each answer will connect the top of the grid to the bottom.

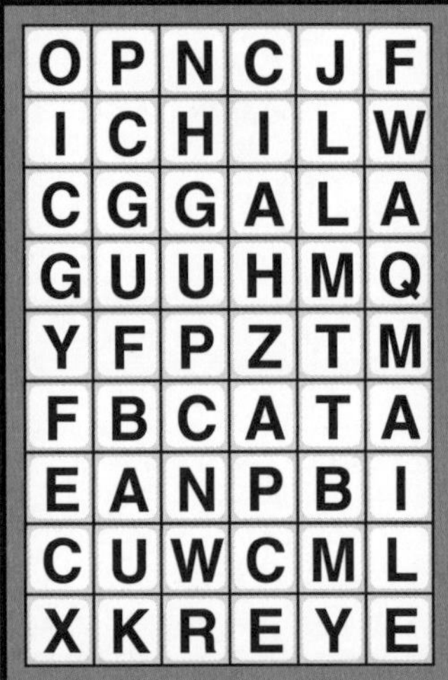

O	P	N	C	J	F
I	C	H	I	L	W
C	G	G	A	L	A
G	U	U	H	M	Q
Y	F	P	Z	T	M
F	B	C	A	T	A
E	A	N	P	B	I
C	U	W	C	M	L
X	K	R	E	Y	E

Find five words containing double consonants word-winding their way from top to bottom.

340 | DIFFICULTY: ●●●●●●○○○○
COMPLETION: ☐ TIME: ______

DICTIONARY UNSCRAMBLE

Unscramble the letters below to form words that match the Merriam-Webster definitions.

adjective
Having a very rich and expensive quality

HAVLSI= ☐☐☐☐☐☐

transitive verb
To grow or become bigger or more advanced

PLODVEE= ☐☐☐☐☐☐☐

noun
Strong approval or praise

LAMCICA= ☐☐☐☐☐☐☐

transitive verb To cover (something) with a thin layer of clear plastic for protection

EMTLIANA= ☐☐☐☐☐☐☐☐

noun
An unbound printed publication with no cover

HAPPMELT= ☐☐☐☐☐☐☐☐

adjective
Careful about avoiding danger or risk

OSTCUUAI= ☐☐☐☐☐☐☐☐

341 | DIFFICULTY: ●●●●●●●●●○○
COMPLETION: ☐ TIME: ______

SYNONYM FINDER

Find and circle the seven pairs of SYNONYMS divided between the letter grids below.

U H A C P T W A
E C O V X J T D
D U O N A N D O
E R F N E L M R
P I B G F S U N
M O R Y C E T E
I U B G P H S U
L S D Y K N C S

=

P R E V E N T E
S D G V A W S H
P I A J D O J S
T R N P L R X I
G W Y C Y T B N
J L S I E H F R
Z I K H N R K A
D N L F M G E G

○ ○ ○ ○ ○ ○ ○

342 | DIFFICULTY: ●●●●●●●●●○○ COMPLETION: ☐ TIME: ______

ANTONYM FINDER

Find and circle the six pairs of ANTONYMS, one on each side, in the letter grids below.

S	T	U	P	I	D
D	G	H	J	H	R
R	R	L	M	E	T
U	X	E	G	A	S
N	H	A	A	P	U
K	E	Z	N	M	J

R	C	F	P	W	G
E	A	C	A	N	K
B	L	H	O	C	D
O	M	R	E	J	T
S	W	P	B	G	L
F	S	H	A	R	P

○○○○○○

343 | DIFFICULTY: ●●●●●●●●○○○ COMPLETION: ☐ TIME: ______

COLOR WORD CHAINS

Use the clues and letters below to make word paths between like colors to fill the board.

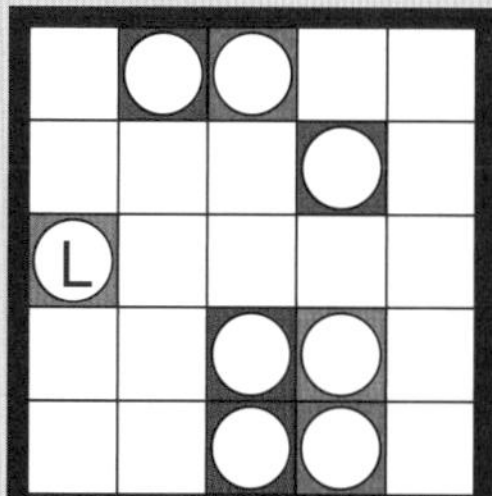

- A large glandular organ
- The way someone acts
- An empty space without air or other gases
- To slow the progress of

A	A	B	C	D	E
E	E	H	H	I	I
I	M	N	O	R	R
R	U	U	V	V	V

344 | DIFFICULTY: ●●●●●●●●●○○
COMPLETION: ☐ TIME: ______

ANTONYM UNSCRAMBLE

Unscramble the letters below to form pairs of ANTONYMS. Note: Some words can be unscrambled more than one way!

D R O N A M ≠ D E P N A N L

G L Y U ≠ T R Y P T E

C I D D A R S ≠ T R A I N E

S T O H O M ≠ U H R O G

B U D M ≠ G R H B I T

D E E P X E T I ≠ L D A E Y

C D C S E U E ≠ A L F I

345 | DIFFICULTY: ●●●●●●○○○○
COMPLETION: ☐ TIME: ______

CROSS'D WORD CONNECTIONS

The crosswords below share common letters as indicated by the colored boxes. Use the clues to solve the puzzles.

ACROSS
1 A table at which a person works
4 A place sheltered from the sun
5 Partially carbonized vegetable tissue

DOWN
1 The darker part of twilight
2 A raised platform in a theater
3 A depression or hollow made by a blow or by pressure

ACROSS
1 Something said to cause laughter
4 An electronic device that allows electric current to flow in only one direction
5 A skin stripped of hair or wool for tanning

DOWN
1 Olympic martial art originating in Japan
2 To poke or stir up (as a fire)
3 Not straight

ACROSS
1 To sell or distribute something as a business
4 The place where someone lives
5 A positive factor or quality

DOWN
1 Having two different parts, uses, etc.
2 An island that is made of coral and shaped like a ring
3 A clear, curved piece of glass or plastic

346 | DIFFICULTY: ●●●●●●●○○○
COMPLETION: ☐ TIME: ______

SYLLABARY

Link word segments together in the grid below to create words, and enter them in the blanks.

TOR	COR	AU	THOR	DI
RY	A	RI	GES	IZE
ER	TO	DOR	TION	LY
OP	DA	ME	DI	ATE
MAN	IM	ER	COV	DIS

Three-Syllable Noun: _ O _ _ _ _ _

Three-Syllable Verb: _ _ _ _ _ _ E _

Four-Syllable Adjective: _ _ _ D _ _ _ _ _

Three-Syllable Verb: _ _ T _ _ _ _ _ _

Five-Syllable Adverb: _ _ _ _ _ I _ _ _ _ _

Four-Syllable Noun: _ _ _ _ A _ _ _

Three-Syllable Noun: _ _ _ _ _ _ _ O _

347 | DIFFICULTY: ●●●●●●●●○○○
COMPLETION: ☐ TIME: ________

PRISM CROSS'D WORDS

Use the color-coded clues below to find words that fit in the like-colored portions of the puzzle grid below.

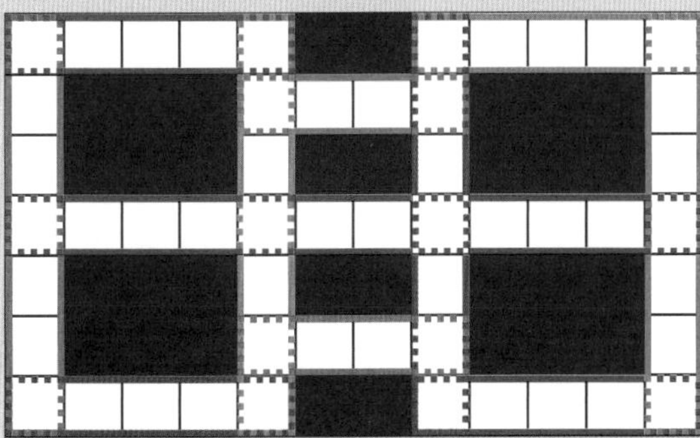

- To choose by vote (2-syllable verb)
- Contest to determine the best (4-syllable noun)
- To mend a hole or weak spot (1-syllable verb)

- Having had a previous owner (1-syllable adjective)
- Having strange mental abilities (2-syllable adjective)

- Making it easier to do a job (2-syllable adjective)
- Painful involuntary muscle spasm (1-syllable noun)

- An artificial waterway (2-syllable noun)
- A very poisonous chemical (3-syllable noun)

- A holy messenger (2-syllable noun)
- Nervous and tense (2-syllable adjective)

348 | DIFFICULTY: ●●●●●●●●○○○
COMPLETION: ☐ TIME: ______

DICTIONARY WORD WINDER

Use the clues below to help you find the answers word-winding their way through the grid. Each answer will connect one side of the grid to the other—left to right, top to bottom, right to left, and bottom to top.

P	E	B	C	I	P
C	R	K	Q	H	F
I	E	U	N	I	T
T	V	I	D	W	O
O	P	O	F	E	N
J	N	T	N	K	V

→ A view, judgment, or appraisal formed in the mind about a particular matter ______

↓ Having or showing careful good judgment ______

← A group of bushes or small trees that grow close together ______

↑ A person who has just started learning or doing something ______

349 | DIFFICULTY: ●●●●●●●●●○○
COMPLETION: ☐ TIME: ______

SYNONYM UNSCRAMBLE

Unscramble the letters below to form pairs of SYNONYMS. Watch out—some words can be unscrambled more than one way!

R E B V A = G R N A I D

W O D Y D = M U P K T E N

F R U M I O N = Q A L U E

S T L R U E = T O O E U M C

C L K B O = T E E P N R V

H M O E D T = T M E S S Y

T A E E B D = S S D U S C I

350 | DIFFICULTY: ●●●●●●●○○○
COMPLETION: ☐ TIME: ______

ANTONYM FINDER

Find and circle the six pairs of ANTONYMS, one on each side, in the letter grids below.

D	B	M	P	E	Y
A	N	B	S	R	E
L	W	A	E	V	L
G	E	I	A	G	B
C	F	R	C	L	A
K	B	T	D	R	F

C	F	L	B	D	N
I	A	V	K	I	D
T	C	J	G	M	S
C	T	E	R	I	A
R	B	C	G	T	D
A	G	I	V	E	B

○○○○○○

351 | DIFFICULTY: ●●●●●●○○○○
COMPLETION: ☐ TIME: ______

SYNONYM FINDER

Find and circle the six pairs of SYNONYMS, one on each side, in the letter grids below.

D	R	I	N	K	P
R	E	P	H	L	A
N	A	F	L	D	N
C	M	I	E	G	I
D	T	P	D	C	C
S	F	E	U	D	T

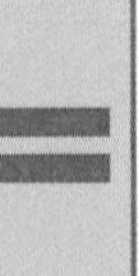

I	M	B	I	B	E
W	C	Y	M	Y	W
P	W	A	A	A	P
C	W	R	L	N	B
N	O	F	Y	M	P
F	R	I	G	H	T

○○○○○○

352 | DIFFICULTY: ●●●●●●○○○○
COMPLETION: ☐ TIME: ______

MAKE THE CONNECTION

Fill in the boxes with common two-word phrases with the help of the clues below. The last word in each pair will be the first word in the following pair.

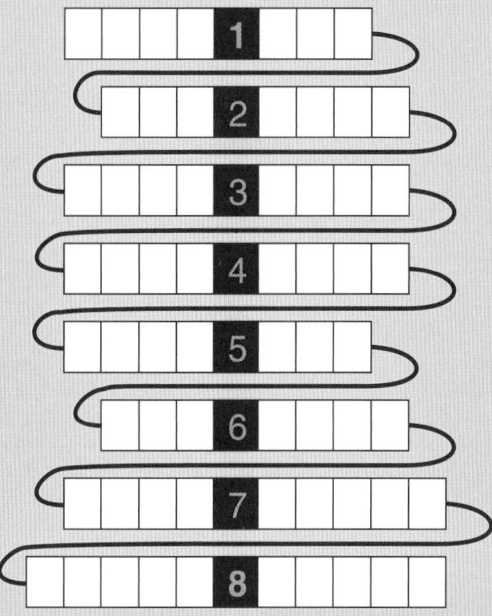

1 Round-tripper, in baseball
2 Leave quickly
3 A team has to travel for this
4 Strategy
5 Prepare
6 Audibly
7 Sledgehammer's output
8 It's measured in decibels

353 | DIFFICULTY: ●●●●●●●○○○
COMPLETION: ☐ TIME: ______

PRISM CROSS'D WORDS

Use the color-coded clues below to find words that fit in the like-colored portions of the puzzle grid below.

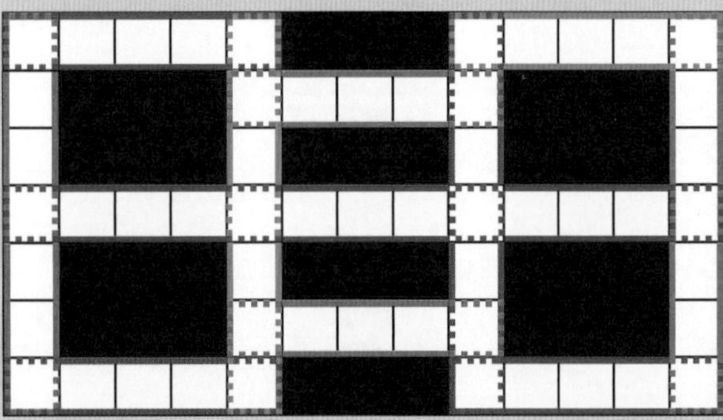

- An ability, talent, or special skill (1-syllable noun)
- To cut food into very small pieces (1-syllable verb)
- Having little life, spirit, or zest (5-syllable adjective)

- Soft-bodied invertebrate animal (2-syllable noun)
- To lay or spread something over (2-syllable verb)

- To increase or improve (2-syllable verb)
- A shout of approval (2-syllable noun)

- A tricky, deceitful fellow (1-syllable noun)
- Crazy and violent (2-syllable adjective)

- Deficient in worldly wisdom (2-syllable adjective)
- The prospect for the future (2-syllable noun)

354 | DIFFICULTY: ●●●●●●●●●○○
COMPLETION: ☐ TIME: ______

DEFINITION FINDER

Using the clues below, find and circle the words concealed in the letter grid.

C	R	A	N	K	Y	Y	Q	X
J	F	X	L	A	F	Z	J	Y
F	Q	A	D	I	V	E	R	T
Z	O	Y	T	Q	E	I	X	H
M	E	R	C	H	A	N	T	G
H	O	X	B	P	O	Z	K	I
F	Q	Z	M	I	X	M	J	L
F	R	I	G	I	D	Q	X	F

- ○ Someone who buys and sells goods *(noun)*
- ○ The time when someone is most successful *(noun)*
- ○ To make (someone or something) stronger *(verb)*
- ○ To change the direction or use of (something) *(verb)*
- ○ Not like other things you have known *(adjective)*
- ○ Given to fretful fussiness *(adjective)*
- ○ To understand the reason for (something) *(verb)*
- ○ To order (someone) not to do something *(verb)*
- ○ Not serious or dependable *(adjective)*
- ○ To make (something) weaker or worse *(verb)*
- ○ Very cold *(adjective)*

355 | DIFFICULTY: ●●●●●●●●●○○
COMPLETION: ☐ TIME: ______

WORD WINDER

Use the clue to help you find the answers word-winding their way through the grid. Each answer will connect the top of the grid to the bottom.

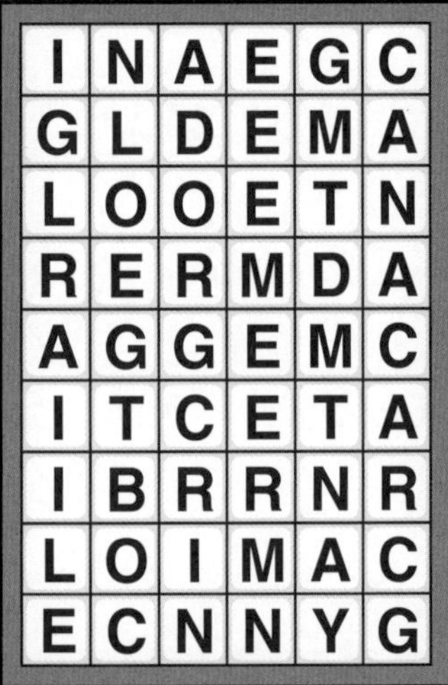

I N A E G C
G L D E M A
L O O E T N
R E R M D A
A G G E M C
I T C E T A
I B R R N R
L O I M A C
E C N N Y G

Find five four-syllable words word-winding their way from top to bottom.

______

______

______

______

______

356 | DIFFICULTY: ●●●●●●●●●○○
COMPLETION: ☐ TIME: ________

CROSS'D WORDS UNSCRAMBLE

Unscramble the letters in each clue to fill in the puzzle grid below.

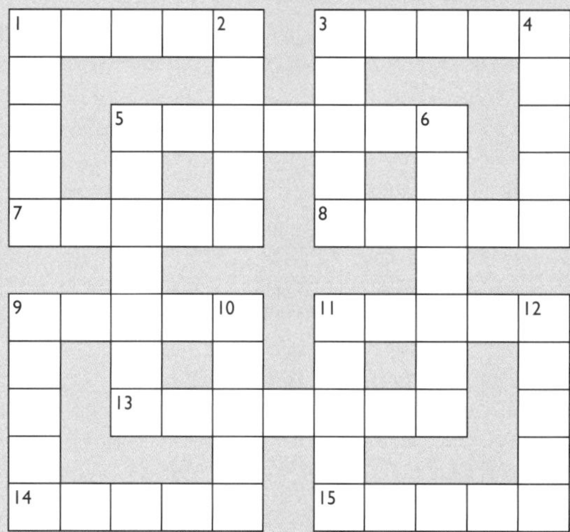

ACROSS

1 THIGM *(one-syllable word)*
3 HUHSS *(one-syllable word)*
5 TROFENU *(two-syllable word)*
7 DAAEH *(two-syllable word)*
8 HADIP *(two-syllable word)*
9 ULEBG *(two-syllable word)*
11 LUVTA *(one-syllable word)*
13 HOTTUGH *(one-syllable word)*
14 SOLOE *(one-syllable word)*
15 TENCA *(two-syllable word)*

DOWN

1 DAIEM *(three-syllable word)*
2 TREDI *(one-syllable word)*
3 BUSAC *(two-syllable word)*
4 ODHAR *(one-syllable word)*
5 GRITFHE *(one-syllable word)*
6 SAXTHEU *(two-syllable word)*
9 VEEBL *(two-syllable word)*
10 KEEOV *(two-syllable word)*
11 AVEUG *(one-syllable word)*
12 PETTM *(one-syllable word)*

357 | DIFFICULTY: ●●●●●●●○○○ COMPLETION: ☐ TIME: _______

ANTONYM FINDER

Find and circle the six pairs of ANTONYMS, one on each side, in the letter grids below.

T	W	C	M	Y	H
P	K	E	L	C	T
E	T	P	A	U	G
N	M	E	O	K	L
I	R	T	H	N	R
J	S	A	V	O	W

A	D	R	O	I	T
E	D	M	L	T	N
T	P	E	R	D	A
A	N	A	N	G	E
T	T	C	W	Y	L
S	T	R	O	N	G

○○○○○○

358 | DIFFICULTY: ●●●●●●○○○○ COMPLETION: ☐ TIME: _______

MIXED-UP DEFINITION

Unscramble the letters below to reveal the definition of the given word.

dis·cern·ing *adjective* \di-ˈsər-niŋ\

bael ot ese dna snaddtrune hstign yrallce adn lniityneeltlg

359 | DIFFICULTY: ●●●●●●○○○○
COMPLETION: ☐ TIME: ______

DICTIONARY UNSCRAMBLE

Unscramble the letters below to form words that match the Merriam-Webster definitions.

transitive verb To fail to take care of or to give attention to (someone or something)

CLEENTG= ☐☐☐☐☐☐☐

adjective
Accepted by Jewish law as fit for eating or drinking

SKEORH= ☐☐☐☐☐☐

adverb
During the period of time that has just passed

NETRYCLE= ☐☐☐☐☐☐☐☐

adjective
Having all necessary parts

MEELOTCP= ☐☐☐☐☐☐☐☐

noun
Someone who has a lot of energy

DOMANY= ☐☐☐☐☐☐

transitive verb To cause (someone) to do something by asking, arguing, or giving reasons

PRUDEEAS= ☐☐☐☐☐☐☐☐

360 | DIFFICULTY: ●●●●●●●○○○
COMPLETION: ☐ TIME: ______

DICTIONARY CROSS'D WORDS

Fill in the puzzle using the Merriam-Webster definition clues below.

Across
1 Something that is very easy to do (1-syllable noun)
3 To make a grant of money (2-syllable verb)
5 The top or highest point of something (2-syllable noun)
6 Appliance for keeping food cool (5-syllable noun)
7 Having very little rain or water (2-syllable adjective)
8 To use strength, ability, etc. (2-syllable verb)
9 A glowing piece of coal (2-syllable noun)

Down
1 Deceptive act or pretense (2-syllable noun)
2 Where something is commonly found (3-syllable noun)
3 To shape by forcing through a hole (2-syllable verb)
4 A person who fights in battles (3-syllable noun)

361 | DIFFICULTY: ●●●●●●●○○○
COMPLETION: ☐ TIME: ______

MISSING DEFINITIONS FINDER

Using the clues below, find and circle the words concealed in the letter grid.

T	Q	S	H	O	R	T	Z	G	B
C	X	O	Z	J	R	X	V	O	C
E	C	J	R	E	Q	E	E	O	I
F	V	L	P	D	M	Q	R	D	N
F	Q	O	E	I	E	O	Y	V	O
E	R	Z	T	V	J	R	N	X	R
P	L	A	C	K	E	Z	K	E	I
A	C	T	I	O	N	R	V	J	Y

brev·i·ty *noun* \ˈbre-və-tē\
the quality or fact of lasting only for a ______ period of ______

de·co·rum *noun* \di-ˈkȯr-əm\
correct or ______ behavior that shows respect and ______ manners

dras·tic *adjective* \ˈdras-tik\
extreme in ______ or ______

hap·haz·ard *adjective* \(ˌ)hap-ˈha-zərd\
marked by ______ of plan, ______, or direction

pros·per *verb* \ˈpräs-pər\
to become ______ successful usually by making a lot of ______

wry *adjective* \ˈrī\
humorous in a ______ and often ______ way

362 | DIFFICULTY: ●●●●●●●○○○
COMPLETION: ☐ TIME: ______

ANTONYM UNSCRAMBLE

Unscramble the letters below to form pairs of ANTONYMS. Note: Some words can be unscrambled more than one way!

A M R ≠ A T E Y U F I B

E B V E E L I ≠ J T E E R C

C A A E V N D ≠ E E R D C E

B D A R ≠ F L E C E U R H

P D U E P ≠ R C D D E E U

T I O I D ≠ S N U G I E

S R E E V E ≠ T E E I L N N

363 | DIFFICULTY: ●●●●●●●●●●○○ COMPLETION: ☐ TIME: ______

PRISM WORD FINDER

Using the color-coded clues below, find and circle the words in the letter grid.

L	Y	R	I	C	A	L	F	G	Y	L
B	C	L	O	U	D	Y	L	D	K	A
H	N	W	O	R	N	A	N	M	L	T
W	R	A	J	Q	U	I	A	X	H	E
L	O	F	L	G	W	G	C	M	J	R
A	B	V	N	F	L	S	A	O	Y	A
C	Z	I	H	A	A	R	U	N	R	L
I	L	W	M	N	G	L	I	N	L	N
G	J	A	R	A	K	A	F	Q	N	M
O	B	O	N	X	R	L	W	A	C	Y
L	T	A	L	I	B	E	R	A	L	P

Find five seven-letter words that start and end with "L" starting with an orange letter ○○○○○

Find four four-letter words that rhyme with "mourn" starting with a blue letter ○○○○

Find four weather-related terms ending in "Y" starting with a purple letter ○○○○

Find three seven-letter words containing three "A's" starting with a red letter ○○○

364 | DIFFICULTY: ●●●●●●●●●●○
COMPLETION: ☐ TIME: ______

WORD WINDER

Use the clue to help you find the answers word-winding their way through the grid. Each answer will connect the top of the grid to the bottom.

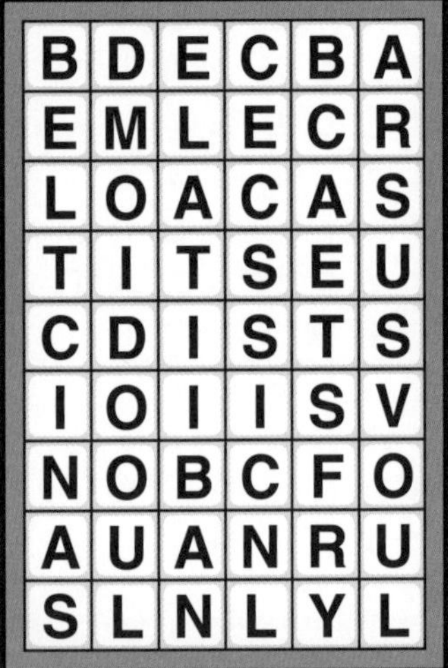

B	D	E	C	B	A
E	M	L	E	C	R
L	O	A	C	A	S
T	I	T	S	E	U
C	D	I	S	T	S
I	O	I	I	S	V
N	O	B	C	F	O
A	U	A	N	R	U
S	L	N	L	Y	L

Find five adjectives word-winding their way from top to bottom.

365 | DIFFICULTY: ●●●●●●●●●●○○ COMPLETION: ☐ TIME: ______

COLOR WORD CHAINS

Use the clues and letters below to make word paths between like colors to fill the board.

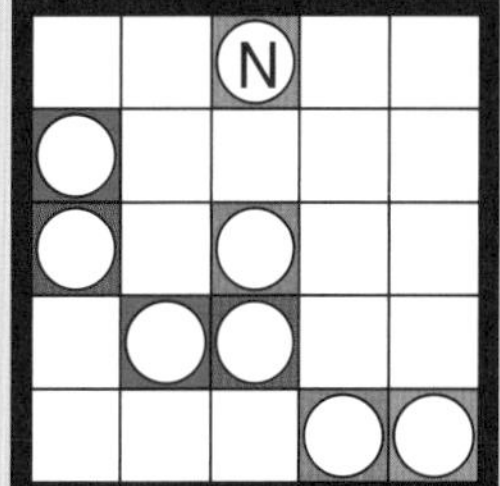

- A very small particle that has no electrical charge
- To suck up or take in
- A man's formal suit
- To support or defend

A	B	B	D	D	E
E	H	L	N	O	O
O	O	P	R	R	S
T	T	U	U	U	X

366 | DIFFICULTY: ●●●●●●●●●●●○ COMPLETION: ☐ TIME: ______

SYNONYM FINDER

Find and circle the six pairs of SYNONYMS, one on each side, in the letter grids below.

P	T	I	N	Y	R
T	R	W	P	E	Y
M	G	I	T	R	E
Y	R	S	S	U	A
T	O	Z	N	O	R
R	W	M	K	S	N

=

N	L	I	S	T	G
C	S	X	N	L	T
J	F	M	I	R	N
E	X	P	A	N	D
K	M	T	G	L	D
L	W	J	A	I	L

○ ○ ○ ○ ○ ○

367 | DIFFICULTY: ●●●●●●●●○○○
COMPLETION: ☐ TIME: ______

SYNONYM FINDER

Find and circle the seven pairs of SYNONYMS divided between the letter grids below.

O	U	T	R	A	G	E	B
N	V	M	I	N	O	R	C
Z	L	E	W	K	U	W	O
E	H	Z	R	T	G	C	M
N	D	Y	S	C	M	K	P
I	A	I	P	B	O	P	O
T	D	L	J	F	N	M	S
H	Q	U	I	V	E	R	E

=

P	I	N	N	A	C	L	E
R	B	D	M	E	G	T	T
E	X	W	K	Y	X	N	R
U	C	A	N	N	O	Y	E
Q	M	H	C	R	N	K	W
N	R	J	F	Q	A	K	O
O	L	F	P	H	P	M	L
C	A	F	S	Z	D	N	C

○○○○○○○

368 | DIFFICULTY: ●●●●●●●●●○
COMPLETION: ☐ TIME: ______

DICTIONARY WORD WINDER

Use the clues below to help you find the answers word-winding their way through the grid. Each answer will connect one side of the grid to the other—left to right, top to bottom, right to left, and bottom to top.

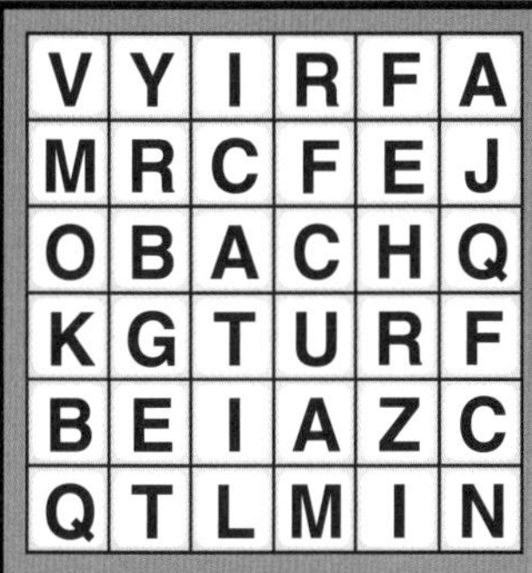

V	Y	I	R	F	A
M	R	C	F	E	J
O	B	A	C	H	Q
K	G	T	U	R	F
B	E	I	A	Z	C
Q	T	L	M	I	N

→ To gain or attain usually by planned action or effort ______

↓ A newly enlisted or drafted member of the armed forces ______

← To say that something is true in a confident way ______

↑ Something transmitted by or received from an ancestor or predecessor or from the past ______

369 | DIFFICULTY: ●●●●●●●●●●○○
COMPLETION: ☐ TIME: ______

SYNONYM UNSCRAMBLE

Unscramble the letters below to form pairs of SYNONYMS. Watch out—some words can be unscrambled more than one way!

T R Y S D U = B U L D E R A

C A V I E D = S L O N C E U

R C E O T V = D H E I N D

O A R V L = V R R B A Y E

D A T T I N S = E E O T R M

I F E R = C R E D A I H G S

F Y S E A T = M Y U A L S

370 | DIFFICULTY: ●●●●●●●●●○○ COMPLETION: ☐ TIME: ______

ANTONYM FINDER

Find and circle the six pairs of ANTONYMS, one on each side, in the letter grids below.

R	H	N	W	G	E
E	I	T	U	F	L
E	C	G	I	D	P
H	M	L	I	D	E
C	S	E	N	D	N
F	F	A	L	S	E

≠

W	G	T	D	S	D
D	E	L	T	M	A
G	E	F	O	E	L
J	O	A	U	O	C
S	B	R	T	C	M
T	T	W	N	H	Y

○○○○○○

371 | DIFFICULTY: ●●●●●●○○○○ COMPLETION: ☐ TIME: ______

MIXED-UP DEFINITION

Unscramble the letters below to reveal the definition of the given word.

pe·riph·er·al *adjective* \pə-ˈri-f(ə-)rəl\
tno trilgane ot eth iman ro smto prittonam tpra

☐☐☐ ☐☐☐☐☐☐☐☐
☐☐ ☐☐☐ ☐☐☐☐
☐☐ ☐☐☐☐
☐☐☐☐☐☐☐☐☐
☐☐☐☐

372 | DIFFICULTY: ●●●●●●●○○○ COMPLETION: ☐ TIME: ______

SYLLABARY

Link word segments together in the grid below to create words, and enter them in the blanks.

LAR	TY	PER	NA	GUA
U	REG	I	MA	I
TES	IR	NENT	AL	TATE
TI	BIG	U	AS	SON
AM	FY	DEV	OUS	PER

Three-Syllable Verb: _ _ _ _ S _ _ _ _

Three-Syllable Adjective: _ _ R _ _ _ _ _ _

Five-Syllable Noun: _ _ _ _ _ _ _ _ _ T _

Three-Syllable Verb: _ E _ _ _ _ _

Four-Syllable Adjective: _ _ _ _ _ _ O _ _

Three-Syllable Noun: _ _ _ A _ _

Four-Syllable Adjective: _ _ _ _ _ _ _ _ R

373 | DIFFICULTY: ●●●●●●●●●●○○
COMPLETION: ☐ TIME: ______

WORD WINDER

Use the clue to help you find the answers word-winding their way through the grid. Each answer will connect the top of the grid to the bottom.

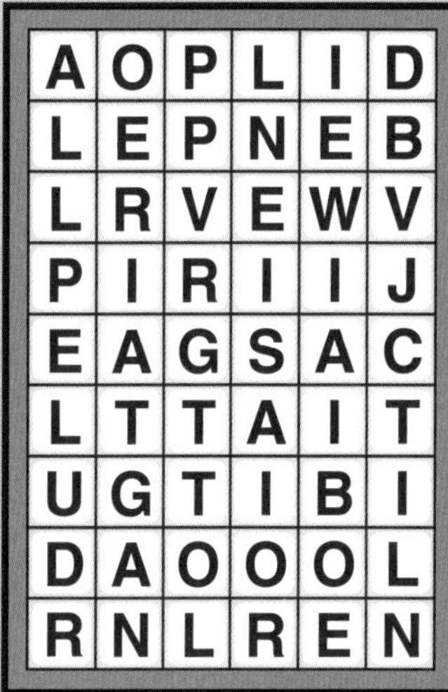

A	O	P	L	I	D
L	E	P	N	E	B
L	R	V	E	W	V
P	I	R	I	I	J
E	A	G	S	A	C
L	T	T	A	I	T
U	G	T	I	B	I
D	A	O	O	O	L
R	N	L	R	E	N

Find five four-syllable words word-winding their way from top to bottom.

374 | DIFFICULTY: ●●●●●●●●●●○
COMPLETION: ☐ TIME: ______

DEFINITION FINDER

Using the clues below, find and circle the words concealed in the letter grid.

- ○ A state in which there is not enough of something *(noun)*
- ○ To change in response to a stimulus *(verb)*
- ○ A government order that limits trade in some way *(noun)*
- ○ To make a quick, rough drawing of (something) *(verb)*
- ○ An individual's part or share of something *(noun)*
- ○ Equal to what is needed *(adjective)*
- ○ To follow regularly or persistently *(verb)*
- ○ A horse that a person rides *(noun)*
- ○ A skilled worker who builds in stone or brick *(noun)*
- ○ A wild horse of western North America *(noun)*
- ○ To fear something that will or might happen *(verb)*

375 | DIFFICULTY: ●●●●●●●●●○
COMPLETION: ☐ TIME: ______

CROSS'D WORD CONNECTIONS

The crosswords below share common letters as indicated by the colored boxes. Use the clues to solve the puzzles.

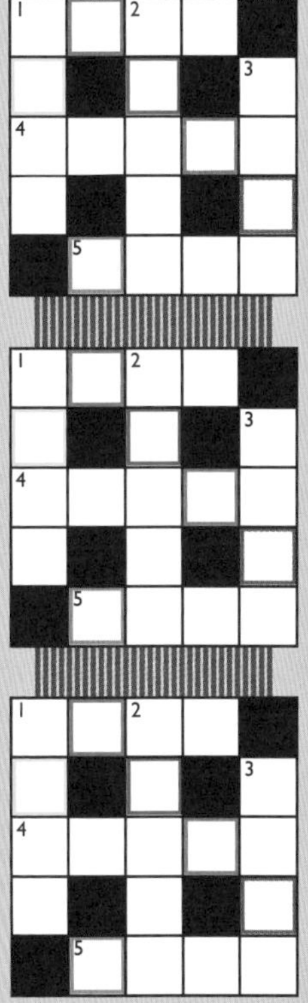

ACROSS
1 To move to a higher position
4 Disposed to inflict pain or suffering
5 Something made or worn to a short or blunt shape

DOWN
1 A tuft, tress, or ringlet of hair
2 A weakness in character
3 Speaking in a smooth, easy way that is not sincere

ACROSS
1 A particular minute or hour
4 Of or relating to a person's mind or spirit
5 To look over or read quickly

DOWN
1 Long strenuous fatiguing labor
2 Very excited, energetic, or emotional
3 To draw back the lips so as to show the teeth especially in amusement

ACROSS
1 Ridges in a knitted or woven fabric
4 A semiaquatic, web-footed carnivore in the weasel family
5 A thin piece of material used to fill in space between things, as for leveling

DOWN
1 The top of a building, vehicle, etc.
2 A group of people or things
3 The top edge of a glass or container

376 | DIFFICULTY: ●●●●●●●●●●○ COMPLETION: ☐ TIME: ______

SYNONYM FINDER

Find and circle the six pairs of SYNONYMS, one on each side, in the letter grids below.

A	Z	T	O	W	R
X	C	R	A	U	T
D	E	C	C	X	E
Z	T	N	U	P	A
R	O	Z	C	S	S
C	X	T	R	U	E

=

A	N	N	O	Y	T
G	D	B	V	H	E
R	I	C	G	L	M
E	L	U	X	E	A
E	A	H	N	V	L
N	V	Z	D	Y	B

○○○○○○

377 | DIFFICULTY: ●●●●●●●●○○○ COMPLETION: ☐ TIME: ______

ANTONYM FINDER

Find and circle the six pairs of ANTONYMS, one on each side, in the letter grids below.

I	A	B	O	U	T
N	R	C	L	S	B
C	G	A	I	A	E
I	D	L	P	G	W
T	N	K	D	I	H
E	B	E	W	F	D

A	F	A	R	N	R
M	C	W	U	E	Y
T	L	H	T	L	W
F	S	E	A	Z	O
R	D	K	N	O	L
F	L	A	T	P	S

○○○○○○

378 | DIFFICULTY: ●●●●●●●○○○
COMPLETION: ☐ TIME: ______

MAKE THE CONNECTION

Fill in the boxes with common two-word phrases with the help of the clues below. The last word in each pair will be the first word in the following pair.

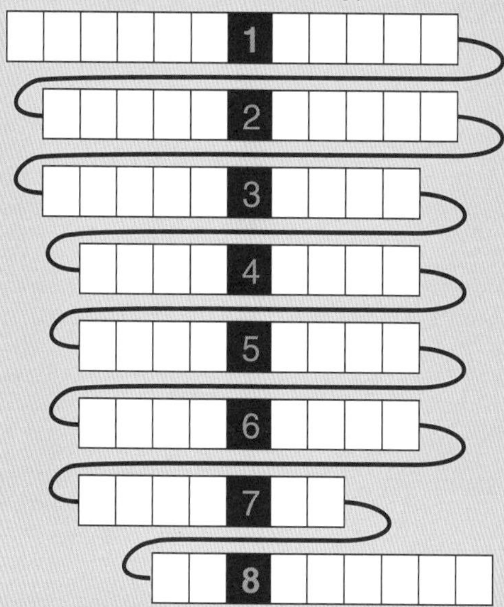

1 Celebratory evening meal
2 Invited person
3 Temporary gym membership
4 Defensive football play
5 Peak drive time
6 Part of a clock
7 Relinquish
8 Shared, as interests

379 | DIFFICULTY: ●●●●●●●●●○○ COMPLETION: ☐ TIME: ______

CROSS'D WORDS UNSCRAMBLE

Unscramble the letters in each clue to fill in the puzzle grid below.

ACROSS

1 ULAMR *(two-syllable word)*
3 PSURY *(two-syllable word)*
5 SMANGTY *(two-syllable word)*
7 RUHYR *(two-syllable word)*
8 RETXA *(two-syllable word)*
9 DASEH *(one-syllable word)*
11 LEVVA *(one-syllable word)*
13 LULQYAE *(three-syllable word)*
14 LIITM *(two-syllable word)*
15 PRYLE *(two-syllable word)*

DOWN

1 CUMHN *(one-syllable word)*
2 PULYM *(two-syllable word)*
3 HEAKS *(one-syllable word)*
4 ZAPZI *(two-syllable word)*
5 RAGEBAG *(two-syllable word)*
6 LOTTYAL *(three-syllable word)*
9 ELWLS *(one-syllable word)*
10 PRETU *(two-syllable word)*
11 LOVRA *(two-syllable word)*
12 SEYSA *(two-syllable word)*

380 | DIFFICULTY: ●●●●●●●●●○○
COMPLETION: ☐ TIME: ________

DICTIONARY UNSCRAMBLE

Unscramble the letters below to form words that match the Merriam-Webster definitions.

transitive verb To search (a place) for something in a way that causes disorder or damage

KANSRCA= ☐☐☐☐☐☐☐

noun
A number that is greater than half of a total

JAMYTRIO= ☐☐☐☐☐☐☐☐

adjective
Having or showing an ability to make new things

ITRACVEE= ☐☐☐☐☐☐☐☐

adjective
Of higher rank, quality, or importance

URRSOIEP= ☐☐☐☐☐☐☐☐

noun
The highest point reached in the sky by the sun

EZTNIH= ☐☐☐☐☐☐

intransitive verb To have a lot of curves instead of going in a straight or direct line

ADREEMN= ☐☐☐☐☐☐☐

381 | DIFFICULTY: ●●●●●●●●●●○
COMPLETION: ☐ TIME: ______

MISSING DEFINITIONS FINDER

Using the clues below, find and circle the words concealed in the letter grid.

H	Z	W	Q	S	Y	G	V	Z	Y
J	A	X	O	L	P	X	O	L	Q
S	V	R	E	R	T	E	K	O	E
Q	O	K	M	N	D	C	E	M	D
F	I	U	E	M	I	S	I	C	X
L	U	V	R	U	O	T	E	Z	H
Z	E	L	Q	C	V	O	Q	N	V
J	K	J	L	Z	E	X	N	J	D

bane *noun* \ˈbān\
a ______ of ______ or ruin

dis·patch *verb* \di-ˈspach\
to ______ (someone or something) ______ to a particular place for a particular purpose

era *noun* \ˈer-ə, ˈe-rə, ˈir-ə\
a period of ______ that is associated with a particular quality, ______, person, etc.

la·con·ic *adjective* \lə-ˈkä-nik\
using few ______ in ______ or writing

sa·lu·bri·ous *adjective* \sə-ˈlü-brē-əs\
making ______ health possible or ______

wane *intransitive verb* \ˈwān\
of the ______ : to appear to become thinner or less ______

382 | DIFFICULTY: ●●●●●●●●●●○ COMPLETION: ☐ TIME: ______

ANTONYM FINDER

Find and circle the six pairs of ANTONYMS, one on each side, in the letter grids below.

B	R	I	G	H	T
B	L	E	A	V	E
L	T	K	C	H	L
G	S	T	Y	F	D
H	A	R	D	Y	I
F	L	D	P	W	N

L	E	A	N	T	B
B	D	W	S	R	W
M	U	R	T	C	E
L	I	S	A	P	A
F	D	C	Y	N	K
S	O	M	B	E	R

○○○○○○

383 | DIFFICULTY: ●●●●●●●●○○○ COMPLETION: ☐ TIME: ______

SYNONYM FINDER

Find and circle the six pairs of SYNONYMS, one on each side, in the letter grids below.

T	L	R	U	S	E
H	C	Y	M	H	D
A	C	T	U	A	L
R	N	D	A	R	K
W	E	A	G	E	R
O	R	D	E	R	H

K	G	F	Y	Y	T
T	Y	I	K	V	R
M	R	R	V	X	U
K	U	I	E	E	L
M	Y	G	C	A	E
K	E	E	N	K	L

○○○○○○

384 | DIFFICULTY: ●●●●●●●●○○○
COMPLETION: ☐ TIME: ______

DICTIONARY WORD WINDER

Use the clues below to help you find the answers word-winding their way through the grid. Each answer will connect one side of the grid to the other—left to right, top to bottom, right to left, and bottom to top.

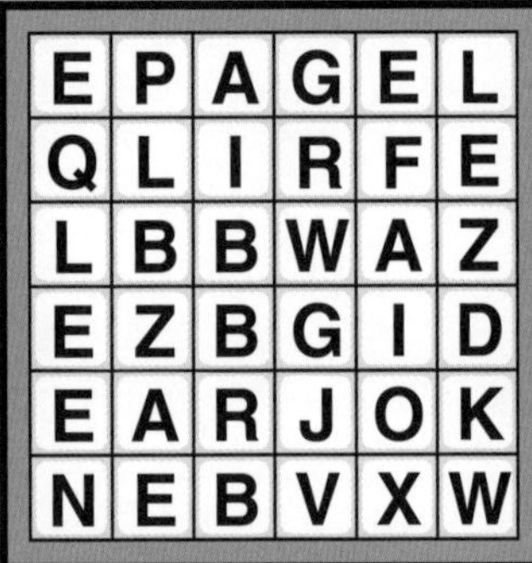

E	P	A	G	E	L
Q	L	I	R	F	E
L	B	B	W	A	Z
E	Z	B	G	I	D
E	A	R	J	O	K
N	E	B	V	X	W

→ To apply voltage to ______

↓ A statement that seems to say two opposite things but that may be true ______

← Capable of being read or deciphered ______

↑ To make speech sounds that do not make sense to the hearer ______

385 | DIFFICULTY: ●●●●●●●●●○
COMPLETION: ☐ TIME: ______

ANTONYM UNSCRAMBLE

Unscramble the letters below to form pairs of ANTONYMS. Note: Some words can be unscrambled more than one way!

K A E M ≠ S L A D N E M I T

Y R W A ≠ S L A E E C R S

R I O M N ≠ J A R O M

G R I E N L ≠ P R E T D A

G N E B I ≠ L E C C U N D O

T S E E T D ≠ I L E K

E R R Y O D L ≠ S E Y S M

386 | DIFFICULTY: ●●●●●●●●●○
COMPLETION: ☐ TIME: ______

PRISM CROSS'D WORDS

Use the color-coded clues below to find words that fit in the like-colored portions of the puzzle grid below.

- Something that causes difficulty (4-syllable noun)
- A small hill (1-syllable noun)
- Monetary unit of India (2-syllable noun)

- Similar in nature or character (2-syllable adjective)
- Showing good judgment (1-syllable adjective)

- A two-footed animal (2-syllable noun)
- A disappointment (2-syllable noun)

- To make a careless mistake (2-syllable verb)
- To become empty of a liquid (1-syllable verb)

- A member of the British peerage (1-syllable noun)
- Composed of unlike elements (2-syllable adjective)

387 | DIFFICULTY: ●●●●●●●●●●○
COMPLETION: ☐ TIME: ______

SYNONYM FINDER

Find and circle the six pairs of SYNONYMS, one on each side, in the letter grids below.

C	R	C	H	T	S
N	O	E	I	P	T
M	S	M	A	E	E
G	D	E	P	P	A
A	L	O	N	E	L
P	H	F	K	D	L

W	R	F	E	E	W
G	T	K	C	O	G
E	A	R	L	H	C
T	O	L	U	K	W
F	A	Q	H	S	G
G	C	A	S	T	T

○○○○○○

388 | DIFFICULTY: ●●●●●●●●○○○
COMPLETION: ☐ TIME: ______

ANTONYM FINDER

Find and circle the six pairs of ANTONYMS, one on each side, in the letter grids below.

C	E	P	F	C	E
H	O	M	H	D	C
K	T	M	I	E	A
G	N	V	P	T	E
D	I	O	X	E	P
D	H	R	W	K	L

N	D	C	H	Z	N
I	B	O	L	F	I
A	A	R	U	R	O
T	L	W	A	B	J
E	K	E	B	W	T
R	F	G	D	Y	L

○○○○○○

389 | DIFFICULTY: ●●●●●●●●○○○
COMPLETION: ☐ TIME: ______

WORD WINDER

Use the clue to help you find the answers word-winding their way through the grid. Each answer will connect the top of the grid to the bottom.

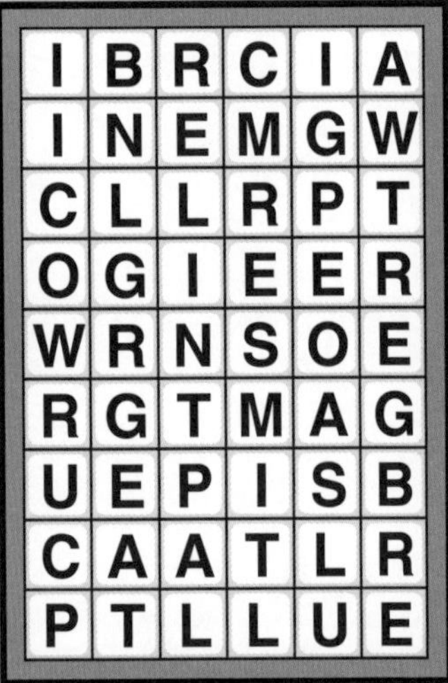

I	B	R	C	I	A
I	N	E	M	G	W
C	L	L	R	P	T
O	G	I	E	E	R
W	R	N	S	O	E
R	G	T	M	A	G
U	E	P	I	S	B
C	A	A	T	L	R
P	T	L	L	U	E

Find five adjectives word-winding their way from top to bottom.

390 | DIFFICULTY: ●●●●●●●●●○
COMPLETION: ☐ TIME: ______

DICTIONARY CROSS'D WORDS

Fill in the puzzle using the Merriam-Webster definition clues below.

Across
1 Marshy or sluggish body of water (2-syllable noun)
3 To trouble mentally or emotionally (2-syllable verb)
5 Having a full, rounded shape (1-syllable adjective)
6 Occurring between countries (5-syllable adjective)
7 A mixture that is baked to make bread (1-syllable noun)
8 A row of shrubs or small trees (1-syllable noun)
9 Lacking in courage or self-confidence (2-syllable adjective)

Down
1 To cast a spell over (2-syllable verb)
2 To raise the quality of (2-syllable verb)
3 Always behaving in an honest way (2-syllable adjective)
4 Newspaper with half-sized pages (2-syllable adjective)

391 | DIFFICULTY: ●●●●●●●●●○ COMPLETION: ☐ TIME: ______

ANTONYM FINDER

Find and circle the six pairs of ANTONYMS, one on each side, in the letter grids below.

E	B	M	R	E	R
T	V	P	Z	Z	E
S	G	A	Y	I	D
H	R	E	D	C	N
O	W	H	P	E	I
W	F	C	N	K	H

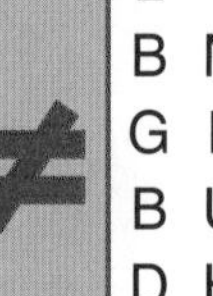

L	I	V	E	H	N
B	N	M	E	E	T
G	L	P	D	K	M
B	U	I	L	D	F
D	H	E	L	P	C
C	O	S	T	L	Y

○○○○○○

392 | DIFFICULTY: ●●●●●●●●○○○ COMPLETION: ☐ TIME: ______

MIXED-UP DEFINITION

Unscramble the letters below to reveal the definition of the given word.

e·qui·lib·ri·um *noun* \ˌē-kwə-ˈli-brē-əm, ˌe-\

a attse ni cwihh spgoonpi scoefr ro osciant rea caadlben

393 | DIFFICULTY: ●●●●●●●●●○○
COMPLETION: ☐ TIME: ______

PRISM WORD FINDER

Using the color-coded clues below, find and circle the words in the letter grid.

S	C	A	R	N	A	T	I	O	N	T
S	W	L	I	B	E	R	A	T	E	W
T	E	I	B	L	A	B	B	E	R	K
O	L	V	M	J	C	R	Q	L	B	L
M	B	R	Z	M	E	V	A	W	A	B
P	B	X	O	V	I	N	V	C	E	L
I	A	M	I	T	I	N	O	O	L	U
N	B	V	J	M	A	F	G	I	B	B
G	E	B	R	V	I	T	C	D	B	B
R	F	E	Z	B	Q	P	O	A	U	E
S	T	R	A	C	E	C	A	R	B	R

Find five three-syllable words starting with an orange letter ○○○○○

Find four words with three "B's" starting with a blue "B" ○○○○

Find three seven-letter palindromes starting with a purple letter ○○○

Find two eight-letter verbs ending in "ING" starting with a red letter ○○

394 | DIFFICULTY: ●●●●●●●●●○ COMPLETION: ☐ TIME: ______

MISSING DEFINITIONS FINDER

Using the clues below, find and circle the words concealed in the letter grid.

F	I	R	S	T	Z	E	J	E	K
A	X	P	Q	T	V	X	R	O	Q
N	M	V	R	I	Y	U	O	G	U
G	A	O	E	E	S	L	N	K	A
R	R	C	V	A	V	O	E	C	L
Y	E	V	E	I	R	E	Q	I	I
D	A	L	Z	T	N	X	N	R	T
J	P	Q	S	Z	V	G	B	T	Y

an·tic·i·pate *verb* \an-ˈti-sə-ˌpāt\
to expect or ________ ahead to (something) with ________

flair *noun* \ˈfler\
an unusual and appealing ________ or ________

hoax *noun* \ˈhōks\
an act that is meant to ________ or ________ people

pi·o·neer *noun* \ˌpī-ə-ˈnir\
someone who is one of the ________ people to move to and live in a new ________

re·strain *transitive verb* \ri-ˈstrān\
to ________ (a person or animal) from ________ by using physical force

ve·he·ment *adjective* \ˈvē-ə-mənt\
showing ________ and often ________ feelings

395 | DIFFICULTY: ●●●●●●●●●○
COMPLETION: ☐ TIME: ________

CROSS'D WORDS UNSCRAMBLE

Unscramble the letters in each clue to fill in the puzzle grid below.

1				2		3				4
		5						6		
7						8				
9				10		11				12
		13								
14						15				

ACROSS

1 AMHSS *(one-syllable word)*
3 WEBLO *(two-syllable word)*
5 SLUCEPA *(two-syllable word)*
7 KNFYU *(two-syllable word)*
8 TUZKL *(one-syllable word)*
9 RYSLU *(two-syllable word)*
11 ACCKR *(one-syllable word)*
13 NIXEEMA *(three-syllable word)*
14 WAPNR *(one-syllable word)*
15 LEEXI *(two-syllable word)*

DOWN

1 CFSUF *(one-syllable word)*
2 SHYUK *(two-syllable word)*
3 NABKL *(one-syllable word)*
4 TAZWL *(one-syllable word)*
5 NEEVUNR *(two-syllable word)*
6 MEELUTA *(three-syllable word)*
9 AWPSM *(one-syllable word)*
10 NAREY *(one-syllable word)*
11 HECMI *(one-syllable word)*
12 FENKI *(one-syllable word)*

396 | DIFFICULTY: ●●●●●●●●●○ COMPLETION: ☐ TIME: ______

SYNONYM FINDER

Find and circle the six pairs of SYNONYMS, one on each side, in the letter grids below.

T	K	C	G	T	P
E	R	D	E	A	R
G	L	A	E	K	P
D	K	H	C	E	M
E	C	D	K	E	F
D	A	N	G	E	R

=

○ ○ ○ ○ ○ ○

397 | DIFFICULTY: ●●●●●●●○○○ COMPLETION: ☐ TIME: ______

COLOR WORD CHAINS

Use the clues and letters below to make word paths between like colors to fill the board.

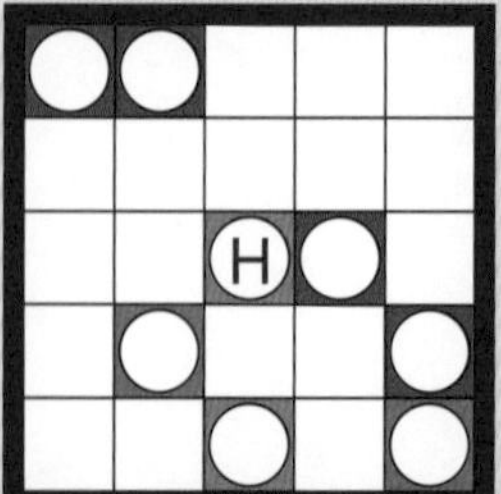

- To supply with water
- A special heated room
- The point or place where something begins
- Different from each other

A A A A D E
G I I I N N
O O R R R S
S T U U V Y

398 | DIFFICULTY: ●●●●●●●●●● COMPLETION: ☐ TIME: ______

WORD WINDER

Use the clue to help you find the answers word-winding their way through the grid. Each answer will connect the top of the grid to the bottom.

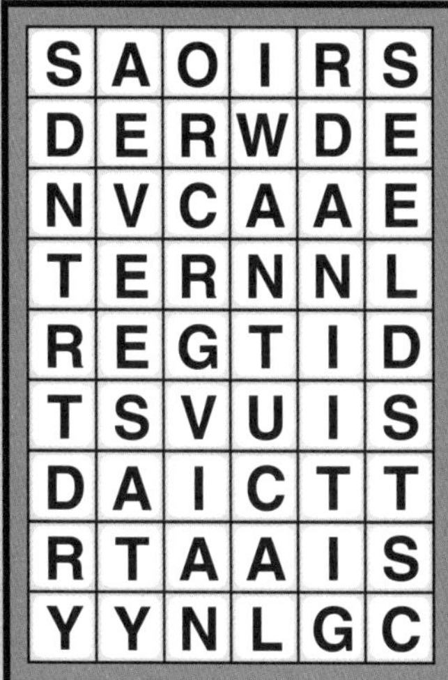

S A O I R S
D E R W D E
N V C A A E
T E R N N L
R E G T I D
T S V U I S
D A I C T T
R T A A I S
Y Y N L G C

↓ Find five four-syllable words word-winding their way from top to bottom.

______

______

______

______

______

399 | DIFFICULTY: ●●●●●●●●●○ COMPLETION: ☐ TIME: ______

ANTONYM FINDER

Find and circle the seven pairs of ANTONYMS divided between the letter grids below.

J	S	X	L	Z	P	E	J
T	X	U	Q	E	T	C	L
C	C	Z	P	E	G	A	Q
E	K	O	L	P	E	A	X
T	D	P	N	C	O	P	L
O	E	W	N	C	T	R	Z
R	N	O	J	X	U	W	T
P	C	M	O	D	E	R	N

S	T	A	R	V	E	D	Q
Z	D	J	V	S	F	L	G
B	Q	I	O	H	I	R	N
N	E	P	S	R	Z	D	O
L	X	T	E	S	E	G	R
E	C	P	R	T	E	V	W
S	M	T	A	A	X	N	F
I	X	D	J	Q	Y	V	T

○ ○ ○ ○ ○ ○ ○

400 | DIFFICULTY: ●●●●●●●●●●○
COMPLETION: ☐ TIME: ______

SYLLABARY

Link word segments together in the grid below to create words, and enter them in the blanks.

EL	GI	BLE	RI	HOR
I	PER	A	BLY	ATE
TEM	TO	RA	TURE	SUL
RY	PRIN	O	IN	LU
PAL	CI	LAB	TIC	NA

Three-Syllable Noun: _ _ _ _ _ _ P _ _

Three-Syllable Verb: _ N _ _ _ _ _ _

Four-Syllable Noun: _ _ _ _ _ _ _ _ _ R _

Three-Syllable Noun: _ _ N _ _ _ _

Four-Syllable Adjective: _ _ _ _ I _ _ _

Five-Syllable Noun: _ _ _ _ _ _ _ O _ _

Three-Syllable Adverb: _ _ _ R _ _ _ _

401 | DIFFICULTY: ●●●●●●●●●●
COMPLETION: ☐ TIME: ______

DICTIONARY UNSCRAMBLE

Unscramble the letters below to form words that match the Merriam-Webster definitions.

adjective
Having a sick feeling in the stomach

SQUYAE= ☐☐☐☐☐☐

transitive verb To directly question the action or authority of (someone)

NNOFORTC= ☐☐☐☐☐☐☐☐

adjective
Able to be trusted to do or provide what is needed

ALLIBEER= ☐☐☐☐☐☐☐☐

noun
A narrow opening or crack

SERFIUS= ☐☐☐☐☐☐☐

transitive verb
To try to influence (someone) by words or advice

THEROX= ☐☐☐☐☐☐

noun
A system of rules that explain the correct conduct

CLOTROOP= ☐☐☐☐☐☐☐☐

402 | DIFFICULTY: ●●●●●●●●●●○ COMPLETION: ☐ TIME: ______

ANTONYM FINDER

Find and circle the six pairs of ANTONYMS, one on each side, in the letter grids below.

D	E	F	E	R	D
X	C	Y	X	I	T
N	R	P	U	W	H
D	M	Q	L	D	A
L	I	Y	T	B	W
L	P	E	T	T	Y

F	S	O	L	I	D
O	R	L	W	N	T
R	D	E	R	A	P
C	P	U	E	M	Y
E	O	R	A	Z	M
M	G	D	N	F	E

○○○○○○

403 | DIFFICULTY: ●●●●●●●●●○○ COMPLETION: ☐ TIME: ______

SYNONYM FINDER

Find and circle the six pairs of SYNONYMS, one on each side, in the letter grids below.

C	A	S	T	E	Y
D	H	B	D	L	R
W	G	U	L	G	H
C	R	A	N	E	T
B	D	L	K	C	F
S	T	E	R	N	H

C	R	O	B	L	G
I	L	I	M	H	R
D	H	A	G	E	T
L	C	U	S	I	N
E	O	G	G	S	D
R	O	B	U	S	T

○○○○○○

404 | DIFFICULTY: ●●●●●●●●●●○○
COMPLETION: ☐ TIME: ______

DICTIONARY WORD WINDER

Use the clues below to help you find the answers word-winding their way through the grid. Each answer will connect one side of the grid to the other—left to right, top to bottom, right to left, and bottom to top.

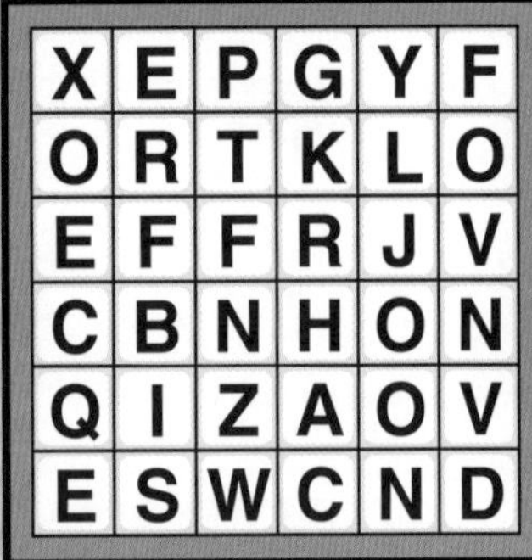

X	E	P	G	Y	F
O	R	T	K	L	O
E	F	F	R	J	V
C	B	N	H	O	N
Q	I	Z	A	O	V
E	S	W	C	N	D

→ Without premeditation or preparation ______

↓ Very careful and exact about the details of something ______

← A mass of spinning air, liquid, etc., that pulls things into its center ______

↑ A group of vehicles or ships that are traveling together usually for protection ______

DICTIONARY CROSS'D WORDS

Fill in the puzzle using the Merriam-Webster definition clues below.

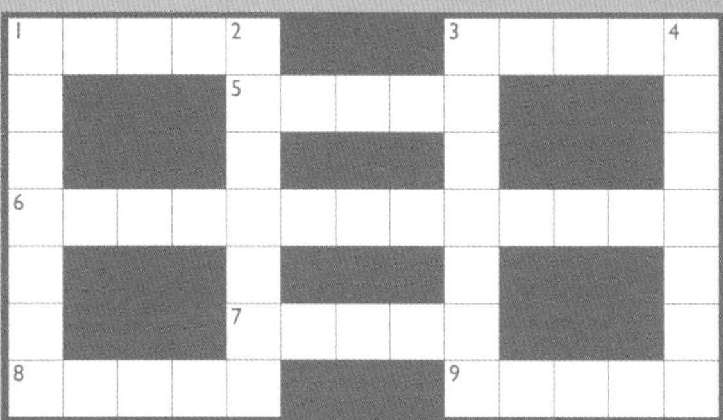

Across
1 A funny or amusing quality (2-syllable noun)
3 To push something out (2-syllable verb)
5 A powerful illegal drug (3-syllable noun)
6 To cause to pass from one to another (4-syllable adjective)
7 To force to leave (2-syllable verb)
8 One that avoids others (2-syllable noun)
9 To be uncertain about something (1-syllable verb)

Down
1 Causing injury or emotional pain (2-syllable adjective)
2 An adult male chicken (2-syllable noun)
3 A bright green stone (3-syllable noun)
4 Food eaten away from its place of sale (2-syllable noun)

406 | DIFFICULTY: ●●●●●●●●●●○ COMPLETION: ☐ TIME: _______

ANTONYM FINDER

Find and circle the six pairs of ANTONYMS, one on each side, in the letter grids below.

F	P	L	A	Y	B
R	E	M	I	T	L
L	G	Q	H	P	E
R	U	X	M	C	D
N	H	I	I	A	N
T	L	N	B	M	G

Y	H	X	D	K	C
Z	Q	O	R	M	Y
X	O	O	L	N	J
G	W	J	I	D	W
D	S	T	I	F	F
Y	N	U	G	L	Y

○○○○○○

407 | DIFFICULTY: ●●●●●●●●●○○ COMPLETION: ☐ TIME: _______

COLOR WORD CHAINS

Use the clues and letters below to make word paths between like colors to fill the board.

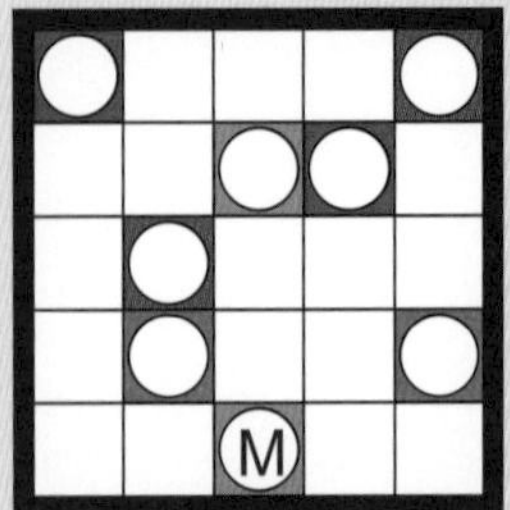

- A long-distance foot race
- A shiny metallic covering
- The skin on the back of the neck
- The number two in cards

A	A	C	C	C	D
E	E	E	F	F	H
H	M	N	O	O	R
R	R	S	T	U	U

408 | DIFFICULTY: ●●●●●●●●●○
COMPLETION: ☐ TIME: ______

SYNONYM FINDER

Find and circle the seven pairs of SYNONYMS divided between the letter grids below.

L	E	A	V	E	L	E	A
G	W	Y	D	A	G	M	R
L	C	G	G	R	G	E	P
I	F	E	A	I	D	A	T
S	L	L	N	N	H	K	B
T	N	E	U	S	W	C	M
E	M	L	I	N	F	Y	P
N	P	M	C	H	J	L	W

P	I	L	L	A	G	E	B
A	H	P	D	R	L	J	W
M	U	K	S	K	B	E	T
G	N	G	R	L	L	H	R
L	C	A	M	Z	I	T	E
R	P	Z	Z	E	J	P	S
S	T	U	F	W	N	G	E
Y	P	R	I	G	H	T	D

○ ○ ○ ○ ○ ○ ○

409 | DIFFICULTY: ●●●●●●●●●●○
COMPLETION: ☐ TIME: ________

ANTONYM UNSCRAMBLE

Unscramble the letters below to form pairs of ANTONYMS. Note: Some words can be unscrambled more than one way!

T E E B R T ≠ S W E R O

O S F L I O H ≠ S I E W

D R A A I F ≠ C R I E O H

L E E P X ≠ E E R I C E V

P L I S G E N E ≠ K W A A E

S T O E B U ≠ T A U E C

S M U F O A ≠ O N N U K N W

410 | DIFFICULTY: ●●●●●●●●●●○ COMPLETION: ☐ TIME: ______

SYNONYM FINDER

Find and circle the six pairs of SYNONYMS, one on each side, in the letter grids below.

C	S	H	U	N	V
S	W	R	E	P	Y
M	E	R	O	N	R
Y	A	V	O	A	W
R	E	G	E	V	M
W	A	I	T	R	N

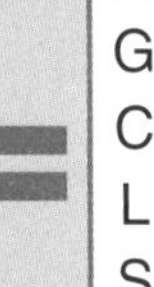

W	A	N	D	E	R
G	A	H	D	E	T
C	V	D	G	P	I
L	O	N	F	A	L
S	I	D	M	I	P
L	D	G	R	N	S

○○○○○○

411 | DIFFICULTY: ●●●●●●●●○○○ COMPLETION: ☐ TIME: ______

ANTONYM FINDER

Find and circle the six pairs of ANTONYMS, one on each side, in the letter grids below.

Y	D	E	A	D	N
W	K	N	V	J	H
H	R	I	Y	I	O
D	P	U	N	M	L
K	B	G	J	D	D
M	F	A	L	L	T

G	H	L	D	N	C
D	J	N	O	G	R
M	V	R	L	S	U
T	A	L	I	V	E
B	E	C	L	S	L
S	G	O	O	D	E

○○○○○○

412 | DIFFICULTY: ●●●●●●●●●○○○ COMPLETION: ☐ TIME: ______

CROSS'D WORD CONNECTIONS

The crosswords below share common letters as indicated by the colored boxes. Use the clues to solve the puzzles.

ACROSS
1 An interrogative expressing inquiry
4 Quietly—used as a direction in music
5 A self-luminous, gaseous, spheroidal celestial body

DOWN
1 To move (something) over a surface
2 To remain in abeyance until
3 Not good in quality or condition

ACROSS
1 The loud, deep sound made by an owl
4 A person who is eating in a restaurant
5 A metric unit of mass

DOWN
1 To put out of sight
2 One who legally possesses (something)
3 A formal dance given by a high school or college class

ACROSS
1 The place where a bird lays its eggs
4 Something unusually large or powerful
5 To return to a normal temperature after being very cold

DOWN
1 Near in place, time, or relationship
2 A long, wide strip of land
3 To put away for future use

413 | DIFFICULTY: ●●●●●●●●●●○ COMPLETION: ☐ TIME: ______

MISSING DEFINITIONS FINDER

Using the clues below, find and circle the words concealed in the letter grid.

C	Z	E	F	F	O	R	T	Z	Q
G	O	J	S	T	E	A	D	Y	U
N	C	P	X	P	Q	R	X	E	N
I	R	Q	Y	V	E	J	V	A	T
V	I	N	Z	Y	C	E	Z	T	I
O	M	E	W	J	A	K	C	S	D
M	E	A	X	V	L	Q	V	H	Y
Q	L	T	Z	J	P	M	U	C	H

dil·i·gent *adjective* \ˈdi-lə-jənt\
characterized by ______, earnest, and energetic ______

glut·ton *noun* \ˈglə-tən\
a person who ______ too ______

mimic *transitive verb* \ˈmi-mik\
to ______ (someone or someone's behavior or ______) especially for humor

pros·e·cute *verb* \ˈprä-si-ˌkyüt\
to work as a ______ to try to prove a case against someone accused of a ______

sta·tion·ary *adjective* \ˈstā-shə-ˌner-ē\
not ______ : staying in one ______ or position

un·kempt *adjective* \-ˈkem(p)t\
not ______ or orderly : messy or ______

414 | DIFFICULTY: ●●●●●●●●●●● COMPLETION: ☐ TIME: ______

CROSS'D WORDS UNSCRAMBLE

Unscramble the letters in each clue to fill in the puzzle grid below.

ACROSS

1 LUMQA *(one-syllable word)*
3 HACPE *(one-syllable word)*
5 SOONNPT *(two-syllable word)*
7 SOYLU *(two-syllable word)*
8 WORPE *(two-syllable word)*
9 SWITT *(one-syllable word)*
11 ASMTE *(one-syllable word)*
13 PHIPYLA *(three-syllable word)*
14 TIBZL *(one-syllable word)*
15 OVYNE *(two-syllable word)*

DOWN

1 LIQLU *(one-syllable word)*
2 NYLMA *(two-syllable word)*
3 TUUPC *(two-syllable word)*
4 ORRPI *(two-syllable word)*
5 SRIHNUO *(two-syllable word)*
6 DROPWYE *(three-syllable word)*
9 MUTBH *(one-syllable word)*
10 AZOTP *(two-syllable word)*
11 ZEESI *(one-syllable word)*
12 CRYME *(two-syllable word)*

415 | DIFFICULTY: ●●●●●●●●●●●
COMPLETION: ☐ TIME: ______

MIXED-UP DEFINITION

Unscramble the letters below to reveal the definition of the given word.

wan·ton *adjective* \ˈwȯn-tən, ˈwän-\
snoigwh on eacr orf het trsihg, slegiefn, ro taeyfs fo shorte

☐☐☐☐☐☐☐ ☐☐ ☐☐☐☐
☐☐☐ ☐☐☐ ☐☐☐☐☐☐,
☐☐☐☐☐☐☐☐,
☐☐ ☐☐☐☐☐☐
☐☐ ☐☐☐☐☐☐

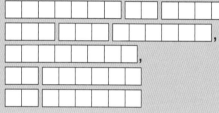

416 | DIFFICULTY: ●●●●●●●●●●●
COMPLETION: ☐ TIME: ______

COLOR WORD CHAINS

Use the clues and letters below to make word paths between like colors to fill the board.

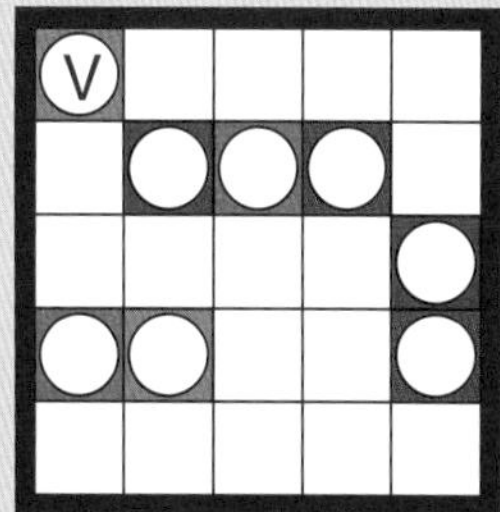

- Poison secreted by animals
- Emotionally out of control
- To cause something to not be effective
- The chemical in liquor

A	A	A	C	C	E
E	E	F	G	H	I
L	L	M	N	N	N
O	O	O	R	T	T

417 | DIFFICULTY: ●●●●●●●●●●○
COMPLETION: ☐ TIME: ______

PRISM WORD FINDER

Using the color-coded clues below, find and circle the words in the letter grid.

S	O	R	D	I	N	A	R	Y	W	Y
B	A	R	B	E	R	R	H	G	W	P
Q	V	B	X	B	E	S	M	P	Y	P
P	C	L	U	Y	A	E	O	T	C	A
Q	G	M	W	D	L	N	I	R	G	H
E	U	A	E	B	D	N	K	N	R	S
U	L	E	M	A	R	Y	O	E	S	Y
Q	J	I	A	E	G	L	W	E	R	B
A	N	L	T	S	B	E	R	Z	P	G
P	V	E	N	O	Y	P	R	H	L	S
O	R	W	E	Q	U	A	L	I	T	Y

Find five six-letter adjectives starting with an orange letter ○○○○○

Find four five-letter words with double consonants starting with a blue letter ○○○○

Find three four-syllable words ending in "Y" starting with a purple letter ○○○

Find three six-letter occupations starting with a red letter ○○○

418 | DIFFICULTY: ●●●●●●●●●●● COMPLETION: ☐ TIME: ______

DEFINITION FINDER

Using the clues below, find and circle the words concealed in the letter grid.

C	E	X	C	L	A	I	M	J
Q	H	Z	L	L	X	J	O	Q
F	R	E	Q	U	E	N	C	Y
X	U	V	C	L	N	V	K	T
Q	C	M	B	K	X	A	E	S
K	K	M	B	Z	U	I	R	R
Z	U	J	X	L	U	P	Y	U
J	S	Q	Z	Q	E	X	Z	B

○ The fact or condition of happening often *(noun)*
○ Funny in a way that shows intelligence *(adjective)*
○ Insulting or contemptuous action or speech *(noun)*
○ Making very little noise *(adjective)*
○ To say (something) in an enthusiastic way *(verb)*
○ To handle something in an awkward or clumsy way *(verb)*
○ To break into pieces in a sudden and violent way *(verb)*
○ A general physical examination *(noun)*
○ To end or stop (something) usually by using force *(verb)*
○ A mass of things mingled together without order *(noun)*
○ Of or relating to the moon *(adjective)*

419 | DIFFICULTY: ●●●●●●●●●●
COMPLETION: ☐ TIME: ______

DICTIONARY CROSS'D WORDS

Fill in the puzzle using the Merriam-Webster definition clues below.

Across
1 A lively dance for couples (2-syllable noun)
3 To propel through the air (1-syllable verb)
5 A large musical instrument (3-syllable noun)
6 Including many, most, or all things (4-syllable adjective)
7 Not lively or interesting (2-syllable adjective)
8 To push something with force (1-syllable verb)
9 Not younger (2-syllable adjective)

Down
1 A series of actions (2-syllable noun)
2 To accept as satisfactory (2-syllable verb)
3 Destructive whirling wind (3-syllable noun)
4 Any person at all (3-syllable pronoun)

420 | DIFFICULTY: ●●●●●●●●●●● COMPLETION: ☐ TIME: ______

DICTIONARY UNSCRAMBLE

Unscramble the letters below to form words that match the Merriam-Webster definitions.

noun
A state of confusion or disorder

ORMULTI= ☐☐☐☐☐☐☐

adjective
Marked by greatness especially in size or degree

MSEENIM= ☐☐☐☐☐☐☐

transitive verb
To count, record, or list systematically

UBETTAAL= ☐☐☐☐☐☐☐☐

noun
One of the four front teeth of the upper or lower jaw

NICROSI= ☐☐☐☐☐☐☐

transitive verb To make less by or as if by cutting off or away some part

CRITALU= ☐☐☐☐☐☐☐

adjective
Very large or wide open

GWIYANN= ☐☐☐☐☐☐☐

421 | DIFFICULTY: ●●●●●●●●●●● COMPLETION: ☐ TIME: ______

ANTONYM FINDER

Find and circle the six pairs of ANTONYMS, one on each side, in the letter grids below.

C	G	H	Y	H	T
L	N	R	C	G	N
G	E	A	I	I	E
M	E	V	O	M	B
R	W	J	E	D	I
H	F	O	I	L	J

R	M	I	L	D	H
E	E	M	D	G	X
V	P	X	U	Q	A
E	H	O	A	K	B
S	R	C	N	L	E
B	E	G	I	N	T

○○○○○○

422 | DIFFICULTY: ●●●●●●●●●●● COMPLETION: ☐ TIME: ______

COLOR WORD CHAINS

Use the clues and letters below to make word paths between like colors to fill the board.

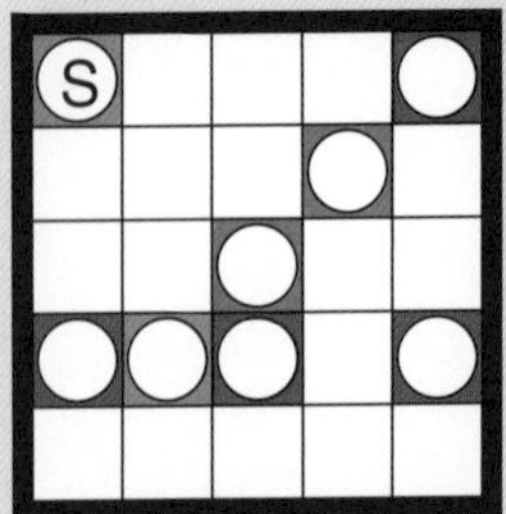

- To walk heavily or noisily
- Not paid at an expected or required time
- A milk substitute for infants
- A financial plan

A	A	B	D	D	E
E	E	F	G	L	M
M	O	O	P	R	R
T	T	U	U	U	V

423 | DIFFICULTY: ●●●●●●●●●○○
COMPLETION: ☐ TIME: ______

DICTIONARY WORD WINDER

Use the clues below to help you find the answers word-winding their way through the grid. Each answer will connect one side of the grid to the other—left to right, top to bottom, right to left, and bottom to top.

B	V	E	J	E	D
L	H	T	N	I	L
K	A	R	Q	F	X
G	E	T	F	O	N
E	H	U	O	Z	S
E	N	S	E	W	K

→ One of the yellow seeds that cover an ear of corn ______

↓ Not concentrated in one area ______

← To bring comfort, solace, or reassurance to ______

↑ To cause to be ineffective or invalid ______

424 | DIFFICULTY: ●●●●●●●○○○
COMPLETION: ☐ TIME: ______

PRISM CROSS'D WORDS

Use the color-coded clues below to find words that fit in the like-colored portions of the puzzle grid below.

- A recorded count of scores (2-syllable noun)
- Relating to a person's job (5-syllable adjective)
- Formal process used in thinking (2-syllable noun)

- The middle of the day (1-syllable noun)
- Person who does physical work (3-syllable noun)

- A business organization (3-syllable noun)
- Extremely bad or unpleasant (2-syllable adjective)

- Relating to a remote period (2-syllable adjective)
- Attended with danger (2-syllable adjective)

- A song to quiet children (3-syllable noun)
- A chamber used for baking (2-syllable noun)

425 | DIFFICULTY: ●●●●●●●●●●● COMPLETION: ☐ TIME: ______

ANTONYM FINDER

Find and circle the six pairs of ANTONYMS, one on each side, in the letter grids below.

D	K	T	W	D	E
T	V	B	N	S	T
A	X	I	N	C	A
E	B	E	L	D	H
N	D	N	W	E	F
H	K	L	O	S	E

T	G	A	I	N	Y
N	U	K	F	S	N
E	M	N	S	I	I
C	L	E	T	N	H
E	M	G	C	I	T
D	Y	L	O	V	E

○○○○○○

426 | DIFFICULTY: ●●●●●●●●●●● COMPLETION: ☐ TIME: ______

COLOR WORD CHAINS

Use the clues and letters below to make word paths between like colors to fill the board.

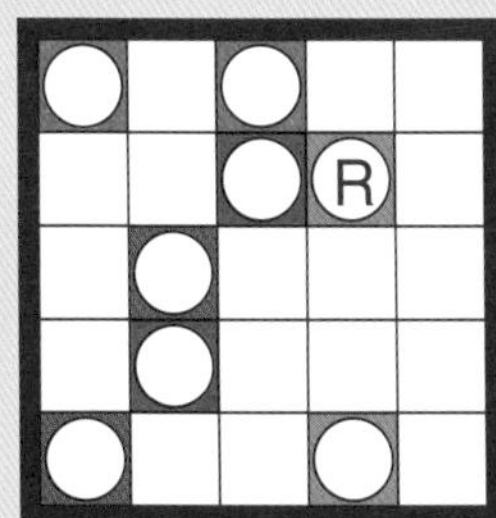

- To confine within bounds
- An offer at auction
- A bridge that allows a road to cross above another road
- Put money into a venture

A	B	C	D	E	E
E	I	I	I	N	O
P	R	R	S	S	S
S	T	T	T	V	V

427 | DIFFICULTY: ●●●●●●●●●○○
COMPLETION: ☐ TIME: ______

CROSS'D WORDS UNSCRAMBLE

Unscramble the letters in each clue to fill in the puzzle grid below.

ACROSS

1 SPESR *(one-syllable word)*
3 NIACP *(two-syllable word)*
5 ACBELNA *(two-syllable word)*
7 SOCID *(two-syllable word)*
8 NEAHY *(three-syllable word)*
9 SBHUR *(one-syllable word)*
11 EQNEU *(one-syllable word)*
13 MEETSTP *(two-syllable word)*
14 ILDPA *(one-syllable word)*
15 OTHCU *(one-syllable word)*

DOWN

1 UNODP *(one-syllable word)*
2 VASOL *(two-syllable word)*
3 CPHNI *(one-syllable word)*
4 MAMCO *(two-syllable word)*
5 STIBUCI *(two-syllable word)*
6 NEEETLM *(three-syllable word)*
9 PLIBM *(one-syllable word)*
10 MUIDH *(two-syllable word)*
11 SQETU *(one-syllable word)*
12 THONC *(one-syllable word)*

428 | DIFFICULTY: ●●●●●●●●●●●
COMPLETION: ☐ TIME: ______

SYLLABARY

Link word segments together in the grid below to create words, and enter them in the blanks.

TION	RY	ENT	HON	ATE
TO	TA	DI	DI	EST
A	U	BE	LY	ME
PRED	TION	REP	O	FY
COM	MO	VER	I	DIS

Three-Syllable Adverb: _ _ _ E _ _ _ _

Five-Syllable Adjective: _ _ _ _ _ E _ _ _ _ _

Three-Syllable Noun: _ O _ _ _ _ _ _ _

Four-Syllable Adjective: _ _ _ _ A _ _ _ _

Three-Syllable Verb: _ _ _ _ _ T _

Four-Syllable Noun: _ _ _ _ _ _ _ I _ _

Three-Syllable Verb: _ _ _ I _ _

429 | DIFFICULTY: ●●●●●●●●●●●
COMPLETION: ☐ TIME: ________

COLOR WORD CHAINS

Use the clues and letters below to make word paths between like colors to fill the board.

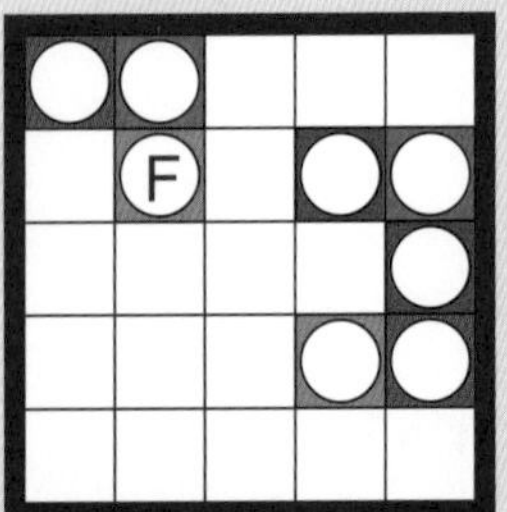

- To make or imitate falsely
- A visual representation
- The way someone's face looks that shows emotion
- Fierce competitor

A	A	E	E	E	E
G	G	I	I	I	L
M	N	O	O	P	R
R	R	S	S	V	X

430 | DIFFICULTY: ●●●●●●●●●●●
COMPLETION: ☐ TIME: ________

ANTONYM FINDER

Find and circle the six pairs of ANTONYMS, one on each side, in the letter grids below.

L	W	F	B	N	D
A	L	A	R	L	Y
E	N	E	I	R	E
Z	T	U	R	T	C
S	B	O	I	G	R
C	S	C	M	W	T

A	Y	B	W	Y	E
K	P	P	D	R	D
I	H	A	O	R	A
N	M	N	T	U	L
D	G	Y	C	H	G
I	R	U	I	N	Y

○○○○○○

431 | DIFFICULTY: ●●●●●●●●●●
COMPLETION: ☐ TIME: ________

SYNONYM FINDER

Find and circle the seven pairs of SYNONYMS divided between the letter grids below.

V	C	Z	M	P	L	J	M
A	E	H	E	A	Y	E	A
G	Y	N	U	A	K	G	I
U	B	S	T	A	L	E	N
E	U	P	T	U	D	M	T
N	D	S	W	I	R	P	A
W	I	F	R	K	C	E	I
M	L	P	Z	P	X	L	N

=

Y	V	F	E	R	V	O	R
T	A	D	C	P	F	E	L
P	N	W	J	B	D	N	A
M	I	D	Z	N	L	H	M
E	T	W	U	C	O	Y	R
T	Y	L	G	X	H	K	O
T	B	R	M	W	P	G	N
A	D	U	N	S	U	R	E

○ ○ ○ ○ ○ ○ ○

432 | DIFFICULTY: ●●●●●●●●●●○
COMPLETION: ☐ TIME: ______

ANTONYM UNSCRAMBLE

Unscramble the letters below to form pairs of ANTONYMS. Note: Some words can be unscrambled more than one way!

S R E M O O ≠ L O J Y L

O S P U I ≠ S L I U F N

C R E A U A C T ≠ S L E F A

F S I T W ≠ G L I H U S S G

T E F I U A G ≠ G R O V I

C O T I A N ≠ A T R I E I N

F L O A O ≠ D R E F Y I L N

433 | DIFFICULTY: ●●●●●●●●●●● COMPLETION: ☐ TIME: ______

CROSS'D WORDS UNSCRAMBLE

Unscramble the letters in each clue to fill in the puzzle grid below.

ACROSS

1 PRYCT *(one-syllable word)*
3 HRUCN *(one-syllable word)*
5 OXOSINU *(two-syllable word)*
7 ANREV *(two-syllable word)*
8 RYPVI *(two-syllable word)*
9 CLUGH *(one-syllable word)*
11 WHSLA *(one-syllable word)*
13 DHIDIYS *(two-syllable word)*
14 PREOA *(two-syllable word)*
15 NPYOH *(two-syllable word)*

DOWN

1 WOERC *(two-syllable word)*
2 NOTXI *(two-syllable word)*
3 PHMCO *(one-syllable word)*
4 WYENL *(two-syllable word)*
5 TONEYVL *(three-syllable word)*
6 NAPSHIC *(two-syllable word)*
9 MOGZI *(two-syllable word)*
10 AHDRY *(two-syllable word)*
11 PKMSI *(one-syllable word)*
12 YOLLW *(two-syllable word)*

434 | DIFFICULTY: ●●●●●●●●●●○
COMPLETION: ☐ TIME: ______

SYNONYM FINDER

Find and circle the six pairs of SYNONYMS, one on each side, in the letter grids below.

V	Z	G	R	C	E
T	I	A	T	S	D
F	E	S	I	V	O
N	E	O	I	Z	B
Z	P	D	H	O	A
I	R	A	T	E	N

=

C	T	Y	L	E	E
A	L	W	M	T	R
L	N	O	H	Y	I
M	H	G	S	C	S
C	I	Z	R	E	E
S	D	H	G	Y	D

○○○○○○

435 | DIFFICULTY: ●●●●●●●●●●●
COMPLETION: ☐ TIME: ______

ANTONYM FINDER

Find and circle the six pairs of ANTONYMS, one on each side, in the letter grids below.

Y	H	U	R	T	D
L	B	T	Q	E	T
E	F	R	K	H	K
M	Y	A	G	P	S
O	N	I	D	W	A
C	L	T	U	E	D

R	C	L	A	D	Y
A	H	Z	C	L	M
E	Q	E	P	L	U
P	D	E	A	Z	G
P	R	E	X	V	L
A	H	W	P	N	Y

○○○○○○

SOLUTIONS

1 ***Orange Answers***
ELATION, SIMILAR, ANIMAL, ENTERTAIN, AREA
Blue Answers
HORSE, COW, MOUSE, MOOSE, PIG
Purple Answers
GORGEOUS, LOVELY, PRETTY, ATTRACTIVE
Red Answers
YOUNGSTER, KID

2 GROW - EXPAND
BRAVE - BOLD
JOURNEY - TRIP
HARM - DAMAGE
HUMAN - PERSON
STRONG - SECURE
FUNNY - COMICAL

3 WITTY
PERFUME
QUART
SILVER
BUNDLE
THEATER
STRAIGHT
MORAL
MIDWIFE
THROUGH
DANCE

4 ACCLAIM - APPLAUD
CAPTURE - TAKE
CONCISE - COMPACT
DEFEAT - CONQUER
PERKY - JAUNTY
PESTER - TEASE
PLUMP - PORTLY

5 SETTLE
CENTRAL
PRECIOUS
DOLLAR
EXACTLY
BUCKET

6 DOING THINGS THAT REQUIRE PHYSICAL MOVEMENT AND ENERGY

7 EQUAL - MATCH
QUIT - CEASE
CLEAR - BRIGHT
RAGE - ANGER
TURN - SPIN
VOID - EMPTY

8 SHALLOW - PROFOUND
QUESTION - ANSWER
INSULT - RESPECT
GLARE - SHADE
MEAGER - LAVISH
MERRY - BLUE
PERSIST - CEASE

9

10 RADISH
PORTION
ENGINE
HARMONY

11
FULL - EMPTY
SMART - FOOLISH
ABOVE - BELOW
RAISE - LOWER
SILENCE - NOISE
LEAVE - ARRIVE
EXCITED - BORED

12

1 S	W	A	R	2 M		3 P	R	O	V	4 E
K				A		A				A
I		5 P	A	R	S	N	I	6 P		G
R		R		C		D		L		L
7 T	O	O	T	H		8 A	M	U	S	E
		V						M		
9 F	R	E	S	10 H		11 G	U	M	B	12 O
L		R		A		R		E		F
O		13 B	A	N	Q	U	E	T		T
O				D		F				E
14 D	I	M	L	Y		15 F	R	O	W	N

13

14
FASTER - SPEED
GOOD - EFFECTS
ROCKS - LAVA
TIME - WORKING
BLOCKS - PATH
LIGHT - HEAT

15
STICK - ADHERE
PROVE - VERIFY
POWER - FORCE
NATION - COUNTRY
ADORE - LOVE
ABSURD - STUPID
RUSH - HURRY

16
ATHLETIC
HARMLESS
OUTGOING
MAJESTIC
DRAMATIC

17
INTENSIFY
COMMUNITY
DOMESTIC
ESPECIALLY
DILIGENT
SURVIVOR
ENCOURAGING

18
BOLD - TIMID
CALM - ANGRY
DELAY - HURRY
HARD - SOFT
SMART - DUMB
DIM - CLEAR

19

F	F	E	S	A
A	N	O	T	F
R	P	B	I	E
I	Y	E	Z	L
G	H	D	E	Y

20

B	O	N	E	■
A	■	O	■	P
C	H	I	L	I
K	■	S	■	E
■	H	E	I	R

C	O	A	L	■
A	■	R	■	T
S	H	I	N	E
T	■	S	■	E
■	V	E	I	N

M	O	L	E	■
A	■	E	■	D
S	H	A	P	E
S	■	S	■	E
■	S	T	I	R

21

Orange Answers
INDULGE, PERMIT,
ENDURE, ABIDE, BEAR
Blue Answers
FREEZE, STOOGE,
WHOOSH, PEEVED
Purple Answers
GIRAFFE, RABBIT,
ZEBRA, BISON
Red Answers
CAMOUFLAGE,
INCOMPLETE

22

EXAMINE HAMBURGER
COOPERATION NECESSARY
FASCINATE DEDICATION
RIGOROUS

23

JUNGLE MOSTLY
BETTER SECRET
HIGHLY NOTICE

24

J	U	M	P	■	■	S	A	F	E
E	■	■	R	O	O	T	■	■	N
W	■	■	E	■	■	R	■	■	V
E	A	R	T	H	Q	U	A	K	E
L	■	■	Z	■	■	D	■	■	L
R	■	■	E	D	G	E	■	■	O
Y	E	L	L	■	■	L	A	M	P

25

IDLE - STILL
TARDY - LATE
TELL - REVEAL
BAD - WICKED
DIVULGE - INFORM
SOURCE - ORIGIN
EDICT - DECREE

26

JUMPING
CYCLING
HOPPING
BETTING
WAITING
CAPPING
BUMPING

27

AWARD
EARLY
USUAL
COBRA
STEAK
BITTER
HAMMER
SCHOOL
DIPLOMA
SEARCH
UNICYCLE

28
ABHOR - HATE
BOAST - BRAG
CAST - THROW
NICE - FINE
ODOR - SMELL
PLAIN - CLEAR

29
FAIL - WIN
REND - JOIN
SOFT - STIFF
TALL - SHORT
YIELD - DENY
ACUTE - DULL

30
KNIGHT
POLISH
RESCUE
OCTAGON

31
LOVE - LOATHE
CALM - HECTIC
RISE - DECLINE
LAZY - LIVELY
WELL - ILL
CASUAL - FORMAL
OLD - YOUNG

32

33
1 S	C	R	U	2 B		3 B	A	C	O	4 N
O				R		L				E
N		5 A	W	E	S	O	M	6 E		W
I		Q		A		O		L		L
7 C	H	U	N	K		8 M	U	D	D	Y
		A						E		
9 O	P	T	I	10 C		11 C	O	R	A	12 L
N		I		L		H		L		A
I		13 C	L	O	S	E	L	Y		N
O				W		S				K
14 N	Y	L	O	N		15 S	H	Y	L	Y

34
PRESERVE - MAINTAIN
PROCURE - ACQUIRE
QUIET - PLACID
RECALL - BETHINK
REMOTE - ALIEN
RUSTIC - RURAL
SHIELD - DEFEND

35
BITTER	TASTE
EASILY	HEARD
LARGE	RAIN
THINK	GREATER
LANGUAGE	TECHNOLOGY
DECISION	TRIAL

36
ABUSE - DAMAGE
BEAT - STRIKE
CEASE - STOP
GLUM - MOODY
HEAL - CURE
ILL - SICK

37
GENEROUS AND FRIENDLY TO GUESTS OR VISITORS

38

TAKEOUT
TANGENT
TEMPEST
THOUGHT
TONIGHT

39

JUBILANT
SOMEBODY
DIALOGUE
ZEALOUS
UNDULATE
RAPPORT

40

GET - ACQUIRE
FAITH - BELIEF
EMBRACE - HUG
NEW - MODERN
DRY - ARID
PREVIOUS - PRIOR
FAR - DISTANT

41

TRIANGLE
ANYBODY
EASILY
IMPORTANT
ORIGINAL
APPRECIATE
MACARONI

42

43

Orange Answers
LEXICAL, LAUREL, LAWFUL, LEGAL, LABEL
Blue Answers
BEIGE, BROWN, BLUE, PINK, BLACK
Purple Answers
CARVING, HEAVIER, GRAVITY
Red Answers
BREEZY, STORMY, SNOWY

44

45

ARMOR
CROWD
FIRST
MODEL
TOOTH
EDIBLE
INJECT
BEAUTY
ENGRAVE
LUGGAGE
AMBITION

46

COAX - BULLY
FAIR - RAINY
HIGH - LOW
DOUBT - FAITH
LIVE - DIE
MOVE - HALT

47
COOL - CALM
TRAP - SNARE
AGED - OLD
FAST - FLEET
OUST - EVICT
PANT - GASP

48
TICKET
ADMIRE
HYPHEN
GROOVE

49

S	H	E	D	
I		V		B
C	R	E	D	O
K		N		O
	A	T	O	M

F	I	N	D	
I		O		B
T	R	U	C	E
S		N		G
	A	S	K	S

S	A	I	D	
I		C		B
G	R	I	P	E
N		N		T
	A	G	E	S

50
SUCCEED - FORFEIT
STINGY - LIBERAL
YIELD - RESIST
HEROIC - TIMID
HOMELY - SUAVE
KINDLE - QUENCH
VIGILANT - HEEDLESS

51
FIANCEE
MEASURE
INITIAL
ELEVATE
ONEROUS

52
DARK - LIGHT
PERIL - SECURITY
TIDY - SLOPPY
DESPAIR - HOPE
CORRECT - UNTRUE
INSIDE - OUTSIDE
FORMER - LATTER

53
VACUUM
FAMOUS
LOUDLY
MODERN
JIGGLE
ALMOST

54
FIND - LOSE
LOUD - QUIET
PART - WHOLE
FULL - EMPTY
MERIT - VICE
NEAR - FAR

55
OFTEN CHANGING
SUDDENLY IN MOOD
OR BEHAVIOR

56
HIDE - CONCEAL
ELECT - PICK
QUEST - TREK
EASY - SIMPLE
AGREE - CONSENT
SAME - IDENTICAL
ACT - PERFORM

57

ARRANGED
HAPPENED
ATTENTION
GREAT
DISAGREE
OPINION
PREVENT
GROUP
SLOW
LEAVING
MIGHT
FUTURE

58

59

GLIMPSE
SQUEEZE
CLEANSE
FRAUGHT
TWELFTH

60

61

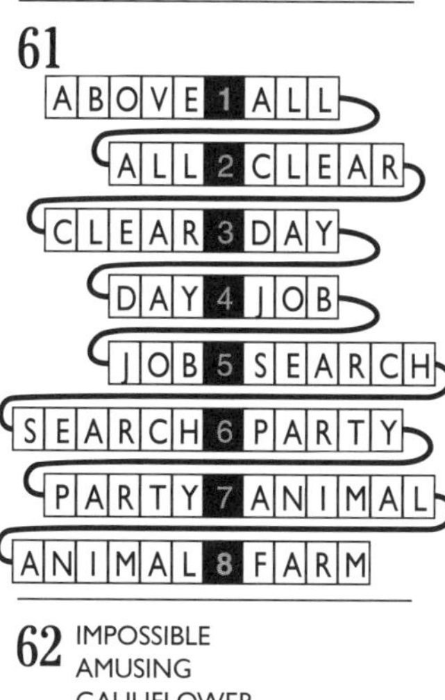

62

IMPOSSIBLE
AMUSING
CAULIFLOWER
GENERALLY
TELEVISION
ORGANIZE
YESTERDAY

63

REFUND
JINGLE
GRAVEL
USEFUL

64

REAP - SOW
POOR - RICH
QUIET - NOISY
SHORT - LONG
MUDDY - CLEAR
TAME - WILD

65

DONE IN A QUIET AND SECRET WAY TO AVOID BEING NOTICED

66

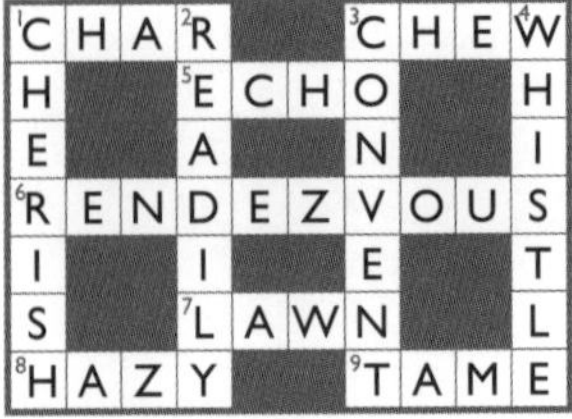

67

FRUIT
RELAX
ISLAND
ISOLATE
JUMBO
OBJECT
LEGAL
DAIRY
NORMAL
GRAFFITI
KENNEL

68

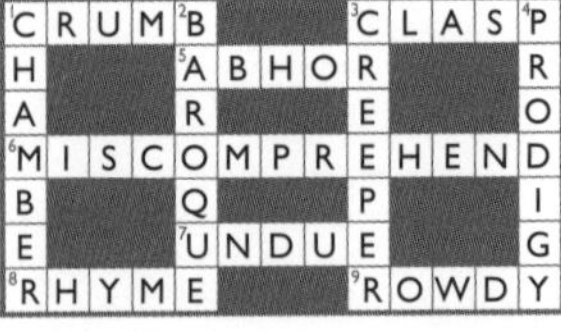

69

70

GOAL - AIM
SHINY - BRIGHT
WANDER - ROAM
FLAW - FAULT
ABIDE - FOLLOW
QUAKE - TREMBLE
FALSE - UNTRUE

71

SICK - STRONG
VALOR - FEAR
BEST - WORST
BAFFLE - AID
ENTRY - EXIT
FOUL - CLEAN

72

QUESTIONABLE OR SUSPECT AS TO TRUE NATURE OR QUALITY

73

VACANT
BEFORE
NARROW
DIAMOND
YOGURT
DAZZLE

74

Orange Answers
APPEASE, PACIFY, SOOTHE, SOFTEN, LULL
Blue Answers
VIVACIOUS, REVOLVE, SAVVY, VIVID, VALVE
Purple Answers
CONJUNCTION, ADVERB, NOUN
Red Answers
TAINT, TAUNT, TIGHT

75

CIRCUIT
LEMMING
MONGREL
FIXTURE
DIFFUSE

76

77

SALARY - WAGES
REVISE - CHANGE
SKEPTIC - DOUBTER
SPARKLE - GLITTER
TAWDRY - SHOWY
UNHAPPY - GLOOMY
RIGHT - PROPER

78

NEW - USED
RIGHT - WRONG
DANGER - SAFETY
HIDE - REVEAL
GIVE - TAKE
GENTLE - COARSE
PEACE - WARFARE

79

ACTIVE - ALERT
BANISH - EXILE
SNARE - TRAP
FEAR - DREAD
KEEP - RETAIN
MOIST - HUMID

80

HEAT - COLD
ADMIT - DENY
MOIST - ARID
GIVE - TAKE
PROFIT - LOSS
GRIEF - JOY

81

82

COMBINATION
BARBARIC
CLARIFY
VEGETARIAN
BELLIGERENT
POLITELY
CONTINUE

83

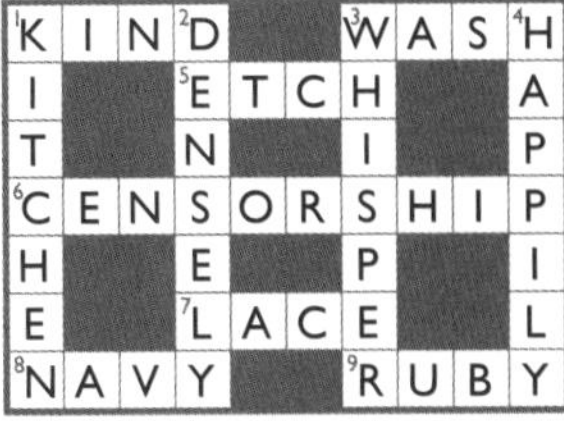

84
IMPROVE
WINDOW
CONNECT
PICKLE

85
ASK - INQUIRE
MIX - SCRAMBLE
SEVERAL - MANY
DIE - PERISH
IMAGE - PICTURE
DOCILE - GENTLE
RARE - UNIQUE

86

1 S	P	E	L	2 L		3 Q	U	I	L	4 T
H				O		U				R
E		5 H	A	Y	W	I	R	6 E		U
L		O		A		R		C		N
7 F	A	T	A	L		8 K	N	O	C	K
		L						L		
9 C	H	I	N	10 A		11 S	C	O	P	12 E
L		N		L		O		G		M
I		13 E	A	G	E	R	L	Y		B
F				A		R				E
14 F	L	A	K	E		15 Y	I	E	L	D

87
BANJO
KNIFE
WHOLE
FORGET
MINIMIZE
COMMENT
HANDY
QUILT
LUNCH
MIDDLE
URGENT

88
DESIRE
CARRY
STRANGE
USUAL
BELIEF
EDGE
FAMOUS
HEAVY
MYSTERIOUS
WORD
GOOD
ROAD

89
AMATEUR - ADEPT
MASTERY - FAILURE
NORMAL - STRANGE
ACTUAL - FALSE
RANSACK - RESTORE
REDUCE - INCREASE
DENY - AFFIRM

90
FINALLY
BORING
LIBRARY
PONDER
GLANCE
HONEST

91
REALIZE
EDITION
AMIABLE
LEISURE
LINEAGE

92
TO CAUSE TO FEEL HOSTILE OR ANGRY: TO IRRITATE OR UPSET

93
ACQUIT - PARDON
BLANK - VOID
JOIN - UNITE
NAME - TITLE
PILE - STACK
RAISE - ERECT

94
ENERGY
IDENTICAL
BENEFIT
COMPETITIVE
AVOCADO
TERRIBLY
REFRIGERATE

95

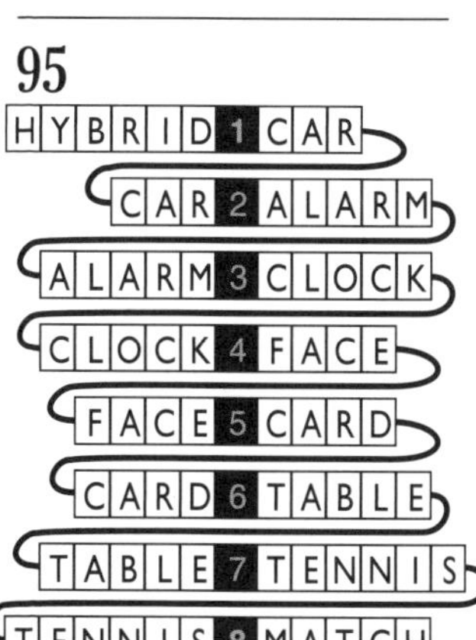

96

ALLOW - PREVENT
EXCLUDE - ADMIT
STRONG - FEEBLE
ENDURE - RESIGN
RUDE - POLITE
EXCITE - SOOTHE
CONFIRM - CANCEL

97

ALTER - SHIFT
REMEDY - CURE
RESIDE - DWELL
SPRY - NIMBLE
UTTER - SPEAK
ENDED - DONE

98

CLEAN - DIRTY
DENY - ADMIT
FEAR - VALOR
LOFTY - LOW
ADD - LESSEN
IMPEL - REACT

99

WISH - DESIRE
HABIT - CUSTOM
ATTEMPT - TRY
IMPEDE - HAMPER
ROUTE - COURSE
HAPPEN - OCCUR
SOLEMN - SERIOUS

100

CHILD
JUDGE
WEIGH
PLEASANT
FLUENT
MYSTERY

FINAL
DETECT
DROUGHT
SNEAK
STATUE

101

P	L	E	A	T		O	V	E	R	T
E				O		F				H
R		C	A	R	E	F	U	L		I
C		O		C		E		I		R
H	U	N	C	H		R	A	B	I	D
		T						R		
W	H	E	E	L		C	R	A	Z	Y
A		X		I		A		R		A
T		T	I	G	H	T	L	Y		C
C				H		C				H
H	A	B	I	T		H	E	A	R	T

102

103

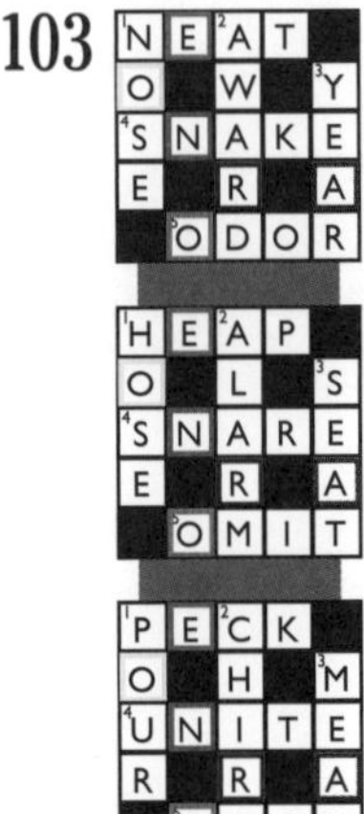

104

105

REAL - ACTUAL
SIMPLE - PLAIN
HAPPY - GLAD
WEIRD - EERIE
VAST - HUGE
SULLEN - GLUM

106

NEEDLE
HOLLOW
PEBBLE
FACTORY

107

PLACE	LIVES
TIME	OFTEN
CHANGE	INDIRECT
WAIT	HIDDEN
MOVE	HANDS
DONE	DETAIL

108

Orange Answers
NERVE, CATCH, MINCE, RANGE, TENSE, CRAVE
Blue Answers
ORDINARY, REGULAR, TYPICAL, AVERAGE, COMMON
Purple Answers
BETTING, BEGGING, WAITING
Red Answers
BOXER, HUSKY

109

WRAPPING ATTITUDE
SQUIGGLE FOLLOWER
CAFFEINE

110

111

112

HACK - CHOP
PHONY - FAKE
HANDY - USEFUL
LAUD - PRAISE
JOLLY - MERRY
CHOOSE - SELECT
TRADE - BARTER

113

ELEVATOR
SIMILAR
CALCULATOR
ANGRILY
ASTROLOGY
DELIVER
NECESSARY

114

QUICKLY ELEGANT
ANSWER HARVEST
YAMMER TENDER

115

ABDICATE - RESIGN
ABSOLUTE - COMPLETE
ABILITY - TALENT
DEPLETE - DRAIN
THRONG - ASSEMBLY
SCOLD - BERATE
TRITE - COMMON

116

117

NORMAL - USUAL
TAUNT - MOCK
REST - SLEEP
SICK - WEAK
SQUARE - CORNY
REVEAL - SHOW

118

A STRONG DESIRE TO SPEND YOUR LIFE DOING A CERTAIN KIND OF WORK

119

DERIDE - INCITE
DISPLAY - CONCEAL
WELCOME - SHUN
REJECT - PERMIT
NEUTRAL - BIASED
COLLECT - SCATTER
WHOLE - PARTIAL

120

MORAL - WICKED
STIFF - FLEXIBLE
SCRAWNY - BRAWNY
ABSENT - PRESENT
REWARD - PENALTY
HIRE - FIRE
DELICATE - ROUGH

121

122

[1]B	I	J	O	[2]U		[3]O	V	E	R	[4]T
A				S		X				E
N		[5]E	X	H	I	B	I	[6]T		M
J		X		E		O		E		P
[7]O	C	C	U	R		[8]W	O	R	S	T
		E						S		
[9]C	U	R	V	[10]E		[11]F	I	E	L	[12]D
O		P		R		I		L		I
U		[13]T	Y	R	A	N	N	Y		T
G				O		C				C
[14]H	O	V	E	R		[15]H	I	T	C	H

123

[1]H	O	[2]P	E	■
O	■	R	■	[3]P
[4]S	P	I	L	L
T	■	O	■	O
■	[5]G	R	I	D

[1]P	A	[2]G	E	■
E	■	R	■	[3]F
[4]S	H	A	W	L
T	■	I	■	O
■	[5]S	L	I	P

[1]L	I	[2]F	E	■
I	■	R	■	[3]S
[4]S	H	I	R	T
T	■	S	■	O
■	[5]S	K	I	P

124

RADIATOR
NOTATION
WITHDRAW
DEADWOOD
MAILROOM

125

Orange Answers
STRAIGHT, SPLASHED,
THRASHED, STRENGTH
Blue Answers
EPEE, ELSE,
EASE, EDGE
Purple Answers
CRACK, SMASH,
BURST, CRUSH
Red Answers
NEVER, LEVER,
SEVER

126 QUARTET NATURAL CHATTY JACKET

127
RENDER - GIVE
SANE - NORMAL
IMPLY - MEAN
AID - HELP
SEIZE - TAKE
BUILD - ERECT

128
ORDER - CHAOS
AGREE - DIFFER
LURE - REPEL
TOAST - CHILL
REAL - FALSE
ABHOR - LOVE

129
BENCH EXPLODE
HONEY FINISH
MINOR ESCAPE
LIMERICK GRUFF
MAGNET REASON
DISMISS

130

LAST 1 NAME
NAME 2 AFTER
AFTER 3 WORK
WORK 4 ON
ON 5 TO
TO 6 GO
GO 7 FISH
FISH 8 FOOD

131 SAPPHIRE LOBBYIST MARRIAGE GLOSSARY BOUILLON

132
MOB - CROWD
OWN - POSSESS
PERFECT - IDEAL
OLD - ANCIENT
RANK - DEGREE
INCITE - URGE
ENDURE - SUFFER

133
ADVENTURE
WONDERFUL
IDENTIFY
INDEPENDENT
ALREADY
MEMORABLE
OBEDIENT

134

1 S	H	R	U	2 G		3 C	H	A	R	4 T
H				I		H				A
A		5 A	M	A	Z	I	N	6 G		L
D		M		N		L		A		O
7 Y	E	A	S	T		8 D	O	Z	E	N
		T						E		
9 P	I	E	C	10 E		11 B	A	T	O	12 N
R		U		N		R		T		A
O		13 R	E	J	O	I	C	E		C
W				O		C				H
14 L	O	F	T	Y		15 K	A	Z	O	O

135

M	O	L	T	T
O	N	S	U	R
C	R	L	M	E
T	A	A	E	A
I	O	N	Y	T

136
SHAPE - FORM
HOAX - TRICK
GREET - HAIL
SLIP - ERROR
ACE - ONE
BOLD - BRAVE

137
LAX - CAREFUL
FRESH - STALE
HAUGHTY - HUMBLE
ACCEPT - REFUSE
IMPART - CONCEAL
LAWFUL - ILLEGAL
IMPAIR - IMPROVE

138
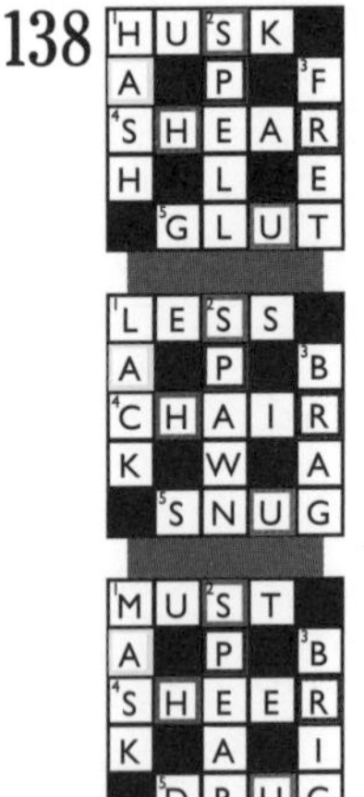

139
REGULAR - COMPLEX
DETACH - UNITE
SAVORY - BITTER
TEDIOUS - AMUSING
PROVE - REFUTE
ABSORB - DISPERSE
EXTEND - LESSEN

140
ULTIMATE - MAXIMUM
INEPT - CLUMSY
UNEQUAL - UNEVEN
RUTHLESS - BRUTAL
SAVORY - PUNGENT
TRUTH - CANDOR
DAINTY - REFINED

141
F	Y	A	C	H
A	L	T	R	I
M	I	F	O	E
H	R	I	T	Y
T	M	E	N	E

142
QUELL - SUBDUE
SNOOP - PROBE
EJECT - EXPEL
SAD - BLUE
ADAPT - SUIT
ALLOT - GIVE

143
SYSTEM
ALWAYS
POPULAR
WELCOME
KINDLE
EXOTIC

144
AMOUNT	OWNING
EASILY	TROUBLE
LARGE	SPACE
SLOW	ACTION
LITTLE	WORTH
CHANGE	FORM

145

Orange Answers
DRAFTEE, ESCAPEE, TRUSTEE, JUBILEE, OVERSEE
Blue Answers
QUALITY, QUART, QUILT, QUALM
Purple Answers
FLOOD, LOOSE, TOOTH, BROOK
Red Answers
IDENTICAL, IRREGULAR

146

DEVOUR
FUTURE
BEACON
GUITAR

147

1 N	E	S	2 T	■	■	3 C	H	E	4 F
E	■	■	5 E	U	R	O	■	■	L
T	■	■	X	■	■	R	■	■	A
6 W	E	A	T	H	E	R	M	A	N
O	■	■	U	■	■	U	■	■	N
R	■	■	7 R	A	M	P	■	■	E
8 K	N	E	E	■	■	9 T	A	I	L

148

ADD - INCREASE
REACH - ATTAIN
HONEST - JUST
FALL - TOPPLE
HARDY - STRONG
OPTION - CHOICE
JUDGE - UMPIRE

149

HUNGRY
DAMAGE
ENTIRE
HUMID
BEFORE
VILLAGE
OPERA
JINGLE
OMNIVORE
RANCH
IMMUNE

150

NECKLACE
HATCHWAY
LOVESICK
FAITHFUL
TIRESOME

151

D	A	M	P	■	■	■	P	A	S	T
I	■	■	O	B	E	S	E	■	■	W
S	■	■	L	■	■	■	N	■	■	I
P	L	A	Y	F	U	L	N	E	S	S
L	■	■	G	■	■	■	A	■	■	T
A	■	■	O	C	E	A	N	■	■	E
Y	A	W	N	■	■	■	T	E	A	R

152

CREDIT 1 CARD
CARD 2 GAME
GAME 3 BOY
BOY 4 SCOUT
SCOUT 5 OUT
OUT 6 WEST
WEST 7 BANK
BANK 8 SHOT

153
ABSOLUTE
CATEGORY
IRONICALLY
REUNION
COOPERATE
NEGATIVE
DEVELOP

154
CHASE - PURSUE
CATCH - GRASP
ALIKE - SAME
DUD - FLOP
ELUDE - EVADE
PICK - SELECT

155
ABLE - WEAK
DIRTY - CLEAN
FAST - SLOW
BEAR - EVADE
FEUD - PEACE
EASY - HARD

156
SLY - CRAFTY
ALLAY - SOOTHE
CIRCULAR - ROUND
KEEN - SHARP
THINK - PONDER
METHOD - SYSTEM
MANY - VARIOUS

157
NORMAL	AVERAGE
RESULT	ACTION
HEAR	SMELL
LIKING	PLEASE
STUDY	LOCATION
LAKES	RIVERS

158
[1]A	M	I	S	[2]S		[3]F	O	R	U	[4]M
M				W		A				A
A		[5]D	R	I	B	B	L	[6]E		Y
S		O		F		L		T		O
[7]S	H	O	U	T		[8]E	T	H	E	R
		R						I		
[9]M	I	M	I	[10]C		[11]F	O	C	U	[12]S
O		A		A		A		A		A
U		[13]T	O	P	I	C	A	L		U
T				E		E				C
[14]H	O	N	O	R		[15]T	R	U	L	Y

159
STOP - CONTINUE
EVEN - ODD
VANITY - MODESTY
POWER - WEAKNESS
WHOLE - DIVIDED
HEIGHTEN - LOWER
SEPARATE - JOIN

160
AN OBJECT USED TO SUGGEST A THING THAT CANNOT BE SHOWN

161
GLOOM - WOE
CRUEL - BRUTAL
FEUD - BRAWL
BRIM - EDGE
CHEAT - DUPE
GLEE - CHEER

162

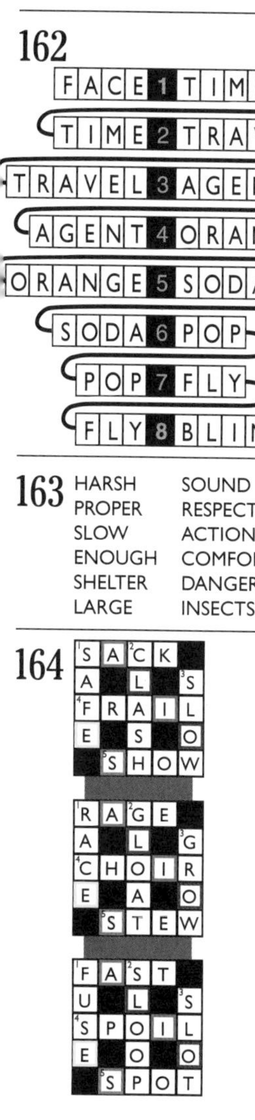

163

HARSH SOUND
PROPER RESPECT
SLOW ACTION
ENOUGH COMFORT
SHELTER DANGER
LARGE INSECTS

164

165

EDGEWISE RATIONAL
ELECTION BEREAVED
EASEMENT

166

VETERAN - NOVICE
ATTEND - NEGLECT
COARSE - DAINTY
MALICE - CHARITY
DAPPER - SLOPPY
AVERAGE - QUIRKY
RECANT - ENDORSE

167

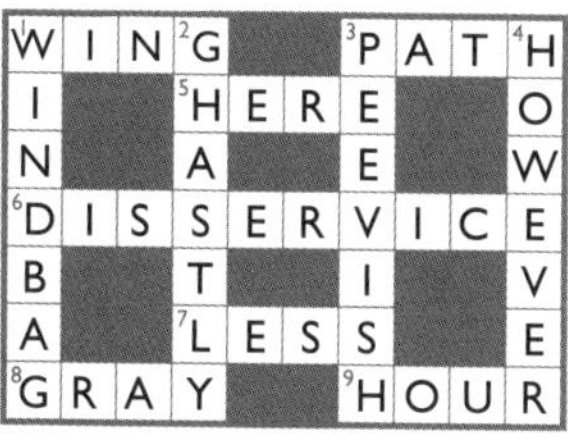

168

HISTORIC
ALLIGATOR
EXPERIMENT
OPERATE
PASSIONATE
WILDERNESS
CAFETERIA

169

GALAXY JEALOUS
ANTIQUE QUIETLY
NERVOUS HAGGLE

170

RAPID WEAVE
AMOUNT JUSTIFY
DOUBT NEVER
COMEDY EXHALE
LUXURY APPROVE
NUMEROUS

171 FAIL - FLUNK
HOIST - ELEVATE
STARDOM - FAME
MONEY - CURRENCY
TEACH - INSTRUCT
BROKEN - SMASHED
SPEECH - ORATION

172 LOCATE
MEMORY
AGENDA
WRENCH

173 ***Orange Answers***
OVERLY, PARTLY, SIMPLY, RARELY, SURELY
Blue Answers
SPEEDY, QUICK, SWIFT, FAST
Purple Answers
OBLIVIOUS, ACTIVATED, MOVIE
Red Answers
EXCEED, NEEDLE, WHEEZE

174

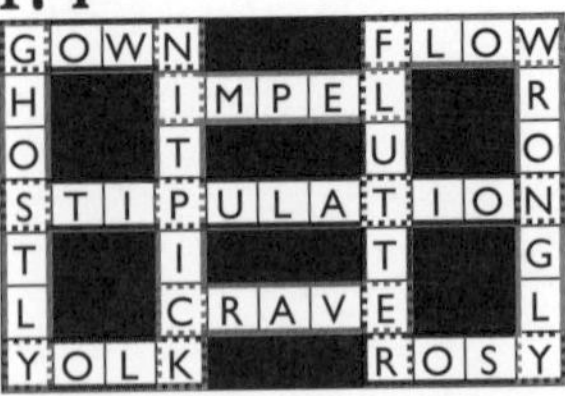

175 FORFEIT OBSTACLE
FRAGRANT WARRANTY
TANGIBLE AUGMENT

176 DRESSING AND ACTING IN AN APPEALING AND SOPHISTICATED WAY

177

D	E	T	A	I
A	N	E	L	C
Y	D	L	E	U
N	O	N	C	R
I	P	A	R	C

178 ABIDE - MOVE
CATCH - MISS
HAPPY - SAD
KEEN - BLUNT
LYING - TRUE
HAZY - CLEAR

179 DEFER - DELAY
ABOUT - NEARLY
ABET - AID
AMEND - REVISE
DESIST - CEASE
CHOOSE - PICK

180 SANCTION - APPROVAL
SCATTER - DISPEL
SUPPOSE - SURMISE
CORRECT - IMPROVE
DETECT - EXPOSE
YIELD - SUBMIT
ENDURE - SUFFER

181

[1]T	R	U	S	[2]S		[3]F	L	A	S	[4]H
H				L		L				O
R		[5]B	O	U	Q	U	E	[6]T		N
O		E		M		I		H		E
[7]B	I	C	E	P		[8]D	I	R	T	Y
		A						I		
[9]B	L	U	N	[10]T		[11]M	A	F	I	[12]A
L		S		E		O		T		W
A		[13]E	X	A	C	T	L	Y		A
N				S		T				R
[14]D	R	O	N	E		[15]O	L	I	V	E

182

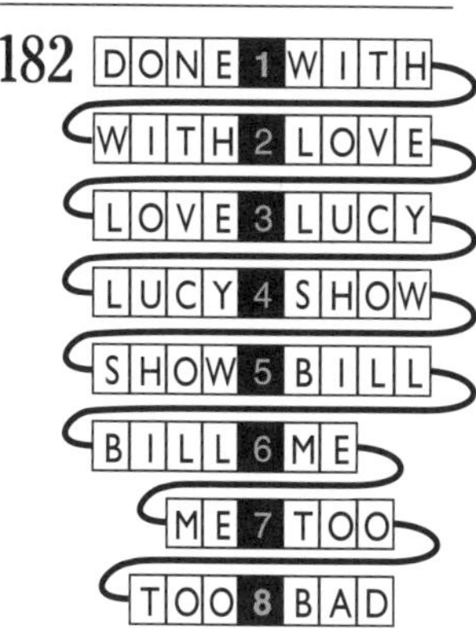

183

RARE - COMMON
WANDER - STAY
FRONT - BACK
SAFETY - DANGER
GIGANTIC - TINY
HEED - IGNORE
SILENCE - CLAMOR

184

DEMOLISH LIBERATE
OPPOSITE PENALIZE
MAGICIAN

185

Orange Answers
ROTOR, KAYAK,
LEVEL, CIVIC, REFER
Blue Answers
BLOOD, MOOSE,
SCOOT, FLOOR, PROOF
Purple Answers
CRUDE, DENSE,
REGAL, INEPT
Red Answers
SNOWFALL, RAINFALL

186

CHANCE - FATE
SLACK - LAX
ALONE - SINGLE
CARE - HEED
BASIC - VITAL
INEPT - UNFIT

187

E	D	U	L	E
H	C	S	S	E
O	P	P	O	R
I	G	N	F	E
E	R	O	O	Y

188

RELATIVE
DECORATIVE
CURIOSITY
ESTIMATE
TOMORROW
APOLOGIZE
FORTUNATE

189

NEAR - ADJACENT
DAWDLE - LOITER
QUALITY - CLASS
UPSET - UNNERVE
SHRINK - DWINDLE
RATIFY - CONFIRM
LOYAL - FAITHFUL

190

191

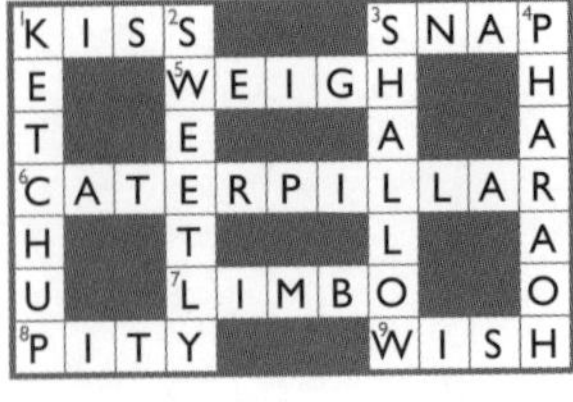

192

HEART
APPARENT
PUPIL
FRUGAL
HICCUP
AWKWARD
ROOKIE
GLEAM
FLOAT
INSPECT
SMALL

193

P	U	C	K	■
L	■	L	■	C
A	L	O	H	A
N	■	N	■	R
■	R	E	S	T

B	U	C	K	■
L	■	H	■	S
A	M	I	G	O
H	■	N	■	R
■	M	A	S	T

C	U	B	E	■
L	■	O	■	W
A	O	R	T	A
P	■	N	■	R
■	M	E	S	S

194

Orange Answers
RECEIVER, RECLINER, RATHER, RENDER, REFER

Blue Answers
CHEER, CHEEP, CREEK, CREED, CREEL

Purple Answers
LEAKY, RANGY, HEAVY, MERRY

Red Answers
ADJECTIVE, PRONOUN

195

HESITATE
MEMORIAL
ABRASIVE
FRUITION
ELEGANCE

196

197

EXACT - WRONG
FANCY - FACT
GAIN - LOSE
HALT - WALK
LONG - SHORT
FAR - NEAR

198

ROAMING ABOUT FROM PLACE TO PLACE AIMLESSLY

199

MEDDLE
SELDOM
BOYCOTT
GRUMPY
EMPLOYEE
QUAINT

200

FEELING	PEOPLE
OCCASION	COVERED
MOON	EARTH
DANGER	RISK
GIVE	POWER
FOLLOW	CAPTURE

201

BIRTH - DEATH
FULL - EMPTY
STORMY - CALM
ADORE - DESPISE
SUNNY - CLOUDY
LOW - HIGH
IMMENSE - MINUTE

202

JAYWALK	FLIMSY
THEORY	HEARTH

203

PRECISE - INEXACT
REVIVE - WEAKEN
SKEPTIC - BELIEVER
BUMPY - FLAT
FORGET - RECALL
SCORN - RESPECT
HASTEN - DELAY

204

ANNOY - IRK
DULL - STUPID
CENTER - FOCUS
GRANT - GIFT
EASE - ALLAY
SLEEK - OILY

205

FOOLISHLY IMPRACTICAL ESPECIALLY IN THE PURSUIT OF IDEALS

206

CANADA 1 GOOSE

GOOSE 2 EGG

EGG 3 ROLL

ROLL 4 CALL

CALL 5 FOR

FOR 6 SALE

SALE 7 PRICE

PRICE 8 WAR

207

Orange Answers
FAULTY, FLASHY, HEARTY, GLOOMY, WINTRY

Blue Answers
VENEER, NEEDED, SECEDE, HEELED, VEERED

Purple Answers
AREA, IDEA, OBOE, ARIA

Red Answers
QUENCHING, REPORTING

208

ADEQUATE ALIENATE
AQUARIUM AUDITION
AVIATION

209

PITY - SYMPATHY
REST - REPOSE
FLAUNT - DISPLAY
OUTLAW - BANDIT
NOTICE - OBSERVE
GENIAL - CORDIAL
CANCEL - RESCIND

210

FIRM - WEAK
RUDE - POLITE
QUICK - SLOW
SOBER - DRUNK
FLOW - STOP
ROAM - REST

211

CHEST - TRUNK
CLING - ADHERE
DARING - BOLD
DAFFY - WACKY
FAIR - HONEST
GIVE - CEDE

212

[1]B	R	A	S	[2]S		[3]L	E	A	R	[4]N
R				T		Y				U
I		[5]Q	U	A	R	R	E	[6]L		D
N		U		S		I		O		G
[7]G	R	A	P	H		[8]C	A	B	L	E
		R						S		
[9]T	O	T	E	[10]M		[11]M	E	T	E	[12]R
H		E		E		O		E		U
I		[13]R	E	A	L	T	O	R		N
E				T		E				N
[14]F	O	L	L	Y		[15]L	O	B	B	Y

213

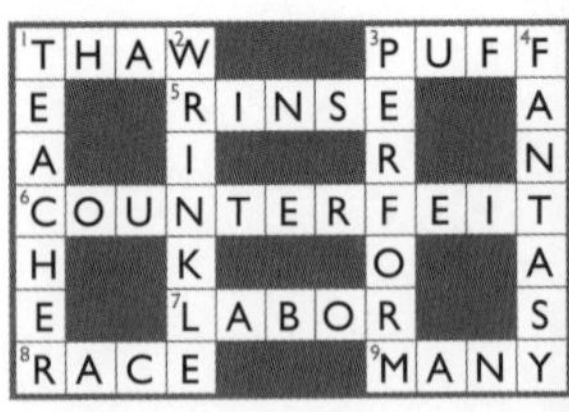

214

KICKOFF
ARREST
BRITTLE
KLUTZ
MUMBLE
CRAVE
NAÏVE
JUNCTION
NOTCH
TABOO
GORGE

215

INFORMATION
IMPULSIVE
EXPERTLY
UNIVERSITY
ALPHABETIZE
MOTIVATE
CONSIDER

216

DIVIDEND
KNAPSACK
ANACONDA
NORTHERN
EMPLOYEE

217

VAST - HUGE
CANCEL - ANNUL
LAST - LEAST
ABYSS - DEPTH
BOUND - HELD
CAUSE - ORIGIN

218

EXPRESSING OPINIONS OR CRITICISM IN A VERY FORCEFUL WAY

219

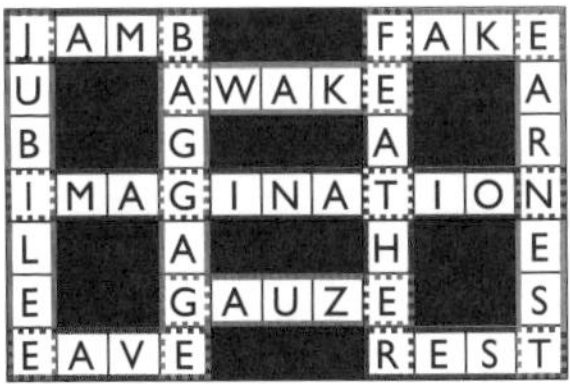

220

FLOURISH - THRIVE
FEELING - PASSION
DILEMMA - PICKLE
LINGER - TARRY
YEARN - DESIRE
ZANY - CLOWN
ALLEGE - STATE

221

T	U	B	E	
I		A		S
R	E	S	E	T
E		I		E
	S	C	A	M

M	U	C	K	
I		I		S
L	E	V	E	L
E		I		O
	F	L	A	P

L	U	S	H	
I		N		S
P	E	A	R	L
S		I		A
	C	L	A	M

222

CHIMNEY
MERCURY
CASHEW
QUAINT

223

JUMP - LEAP
PERMIT - ALLOW
PROTECT - DEFEND
QUALIFIED - ABLE
SHREWD - CUNNING
DETER - DISSUADE
HARMONY - ACCORD

224 SIZZLE, DENTAL, JOINT, HECKLE, PIRATE, POISE, CABOOSE, JADED, HARMONY, DELIVERY, LAVISH

225 FACT - FICTION
TOP - BOTTOM
SHAME - RESPECT
CLEAR - OPAQUE
RAPID - SLOW
LISTEN - IGNORE
ADJOURN - BEGIN

226 SHOWY - GAUDY
ABIDE - BEAR
RIVAL - OPPOSE
ROT - DECAY
SHINE - GLARE
ADORN - DECK

227 CHIC - TACKY
READY - TARDY
FEED - STARVE
HINT - VEIL
RANK - FRESH
MEAN - NICE

228 ***Orange Answers***
HIGHLY, SLOWLY, LOUDLY, BOLDLY, GLADLY
Blue Answers
LEAGUE, UTOPIA, IGUANA, AZALEA
Purple Answers
TERRIER, SPANIEL, BEAGLE, HOUND
Red Answers
CALCIUM, COBALT

229 COHERENT, ORGANIZE, SYCAMORE, CAROUSEL, ARROGANT

230 PERFECT, CALENDAR, INVOLVE, SWIFTLY, AWKWARD, MIGRATE

231 VOCABULARY, SUITABLE, GYMNASIUM, ENERGETIC, MODESTLY, ABANDON, CONFUSION

232 SIMPLE - WISE
KEEP - CEDE
FIERCE - MILD
SIN - VIRTUE
WANT - PLENTY
BREAK - FIX

233 AIRY - LIGHT
VICE - CRIME
DECIDE - SETTLE
COMPLY - AGREE
BEND - MOLD
DEFY - DARE

234

[1] S	I	N	E	[2] W		[3] W	H	I	R	[4] L
A				A		H				E
U		[5] H	Y	G	I	E	N	[6] E		A
N		O		O		A		Q		S
[7] A	R	S	O	N		[8] T	R	U	C	E
		T						A		
[9] S	L	E	E	[10] K		[11] A	T	T	I	[12] C
T		S		N		N		O		A
O		[13] S	N	E	A	K	E	R		N
O				A		L				D
[14] P	O	U	N	D		[15] E	N	E	M	Y

235

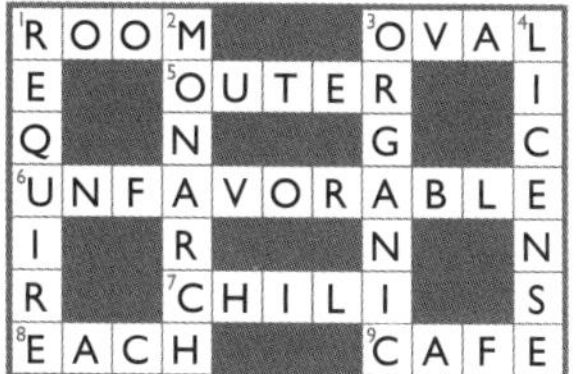

236

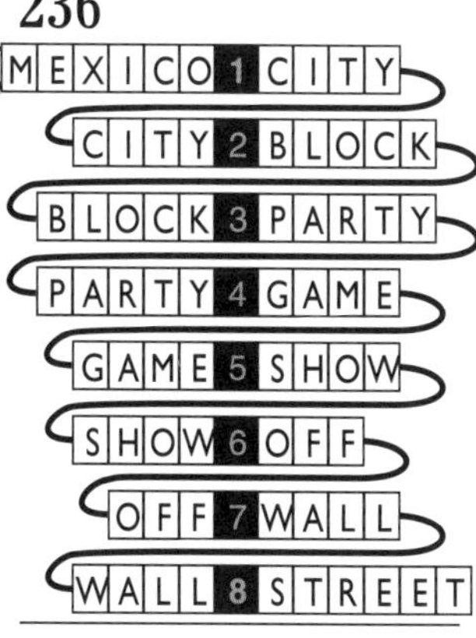

237

SILLY FOOLISH
DIVIDE BLOW
HOLD FIGHT
CAUSE HAVE
EAGER IMPORTANT
TRAVELS HOME

238

DRESS - GARB
DREAM - FANCY
BAFFLE - FOIL
ADO - FUSS
CASTE - CLASS
ANGER - WRATH

239

240

NUPTIAL
ADHERE
REVIEW
DISRUPT

241

MONEY ACCOUNT
FIRE BURN
CATCHING FISH
NUMBER POSSIBLE
SECOND ELECTION
CITIES PEOPLE

242

243

LOOPHOLE
SHEETING
CAREFREE
MONGOOSE
TWEEZERS

244

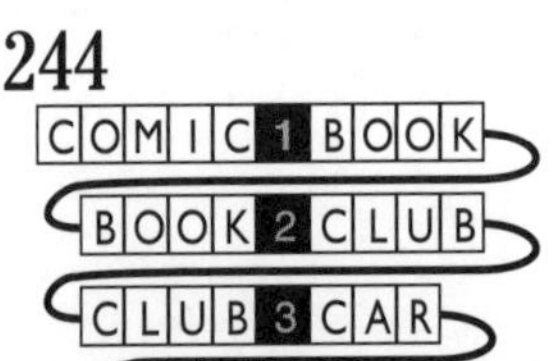

245

Orange Answers
VAINLY, POORLY, WARMLY, LOVELY, MILDLY
Blue Answers
ECONOMIZE, ELONGATE, EMBRACE, ECLIPSE, EAGLE
Purple Answers
ACTIVE, FAST
Red Answers
DODGING, PUMPING

246

YELLOW
PROFIT
NOBLE
UNFOLD
OVERDO
HEXAGON
TWICE
NURSERY
WRECKAGE
BEGIN
ERODE

247

SHUFFLE
HOSPITAL
LIKEABLE
ALREADY
TRAMPLE
MEAGER

248

VERDICT - JUDGMENT
VOCAL - VERBAL
VICTORY - CONQUEST
WARY - CAUTIOUS
ALLOW - ASSENT
DISCLOSE - REVEAL
COMPLEX - MIXED

249

ALONE - SOLITARY
VALID - SOUND
ROTATE - REVOLVE
PARDON - RELEASE
THREAT - MENACE
GOVERN - CONTROL
ERROR - BLOOPER

250

THIN - THICK
FRESH - TIRED
VAGUE - SURE
MEET - AVOID
YELL - STIFLE
WORK - REST

251

BRAWL - FRACAS
EMPTY - BARE
CALM - QUIET
SCARE - ALARM
EFFORT - WORK
BODY - LUMP

252

253

TRUST - DOUBT
BROAD - NARROW
ZEAL - APATHY
POVERTY - WEALTH
PLUNGE - SOAR
MISERY - BLISS
TURMOIL - CALM

254

255

256

GROUP - CLUMP
PAIN - AGONY
INEPT - UNFIT
SACK - LOOT
JEST - QUIP
GROVEL - CRAWL

257

TO GATHER TOGETHER ESPECIALLY FOR BATTLE OR WAR

258

PLAYFULLY
APOLOGETIC
COMPUTER
STAMINA
PARTICIPATE
AMPLIFY
ILLITERATE

259

GLOWINGLY LENIENTLY
ANXIOUSLY UNUSUALLY
INSTANTLY

260

ALTER - MODIFY
OBVIOUS - EVIDENT
PROPER - SUITABLE
RANDOM - CHANCE
PERFECT - SPOTLESS
PROMPT - SWIFT
PLUSH - ELEGANT

261

GULLIBLE
LOCATE
ADVANCE
AVIAN
KNACK
MALICE
UNION
RUGGED
GENERIC
DRONE
DELUXE

262

LAVISH
REFLEX
ORCHARD
DARING

263

WORKS
CAUSE
NOISY
SCENE
CAREFULLY
PLANNED
VERY
SOON
MOVE
COUNTRY
LIVE
CHANGE
IDEAS

264

MAP - PLOT
IMPART - TELL
DREAD - ALARM
CARRY - BRING
AGED - SENILE
TARDY - LATE

265

A	N	T	E	D
H	N	A	C	A
C	E	F	I	S
R	X	U	R	B
E	M	S	H	

266

B	R	E	A	K	1	E	V	E	N	
E	V	E	N	2	T	R	A	D	E	
T	R	A	D	E	3	U	N	I	O	N
U	N	I	O	N	4	J	A	C	K	
J	A	C	K	5	C	H	E	E	S	E
C	H	E	E	S	E	6	B	R	E	A	D
B	R	E	A	D	7	L	I	N	E	
L	I	N	E	8	D	R	I	V	E	

267

GIFT - LOSS
FACE - AVOID
RACKET - STILL
BLEAK - SUNNY
EASE - GRIEF
DWELL - MOVE

268

ADEPT - MASTER
PLOT - PLAN
RAPID - FAST
SCRAP - BRAWL
FAINT - WEAK
HARD - STIFF

269

CHEERFUL - GLOOMY
GENUINE - PHONY
ASSIST - IMPEDE
PATRON - VENDOR
WITTY - SOLEMN
CONDEMN - APPROVE
STURDY - RICKETY

270

Orange Answers
SERVANT, WEAVING, NERVOUS, ELEVATE

Blue Answers
CUMULATIVE, ILLEGIBLE, MUNICIPAL, ALUMINUM

Purple Answers
PUMP, PULP, PEEP, PROP

Red Answers
WEEDED, SEEDED, SETTEE

271

272

DURING
UPBEAT
HARPOON
GROVEL
WICKED
RECLINE

273

MAUSOLEUM
EFFLUENCE
TREATMENT
RACKETEER
NUTRITION

274

INCOME - REVENUE
SHAME - DISGRACE
PACKAGE - PARCEL
LEAN - SCRAWNY
ENLIST - ENROLL
PRAISE - FLATTER
ACCEPT - RECEIVE

275

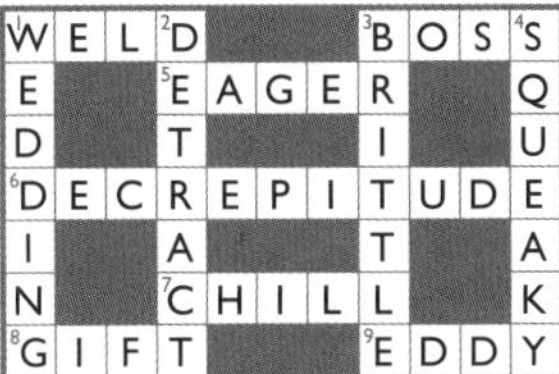

276

DENY - INDULGE
BLUNT - SUBTLE
START - CONCLUDE
TENDER - TOUGH
CHAOS - HARMONY
GLUM - CHEERFUL
CAUSE - EFFECT

277

ABRUPT - SUDDEN
BEAR - CARRY
SOLID - HARD
TIDY - TRIM
WORK - LABOR
FABLE - TALE

278

VERY CAREFUL ABOUT DOING WHAT YOU ARE SUPPOSED TO DO

279

1 S	A	L	A	2 D		3 B	R	I	E	4 F
N				E		L				L
I		5 I	M	P	E	A	C	6 H		A
F		N		T		C		O		S
7 F	I	F	T	H		8 K	I	O	S	K
		L						D		
9 S	K	I	F	10 F		11 P	U	L	P	12 Y
C		C		A		R		U		O
O		13 T	O	U	R	I	S	M		D
L				L		D				E
14 D	R	A	F	T		15 E	Q	U	A	L

280 CONQUER - SUBDUE
ENOUGH - PLENTY
FERVENT - ARDENT
PAUSE - RESPITE
INFINITE - ETERNAL
NOVICE - LEARNER
OCCULT - SECRET

281

282 HOT - COLD
RASH - WARY
LITTLE - LARGE
QUIT - REMAIN
COMMON - RARE
MEND - HARM

283 MANDATORY
IMPORTANT
HEARTFELT
DEFECTIVE
IDENTICAL

284

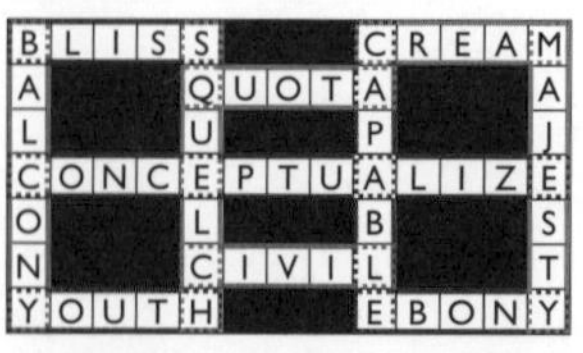

285

T	A	P	E	
I		I		C
L	A	P	E	L
T		E		O
	U	S	E	D

F	A	D	E	
I		O		T
R	A	Z	O	R
M		E		O
	U	N	I	T

H	A	L	F	
I		A		P
C	A	T	E	R
K		E		O
	U	R	N	S

286

CENTER 1 COURT
COURT 2 CASE
CASE 3 STUDY
STUDY 4 HARD
HARD 5 CANDY
CANDY 6 CANE
CANE 7 SUGAR
SUGAR 8 COOKIE

287

PLUMP - LEAN
RAGE - CALM
TAKE - GIVE
SHARP - DULL
USUAL - RARE
VAST - SMALL

288

289

UPPER
MEDIUM
OFFBEAT
ANNEX
AMONG
INFANT
DECIDE
BILLION
BOGEYMAN
PHRASE
AGENT

290

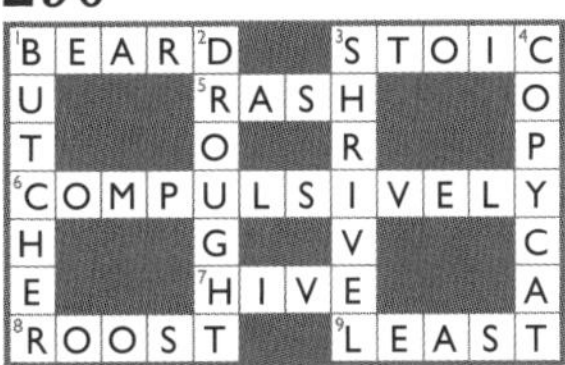

291

VICTOR
GRAPHIC
DEFAME
PRAISE

292

Orange Answers
BANNER, ARRIVE, HOTTER, MUTTER, RIPPLE
Blue Answers
BATTLE, CATTLE, TATTLE, RATTLE
Purple Answers
SULFUR, RADIUM, HELIUM
Red Answers
AROMA, ALPHA, AORTA

293

DRIVE - HALT
BREAK - MEND
LEVEL - ROUGH
EQUAL - UNLIKE
DULL - KEEN
HEAD - BASE

294

THE USE OF CLEVER AND USUALLY DISHONEST METHODS

295

LOYALTY
LARGEST
ESCAPE
SPEAK
CAREFUL
UNLIKE
COUNTRY
HELD
QUICK
WITHOUT
DETAILS
ELSE

296

HELICOPTER
PROBABLY
SECONDARY
ADVANTAGE
EXCITEMENT
UTTERLY
ELEMENTARY

297
HELP - HINDER
DELIGHT - SORROW
STRANGE - COMMON
CAVITY - MOUND
SUPPLY - RESERVE
RESIST - COMPLY
MERCY - CRUELTY

298
ADVANTAGE
TEMPERATE CARNATION
DIFFERENT TELEPHONE

299
GENUINE RECEIPT
ACCURATE OVERDUE
QUIVER INFERIOR

300
CAVITY - HOLLOW
SPEED - VELOCITY
OBTAIN - PROCURE
GIFT - ENDOWMENT
DENSE - COMPACT
FASTEN - BIND
SKILLED - ADROIT

301

302
HINDER - OBSTRUCT
HOSTILE - CONTRARY
ILLEGAL - ILLICIT
COMPLAIN - LAMENT
PIOUS - DEVOUT
IMPART - REVEAL
CONDONE - EXCUSE

303
C	L	A	I	M		F	E	W	E	R
I				O		L				A
V		P	O	N	T	I	F	F		I
I		R		E		N		L		S
C	H	E	W	Y		G	R	I	P	E
		V						G		
W	H	I	N	E		A	C	H	O	O
E		E		A		U		T		U
I		W	O	R	L	D	L	Y		G
R				L		I				H
D	E	L	A	Y		O	R	B	I	T

304

305
EVEN - LUMPY
FAME - SHAME
ANGER - PEACE
ALLOT - DENY
NASTY - SWEET
HASTY - SLOW

306

I	N	E	E	S
F	E	L	E	A
E	R	G	A	R
D	E	C	E	M
P	I	T	N	E

307

WEAKER
STUPID
TIME
EFFECT
LARGE
AGREED

STRENGTH
MISTAKE
LASTS
USELESS
HEAVY
SAME

308

INFECT
EMPATHY
PACKET
INSTEAD

309

SCHOLAR
FOREMAN
DINGY
JARGON
MOLTEN
CANYON

MANOR
LEISURE
BIZARRE
ADORE
GUESS

310

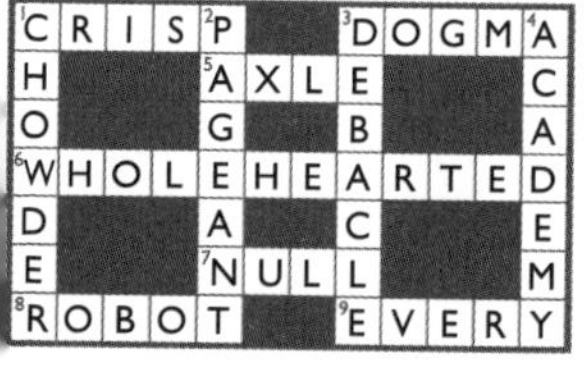

311

Orange Answers
AGENDA, ARMADA, AMOEBA, ASTHMA, ALPACA

Blue Answers
GALAXY, PROXY, EPOXY, FOXY, WAXY

Purple Answers
AMPUTEE, FORESEE, DEVOTEE, GRANTEE

Red Answers
ROOST, LEDGE

312

TRITE - FRESH
PANIC - PEACE
EVADE - MEET
MEEK - HARSH
LACK - PLENTY
HEAVY - LIGHT

313

A FACTOR OR CIRCUMSTANCE OF BENEFIT TO ITS POSSESSOR

314

DASHBOARD
YESTERDAY
TESTAMENT
MAGNESIUM
ELECTRODE

315

BLUFF - GRUFF
GRAND - LOFTY
AMUSE - CHEER
CANDID - FRANK
ACT - PLAY
BLOT - STAIN

316 RIGID - SLACK
RAISE - LOWER
START - END
HIDE - EXPOSE
DISMAL - GLAD
FORM - WRECK

317

EXCHANGE	MONEY
GOOD	LONG
CATEGORY	LITERATURE
TALENT	SKILL
TRYING	ACHIEVE
HAPPEN	AGAIN

318

319 ABATE - LESSEN
BLEAK - BARE
CEDE - YIELD
NEAT - TIDY
OMEN - SIGN
PACE - GAIT

320

G	E	B	R	Y
L	A	N	A	F
H	O	O	L	I
P	Q	U	A	E
Y	T	V	I	C

321 OMIT - INSERT
ENEMY - FRIEND
SQUALID - CLEAN
CLUMSY - HANDY
GRIEVE - REJOICE
RELEASE - ENTRAP
SLANDER - PRAISE

322 DELICACY
CARAVAN
HOWEVER
ACCUMULATE
WEARILY
ELECTRICITY
AFTERWARD

323 RELUCTANT
DEBATABLE
FINANCIAL
PERMANENT
IMPETUOUS

324 UNIFORM
MISSION
HANDSOME
EXCLUDE
BUOYANT
INDULGE

325

326

1 S	H	A	R	2 P		3 A	C	T	O	4 R
H				U		M				O
E		5 V	I	S	I	B	L	6 E		U
E		E		H		E		X		G
7 P	A	R	T	Y		8 R	E	A	C	H
		T						M		
9 S	K	I	L	10 L		11 A	M	P	L	12 E
I		G		A		B		L		N
G		13 O	U	T	C	O	M	E		T
H				E		V				R
14 T	U	T	O	R		15 E	P	O	X	Y

327

WISE - SENSIBLE
STOUT - ROTUND
ACCEDE - CONSENT
HEALTHY - ROBUST
FETCH - PROCURE
HIDDEN - SECRET
ENGROSS - ABSORB

328

MEADOW REPEAT
VELVET AFRAID

329

330

LAME - QUICK
DREAD - VALOR
FAULT - GAIN
VICE - VIRTUE
FLAUNT - HIDE
GLOOM - MIRTH

331

HARM DAMAGE
HARD EXPLAIN
MONEY PAID
GENEROUS KIND
WORST POINT
STRANGE SILLY

332

CEASE - PERSIST
TRUTH - LYING
UNEQUAL - MATCHED
VACANT - FILLED
IMPAIR - BENEFIT
INVOLVE - EXCLUDE
LIFELESS - ALIVE

333

Orange Answers
MOUNTAIN, ARROYO, RAVINE, VALLEY, GORGE
Blue Answers
RANGY, DIRTY, NEEDY, MUSHY, MEATY
Purple Answers
SQUIRREL, COUGAR, BABOON
Red Answers
RIVAL, ENVOY, DIVOT

334

VANISH TWILIGHT
ICONIC BRIGADE
UTOPIA SPLIT
MUSEUM FEAST
TEMPT HERMIT
CHAFE

335

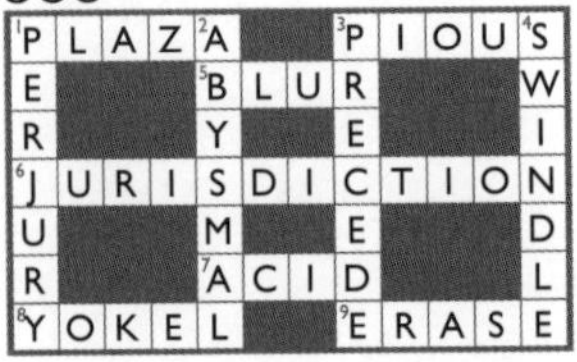

PLAZA
PIOUS
BLUR
JURISDICTION
ACID
YOKEL
ERASE
PERJURY
ABYSMAL
PRICED
SWINDLE

336

FILE 1 CARD
CARD 2 TABLE
TABLE 3 SALT
SALT 4 BATH
BATH 5 WATER
WATER 6 SLIDE
SLIDE 7 OVER
OVER 8 WITH

337

GIANT - PYGMY
WARM - COLD
RACY - TAME
CLEVER - DULL
GLEE - SORROW
ARID - LUSH

338

DRAW - SKETCH
ALIVE - ALERT
CRANKY - CROSS
ENEMY - FOE
FALL - TUMBLE
PROFIT - GAIN

339

OCCUPANCY
PIGGYBACK
NIGHTTIME
CHAUFFEUR
FLAMMABLE

340

LAVISH DEVELOP
ACCLAIM LAMINATE
PAMPHLET CAUTIOUS

341

CURIOUS - PRYING
CONFESS - DISCLOSE
HONEST - SINCERE
VALUE - WORTH
URGENT - GRAVE
ADORN - GARNISH
IMPEDE - PREVENT

342

JUST - WRONG
DRUNK - SOBER
STUPID - SHARP
HEAP - SPECK
DREAM - FACT
EAGER - CALM

343

I H B E H
N D E R A
L I V E Y
C A V R I
U U M R O

344

RANDOM - PLANNED
UGLY - PRETTY
DISCARD - RETAIN
SMOOTH - ROUGH
DUMB - BRIGHT
EXPEDITE - DELAY
SUCCEED - FAIL

345

346 CORRIDOR
DISCOVER
MANDATORY
AUTHORIZE
IMMEDIATELY
OPERATOR
DIGESTION

347

348 OPINION PRUDENT
THICKET NOVICE

349 BRAVE - DARING
DOWDY - UNKEMPT
UNIFORM - EQUAL
RESULT - OUTCOME
BLOCK - PREVENT
METHOD - SYSTEM
DEBATE - DISCUSS

350 FIERY - ARCTIC
GLAD - SAD
BEG - GIVE
CEASE - BEGIN
FABLE - FACT
BRAVE - TIMID

351 RAID - FORAY
DRINK - IMBIBE
FEUD - ROW
DEFECT - FLAW
PANIC - FRIGHT
STILL - CALM

352

353

M	I	N	C	E				B	R	A	V	O
O				N	A	I	V	E				U
L				H				R				T
L	A	C	K	A	D	A	I	S	I	C	A	L
U				N				E				O
S				C	O	V	E	R				O
K	N	A	V	E				K	N	A	C	K

354

MERCHANT
FORTIFY
ALIEN
FATHOM
FLIGHTY
FRIGID
HEYDAY
DIVERT
CRANKY
FORBID
IMPAIR

355

EMERGENCY
CATAMARAN
ILLEGIBLE
GEOMETRIC
ADORATION

356

1M	I	G	H	2T		3S	H	U	S	4H
E				I		C				O
D		5F	O	R	T	U	N	6E		A
I		R		E		B		X		R
7A	H	E	A	D		8A	P	H	I	D
		I						A		
9B	U	G	L	10E		11V	A	U	L	12T
E		H		V		A		S		E
V		13T	H	O	U	G	H	T		M
E				K		U				P
14L	O	O	S	E		15E	N	A	C	T

357

AVOW - DENY
STOUT - LEAN
REACH - START
INEPT - ADROIT
WEAK - STRONG
IMPLY - STATE

358

ABLE TO SEE AND UNDERSTAND THINGS CLEARLY AND INTELLIGENTLY

359

NEGLECT
RECENTLY
DYNAMO
KOSHER
COMPLETE
PERSUADE

360

361

SHORT
PROPER
EFFECT
LACK
VERY
CLEVER
TIME
GOOD
ACTION
ORDER
MONEY
IRONIC

362

MAR - BEAUTIFY
BELIEVE - REJECT
ADVANCE - RECEDE
DRAB - CHEERFUL
UPPED - REDUCED
IDIOT - GENIUS
SEVERE - LENIENT

363 ***Orange Answers***
LOGICAL, LIBERAL, LINGUAL, LYRICAL, LATERAL
Blue Answers
TORN, BORN, CORN, WORN
Purple Answers
CLOUDY, RAINY, SUNNY, WINDY
Red Answers
ALFALFA, AMALGAM, ANAGRAM

---

364 ACCESSORY DELICIOUS
EMOTIONAL BEAUTIFUL
CLASSICAL

365

P	H	N	E	U
U	O	B	S	T
T	L	A	O	R
U	D	O	R	O
X	E	D	B	N

---

366 TINY - SMALL
EARN - GAIN
PRISON - JAIL
SOUR - TART
ROSTER - LIST
GROW - EXPAND

---

367 OUTRAGE - AFFRONT
OVERCOME - CONQUER
ZENITH - PINNACLE
DISTURB - ANNOY
COMPOSE - MAKE
MINOR - LOWER
QUIVER - SHAKE

---

368 OBTAIN RECRUIT
AFFIRM LEGACY

---

369 STURDY - DURABLE
ADVICE - COUNSEL
COVERT - HIDDEN
VALOR - BRAVERY
DISTANT - REMOTE
FIRE - DISCHARGE
SAFETY - ASYLUM

---

370 SEND - GET
FALSE - TRUE
CHEER - GLOOM
LIFE - DEATH
NUDE - CLAD
RIGID - SOFT

---

371 NOT RELATING TO THE MAIN OR MOST IMPORTANT PART

---

372 DEVASTATE
PERMANENT
PERSONALITY
TESTIFY
AMBIGUOUS
IGUANA
IRREGULAR

---

373 OPERATION DEVIATION
PERPETUAL ALLIGATOR
INVISIBLE

---

374 SHORTAGE REACT
EMBARGO SKETCH
PORTION ENOUGH
CHASE STEED
MASON BRONCO
DREAD

375

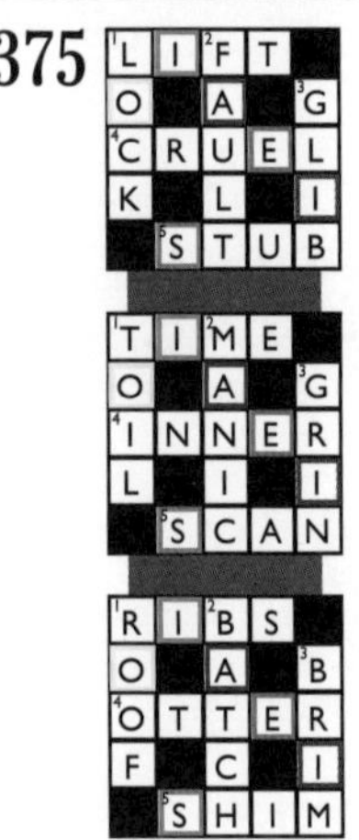

376

TRUE - VALID
ACCUSE - BLAME
CONCUR - AGREE
TAX - LEVY
ZERO - NAUGHT
TEASE - ANNOY

377

ENLIST - SHUN
ABOUT - AFAR
RAPID - SLOW
INCITE - DETER
LAW - CHAOS
EDGE - FLAT

378

379

1M	U	R	A	2L		3S	Y	R	U	4P
U				U		H				I
N		5G	Y	M	N	A	S	6T		Z
C		A		P		K		O		Z
7H	U	R	R	Y		8E	X	T	R	A
		B						A		
9S	H	A	D	10E		11V	A	L	V	12E
W		G		R		A		L		S
E		13E	Q	U	A	L	L	Y		S
L				P		O				A
14L	I	M	I	T		15R	E	P	L	Y

380

RANSACK
MAJORITY
CREATIVE
SUPERIOR
ZENITH
MEANDER

381

SOURCE HARM
SEND QUICKLY
TIME EVENT
WORDS SPEECH
GOOD LIKELY
MOON FULL

382

LAST - FIRST
FAT - LEAN
HARDY - WEAK
BRIGHT - SOMBER
IDLE - BUSY
LEAVE - STAY

383

ACTUAL - REAL
RUSE - TRICK
SHARE - GIVE
DARK - MURKY
EAGER - KEEN
ORDER - RULE

384

ENERGIZE PARADOX
LEGIBLE BABBLE

385

MAKE - DISMANTLE
WARY - CARELESS
MINOR - MAJOR
LINGER - DEPART
BEGIN - CONCLUDE
DETEST - LIKE
ORDERLY - MESSY

386

387

STEAL - TAKE
HOPE - TRUST
ADMIT - ALLOW
COMPEL - FORCE
REAP - GET
SEND - CAST

388

COMPEL - BALK
HOPE - FEAR
EMIT - RETAIN
KNOW - DOUBT
DIVIDE - JOIN
PEACE - BRAWL

389

IMPROMPTU
INCORRECT
AGREEABLE
BILINGUAL
CELESTIAL

390

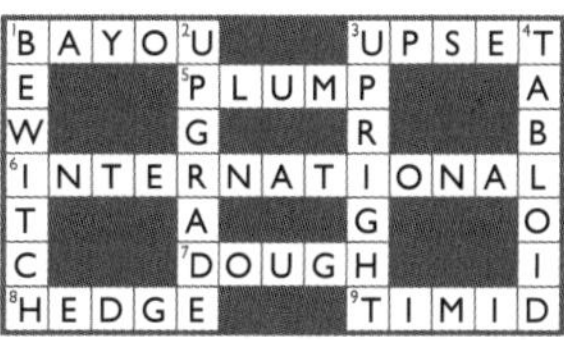

391

EVADE - MEET
RAZE - BUILD
SHOW - HIDE
HINDER - HELP
CHEAP - COSTLY
DIE - LIVE

392

A STATE IN WHICH
OPPOSING FORCES OR
ACTIONS ARE BALANCED

393

Orange Answers
CARNATION, TERMINAL, LIBERATE, BIFOCAL, RADIO
Blue Answers
BLABBER, BLUBBER, BABBLE, BUBBLE
Purple Answers
ROTATOR, RACECAR, REVIVER
Red Answers
SWIMMING, STOMPING

394

LOOK	PLEASURE
QUALITY	STYLE
TRICK	DECEIVE
FIRST	AREA
PREVENT	MOVING
STRONG	ANGRY

395

[1]S	M	A	S	[2]H		[3]B	E	L	O	[4]W
C				U		L				A
U		[5]U	P	S	C	A	L	[6]E		L
F		N		K		N		M		T
[7]F	U	N	K	Y		[8]K	L	U	T	Z
		E						L		
[9]S	U	R	L	[10]Y		[11]C	R	A	C	[12]K
W		V		E		H		T		N
A		[13]E	X	A	M	I	N	E		I
M				R		M				F
[14]P	R	A	W	N		[15]E	X	I	L	E

396

CHEAP - PETTY
TRACE - MARK
DANGER - PERIL
EDGE - BORDER
TAKE - SNATCH
DEAR - COSTLY

397

O	V	A	R	I
R	I	G	I	O
D	Y	H	N	U
R	S	A	U	S
A	T	E	N	A

398

IDENTICAL	SECRETARY
ADVERSITY	ORANGUTAN
REALISTIC	

399

MODERN - DATED
CONCEAL - EXPOSE
CONCUR - DISSENT
REPLETE - STARVED
PROTECT - IMPERIL
SUPPORT - BETRAY
LEGAL - WRONG

400

PRINCIPAL
INSULATE
TEMPERATURE
LUNATIC
ELIGIBLE
LABORATORY
HORRIBLY

401

QUEASY	CONFRONT
RELIABLE	FISSURE
EXHORT	PROTOCOL

402

DRY - DAMP
THAW - FREEZE,
PETTY - GREAT
DEFER - FORCE
LIQUID - SOLID
EXULT - MOURN

403 DALLY - IDLE
ABLE - ROBUST
STERN - RIGID
RUDE - ROUGH
CASTE - CLASS
HUNCH - OMEN

404 OFFHAND PRECISE
VORTEX CONVOY

405

406 HUGE - TINY
PLAY - WORK
LIMP - STIFF
NICE - UGLY
REMIT - HOLD
BAD - GOOD

407

D	E	U	C	F
H	O	N	E	F
T	S	C	R	U
A	C	H	R	E
R	A	M	O	M

408 ENLARGE - AUGMENT
GLISTEN - SPARKLE
PLUNDER - PILLAGE
ENIGMA - PUZZLE
LEGAL - RIGHT
LEAVE - DESERT
MISHAP - SLIP

409 BETTER - WORSE
FOOLISH - WISE
AFRAID - HEROIC
EXPEL - RECEIVE
SLEEPING - AWAKE
OBTUSE - ACUTE
FAMOUS - UNKNOWN

410 ROAM - WANDER
SEVER - SPLIT
WAIT - LINGER
RARE - ODD
AGONY - PAIN
SHUN - AVOID

411 EVIL - GOOD
BUY - SELL
HOLD - LOSE
KIND - CRUEL
DEAD - ALIVE
FALL - RISE

412

413

STEADY	EFFORT
EATS	MUCH
COPY	SPEECH
LAWYER	CRIME
MOVING	PLACE
NEAT	UNTIDY

414

1 Q	U	A	L	2 M		3 C	H	E	A	4 P
U				A		U				R
I		5 N	O	N	S	T	O	6 P		I
L		O		L		U		O		O
7 L	O	U	S	Y		8 P	O	W	E	R
		R						D		
9 T	W	I	S	10 T		11 S	T	E	A	12 M
H		S		O		E		R		E
U		13 H	A	P	P	I	L	Y		R
M				A		Z				C
14 B	L	I	T	Z		15 E	N	V	O	Y

415

SHOWING NO CARE FOR THE RIGHTS FEELINGS OR SAFETY OF OTHERS

416

417

Orange Answers
MEAGER, NIMBLE, OBLONG, OPAQUE, QUEASY
Blue Answers
PRESS, BUDDY, HAPPY, SORRY
Purple Answers
ETERNITY, EQUALITY, ORDINARY
Red Answers
LAWYER, BANKER, BARBER

418

FREQUENCY	CLEVER
MOCKERY	QUIET
EXCLAIM	FUMBLE
BURST	CHECKUP
QUELL	JUMBLE
LUNAR	

419

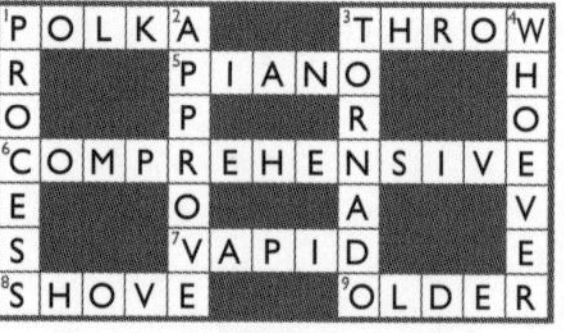

420

TURMOIL	IMMENSE
TABULATE	INCISOR
CURTAIL	YAWNING

421

GRIM - MILD
FOIL - ABET
JIBE - EXALT
LEVEL - ROUGH
JOIN - SEVER
REACH - BEGIN

422

423

KERNEL
DIFFUSE
SOOTHE
NEGATE

424

425

VILE - DECENT
NEAT - MESSY
BIND - UNTIE
DENSE - THIN
HATE - LOVE
LOSE - GAIN

426

427

1 P	R	E	S	2 S		3 P	A	N	I	4 C
O				A		I				O
U		5 B	A	L	A	N	C	6 E		M
N		I		V		C		L		M
7 D	I	S	C	O		8 H	Y	E	N	A
		C						M		
9 B	R	U	S	10 H		11 Q	U	E	E	12 N
L		I		U		U		N		O
I		13 T	E	M	P	E	S	T		T
M				I		S				C
14 P	L	A	I	D		15 T	O	U	C	H

428

HONESTLY
DISOBEDIENT
COMMOTION
PREDATORY
MEDIATE
REPUTATION
VERIFY

429

430

CITE - IGNORE
BUILD - RUIN
SORRY - GLAD
WAIT - HURRY
ZEAL - APATHY
STERN - KIND

431 MAINTAIN - UPHOLD
MISTAKE - BLUNDER
USUAL - NORMAL
VAGUE - UNSURE
VENTURE - ATTEMPT
ZEAL - FERVOR
PRIDE - VANITY

432 MOROSE - JOLLY
PIOUS - SINFUL
ACCURATE - FALSE
SWIFT - SLUGGISH
FATIGUE - VIGOR
ACTION - INERTIA
ALOOF - FRIENDLY

433

[1]C	R	Y	P	[2]T		[3]C	H	U	R	[4]N
O				O		H				E
W		[5]N	O	X	I	O	U	[6]S		W
E		O		I		M		P		L
[7]R	A	V	E	N		[8]P	R	I	V	Y
		E						N		
[9]G	U	L	C	[10]H		[11]S	H	A	W	[12]L
I		T		Y		K		C		O
Z		[13]Y	I	D	D	I	S	H		W
M				R		M				L
[14]O	P	E	R	A		[15]P	H	O	N	Y

434 ABODE - HOME
NEAR - CLOSE
VISION - SIGHT
ZEST - DESIRE
IRATE - ANGRY
POISE - CALM

435 ASK - REPLY
LIGHT - HEAVY
COMELY - UGLY
HURT - HEAL
FADE - APPEAR
NAKED - CLAD

ABOUT THE AUTHORS

David L. Hoyt is the most syndicated puzzle maker in the United States and founder of HoytInteractiveMedia.com. He is the author of *Jumble, USA Today Word Roundup, Up & Down Words, Word Winder,* and more. **Colin Morgan** is an architect, game inventor, and puzzle writer who frequently collaborates with David.

Merriam-Webster has been America's leading and most trusted provider of language information for over 150 years. Publications include *Merriam-Webster's Collegiate® Dictionary* (among the bestselling books in American history) and dictionaries for English-language learners.